Oxford

CHORAL
CLASSICS

European Sacred Music

EDITED BY JOHN RUTTER

ASSOCIATE EDITOR
CLIFFORD BARTLETT

MUSIC DEPARTMENT
OXFORD UNIVERSITY PRESS
OXFORD AND NEW YORK

Oxford University Press, Great Clarendon Street, Oxford OX2 6DP
Oxford University Press Inc., 198 Madison Avenue, New York, NY 10016, USA

Oxford New York Athens
Auckland Bangkok Bombay Calcutta
Cape Town Dar es Salaam Delhi Florence Hong Kong
Istanbul Karachi Kuala Lumpur Madras
Madrid Melbourne Mexico City Nairobi Paris
Singapore Tapei Tokyo Toronto

and associated companies in
Berlin Ibadan

Oxford is a trade mark of Oxford University Press

1 3 5 7 9 10 8 6 4 2

ISBN 0–19–343695–7

Music originated on Sibelius

Printed in Great Britain on acid-free paper by
The Bath Press Ltd., Bath

Orchestral scores and parts are available on rental
(see the Index of vocal and instrumental requirements on p. 378).

CONTENTS

PREFACE

The aim of the *Oxford Choral Classics* series is to offer choirs a practical and inexpensive working library of standard repertoire in new, reliable editions. Where space allows, music that is less widely known but of special value within its genre is also included. Inevitably, any anthology is a personal selection reflecting the perspective of its editor, and it must also be recognized that there are wide national differences of repertoire: what is standard fare for a choir in one country may be little known in another. For this volume of European sacred music it has been a hard task to narrow down an enormous field of marvellous music to fit a 384-page book. In general, I have selected those pieces which are regarded as classics or which, whether famous or not, give me particular pleasure. Hence, familiar cornerstones of the repertoire such as Palestrina's *Sicut cervus* and the Lotti *Crucifixus* are found alongside rarities such as Rheinberger's lovely *Abendlied* and Lassus's serenely soaring *Ave verum Corpus*, which I hope others will enjoy as much as I do. The specific parameters followed have been these:

1. The period covered is from about 1500 up to the twentieth century (though copyright considerations have limited the amount of twentieth-century music included).
2. Sacred music from Britain appears in a separate volume so is excluded here. The English composers Peter Philips and Richard Dering, who lived and worked on the continent, appear in the English volume.
3. Most regretfully, constraints of space and copyright have made it impossible to do justice to the music of every region, notably Scandinavia, Eastern Europe, and the Baltic States. It is hoped that this music may be the subject of later volumes.
3. With one or two exceptions, only complete, self-standing compositions are included, not extracts from larger works such as masses, cantatas, and oratorios. Single movements from cantatas and oratorios are to be found in the *Sacred Choruses* volume.
4. With a few exceptions, pieces with orchestral accompaniment (such as French baroque *grands motets*, Handel's *Zadok the priest*, Mozart's various liturgical compositions, and the Bruckner and Franck settings of Psalm 150) appear in the *Sacred Choruses* volume.
5. With one exception, choral arrangements of music not originally for choir or vocal ensemble are excluded, as is music in less than four voice parts. Franck's *Panis angelicus*, originally for solo tenor, is so widely performed in choral versions as to have become part of the choral repertoire and impossible to leave out.
6. Advent, Christmas and Epiphany motets appear in a separate volume and are excluded.

A few particular editorial decisions call for explanantion:

1. J. S. Bach's six motets have reluctantly been excluded on the grounds of their length. There seemed a stronger case for including his 'seventh motet', the serenely beautiful *O Jesu Christ, meins Lebens Licht*—just as much a motet as the other six, but often overlooked because the old Bach-Gesellschaft edition mistakenly categorized it as a cantata.
2. Schubert's *Psalm 23* is the only upper-voice piece in an otherwise all mixed-voice collection. As the best of Schubert's shorter sacred pieces without orchestra, I felt it had to be included.
3. I have not seen any reason to exclude pieces of doubtful authorship if they are especially good or well known. The pieces concerned are the Buxtehude *Magnificat*, John of Portugal *Crux fidelis*, and Victoria *Ave Maria* and *Jesu, dulcis memoria*.
4. This book being intended as much for church choirs as for concert choirs, I have tried, other things being equal, to pick pieces with texts that are generally useable in church—avoiding, for example, Venetian motets in praise of St Mark and Sweelinck's French psalm settings.

However, choice has been mainly based on the quality of the pieces as musical literature, so no attempt has been made to cover all the occasions of the church's year, to avoid Marian texts which would not find a place in Protestant liturgy, or to avoid including more than one setting of the same text. On this last point, concert choirs could in fact build some effective groups within a programme by juxtaposing, say, the *Ave Maria* settings of Josquin, Bruckner, and Stravinsky.

Translations

Many, perhaps most, of the choirs using this book will never need to make use of the singing translations provided. Others—including, for example, those serving the largest Christian denomination in the United States—have little choice but to sing in English. I do not think it right that they, and their listeners, should be denied the experience of so much of the best choral literature for lack of an English text. That alone seems to me sufficient reason for including singing translations; as for the general arguments for and against singing in translation (where there is a choice), they are familar enough not to need rehearsing here. The policy adopted in this volume is to provide singing translations for everything except the longer Latin pieces such as the Allegri *Miserere* and the Monteverdi *Beatus vir*; these are most likely to be performed either by concert choirs or in churches where Latin is not a problem, and it is hard to imagine that a singing translation for them would be widely useful.

The principles governing the singing translations in the *Oxford Choral Classics* series are: to be as faithful as possible to the meaning and flavour of the originals; to alter the rhythms of the originals as little as possible; to preserve the rhyme schemes of the originals as far as possible; and to make the English texts as singable as possible, with due consideration for vowel sounds on exposed notes. Where these principles come into conflict and one or more of them has to be sacrificed, I have tried to preserve singability. An additional factor in the present volume is that of the style of religious language. I respect the viewpoint of those who believe that all religious texts should be expressed in modern language, but it seems to me, in general, appropriate if the style of an English translation more or less matches the period of the music to which it is set. We are accustomed to hearing the anthems of Gibbons and Purcell or the oratorios of Handel in unmodernized English (in fact, a performance of *Messiah* affords one of the few remaining opportunities to experience in public the language of the 1611 Bible), and I would find it unsettling to hear, say, Palestrina's sixteenth-century polyphony clashing with aggressively twentieth-century words. For that reason, in my translations I have not hesitated to use the 'thou' verb form, or to echo appropriate phrases from older bibles, prayer books, and hymns. In earlier pieces, Zarlino's principles of verbal underlay have generally been adhered to, but with some exceptions allowed.

The four pieces of Russian liturgical music included in this volume are provided with new transliterations. A separate note on these, by David Lloyd-Jones, appears at the end of this preface.

Editorial practice

The policy of the *Oxford Choral Classics* series is to use primary sources wherever possible (except for copyright pieces, which are reprinted as given by their publishers). With the present volume, primary source material, printed or in manuscript, is available in the majority of cases and has been consulted, resulting in the elimination of some long-standing errors in a number of pieces. In presenting our editions, the aim is first and foremost to serve the practical needs of non-specialist choirs, keeping the music pages as clean and uncluttered as possible, though not neglecting the interests of the scholar. Prefatory staves are given for pre-1700 sources. References to clefs and pitch follow the standard conventions. Note values in early pieces have generally been reduced to give a ♩ pulse, pitch transposed to suit standard voice ranges, editorial barring shown in a modern, standard way, and key signatures modernized. Punctuation, capitalization and spelling of texts has been modernized, with the *Liber Usualis* as the point of reference for Latin texts. Psalm numbering follows Protestant usage. Editorially completed text underlay is not shown in italics: this convention presents a confusing appearance when italics are already being used for the singing translation. Indications of ligature and coloration are omitted, though care has been taken with editorial underlay never to move to a new syllable in the middle of a ligature. Obvious scribal or printing errors in sources are silently corrected; cases of doubt or of discrepancy between sources are advertised by footnotes or listed in the commentary. All material in square brackets or printed small is editorial. In pre-1700 pieces, full-size accidentals are those which appear in the source; they are silently omitted when made unnecessary by a modern key signature, and also omitted for immediate repetitions of the same note in the same bar. Small accidentals are editorial. Cautionary accidentals are shown full size in round brackets. Cancelling accidentals customary in modern notation but absent in the source are shown full size in round brackets; in pieces where they are frequently needed, they are shown small without brackets, to avoid a cluttered appearance. Crossed slurs are editorial; dotted slurs have been inserted only where felt to be really necessary, and indicate that the underlay of the translated text and the original text differ. Syllabic slurs in voice parts, as used in modern publishing style, have not generally been added. Beaming and stemming of notes has been modernized.

Not everyone will agree on the desirability of including editorial suggestions of tempo and dynamics in a book such as this one. To some choir directors, they are an imposition and an irritation; to others, they are a lifeline. As a compromise solution, pre-1700 pieces include editorial suggestions in the keyboard reduction only, so they are available for those who want them but easy to ignore for those who do not. These general markings cannot, of course, take account of the differing rises and falls of each voice part in a polyphonic texture. Moreover, music of the past is inevitably viewed through spectacles tinted by one's own era, musical experience, and personality. Ideas on the performance of 'old' music are constantly changing: there can never be a single right way to perform Josquin, or Monteverdi, or even Stravinsky. For these reasons, my editorial markings are to be taken as tentative suggestions and not as prescriptions. Conductors should be encouraged to find their own interpretations, drawn out of the music and its text as they understand them, never arbitrarily imposed. Editorial metronome markings are given where I feel there may be a need for them.

Keyboard parts

Keyboard reductions of *a cappella* pieces are given in their most readable and playable form, without always showing the movement of individual polyphonic voices, especially where these cross. This sometimes results in apparent parallel fifths and octaves, but I consider this preferable to the frequent sight of upstems and downstems crossed. Where all the voices of a texture are impossible to play, the keyboard reduction has been discreetly simplified. Editorial *musica ficta* is incorporated into the reduction without qualification; this standard editorial practice has recently been critically challenged, but I prefer it to the alternative of ultra-small accidentals or forests of brackets. Accidentals generally follow the convention of homophonic keyboard music, not polyphony: they are not duplicated within a bar at the same pitch if in different voices.

Seventeenth-century pieces originally published with a *basso continuo* part (even if this is no more than a *basso seguente*) have been assumed to be intended for accompanied performance. Keyboard parts for these take the form of plain realizations of the bass rather than exact reductions of the vocal texture; these realizations can be played as written, to accompany performances, though experienced continuo players will doubtless wish to add their own embellishments. Original figuring has been editorially supplemented just sufficiently to make the figured basses useable without reference to the editorial realizations. Bach's *O Jesu Christ, meins Lebens Licht*, Franck's *Panis angelicus*, Mendelssohn's *Verleih uns Frieden*, and Mozart's *Ave verum Corpus* have instrumental accompaniments which lend themselves better to organ transcription than to piano reduction, so I have presented them for organ; all these four pieces are very suitable for use in church, so this may well be the most useful option. Other instrumental accompaniments (for the Buxtehude *Magnificat* and Monteverdi *Beatus vir*) are shown as piano reductions.

Full scores and instrumental parts for all instrumentally accompanied items are available on rental from the publisher (see Index of Orchestrations, p. 378).

Acknowledgements

It is a pleasure to record here the names of those who have given advice, help and encouragement at various stages in the preparation of this book. My associate editor Clifford Bartlett has furnished me with the primary sources for my editions, painstakingly gathered from libraries in several countries; he has generously loaned me books and music, drawn my attention to all manner of relevant scholarly writings, and commented perspicaciously on my work. Dr George Guest, who was for many years Organist and Choirmaster of St John's College, Cambridge, has suggested a number of items for inclusion and given most detailed and valuable scrutiny to the entire book at proof stage. His colleagues at St John's College, Professor John Crook and the Revd Andrew Macintosh, and Dr Eamon Duffy of Magdalene College, have kindly assisted with the identification and translation of certain Latin texts. Dr Roger Bowers of Jesus College, Cambridge has elucidated for me the tricky problems of tempo relationships in Monteverdi. Hugh Keyte has shared with me the fruits of his long and detailed research into the Allegri *Miserere*, and given my commentary on this piece the benefit of searching and constructive criticism. Bruce Hamilton has provided expert transliterations of the Russian items. Jenny Wilson has given me meticulous assistance in typesetting the volume. I thank them all.

Acknowledgement is made to the libraries who provided microfilms and photocopies of many items in this volume. We are grateful for their permission to use or consult their sources.

Of my many friends at Oxford University Press, I especially want to thank Julian Elloway, Senior Music Editor, and Paul Keene, editor for this series, whose interest, support, advice, and scrutiny at every stage have once again been invaluable, as they were with the earlier *Opera Choruses* volume. Lastly, I gratefully acknowledge the contribution of Ben and Jonathan Finn, inventors of the Sibelius 7 Music Processor, on which the entire book was computer-typeset; their quest for graphical perfection remains inspiring.

JOHN RUTTER

Russian transliterations

Those who have never sung in Russian using a phonetic spelling of the Cyrillic alphabet should not be discouraged from attempting it. In fact, Russian sounds are surprisingly similar to those found in English (though the vowels are largely Italianate), and no attempt at an 'accent' is necessary. Some choirs may be fortunate enough to have a Russian speaker among their members or friends, who can help to perfect what a transliteration can only broadly suggest. The following remarks have therefore been kept to a minimum in the hope that the undertaking will not appear too daunting.

1. The most 'foreign' sound in Russian is the so-called 'hard i'. Here it is represented by 'yi'. This is pronounced not forward, like the usual English 'i', but backward with an almost adenoidal sound. The main thing is to avoid pronouncing 'yi' as the usual 'i'; try to keep it dark and covered.

2. Clusters of consonants can look intimidating but need not be so. The sound 'kh' is the guttural 'ch' as found in the Scottish word 'loch'; 'zh' is the voiced version of 'sh' and sounds as the 'j' in French 'je'; 'shch' sounds as in 'Engli*sh ch*urch'.

3. The letter 'o' in a pre-stressed syllable (shown in this book as ŏ) is so modified and lightened that it is best pronounced as an 'a'. The letter 'o' in any other unstressed position is pronounced like the 'a' in 'sofa'.

4. Some Russian words, usually verbs, end with a 't' followed by a 'soft sign'. This so softens the 't' that in practice it sounds like 'ts', as in 'rabbi*ts*'. In such cases the 's' is shown in brackets. Otherwise, soft signs in Russian have been ignored as most English speaking is soft anyway.

5. The letter 's' in the middle of words has usually been represented by 'ss' in order to prevent it being mispronounced as a 'z' (i.e. 'Mu*ss*orgsky' and not the regularly mispronounced 'Mu*z*orgsky').

DAVID LLOYD-JONES

1. Miserere

Psalm 51

GREGORIO ALLEGRI
(1582–1652)

*Translation from the 1662 Book of Common Prayer

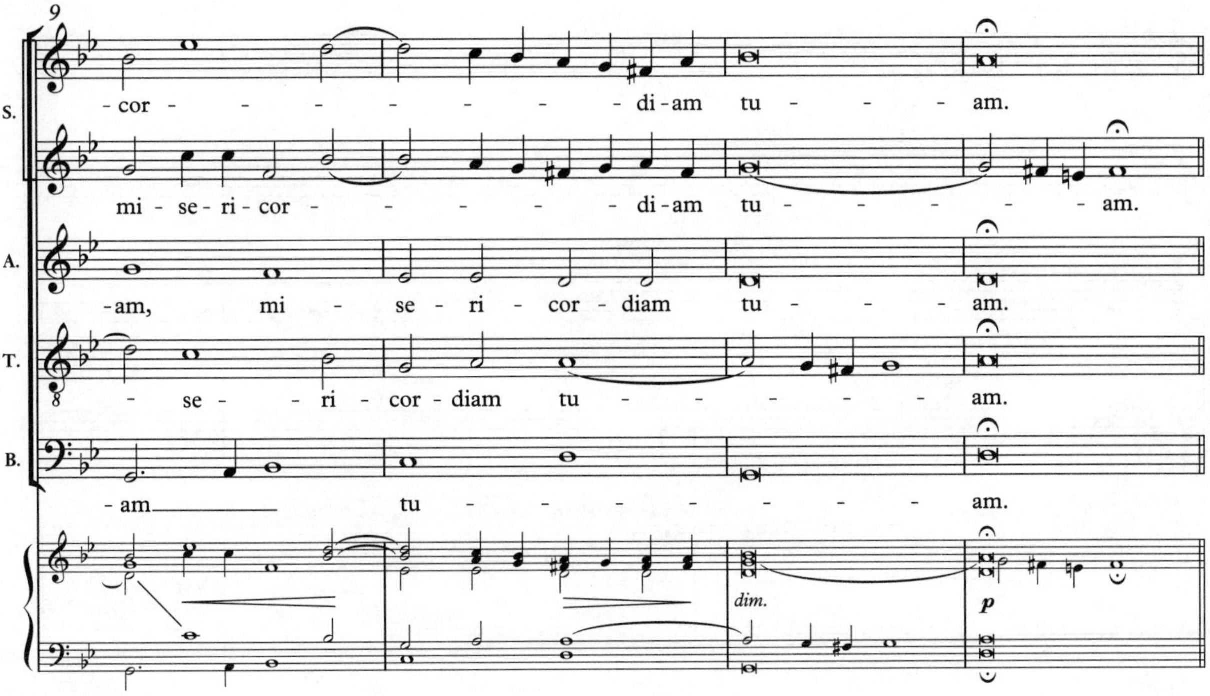

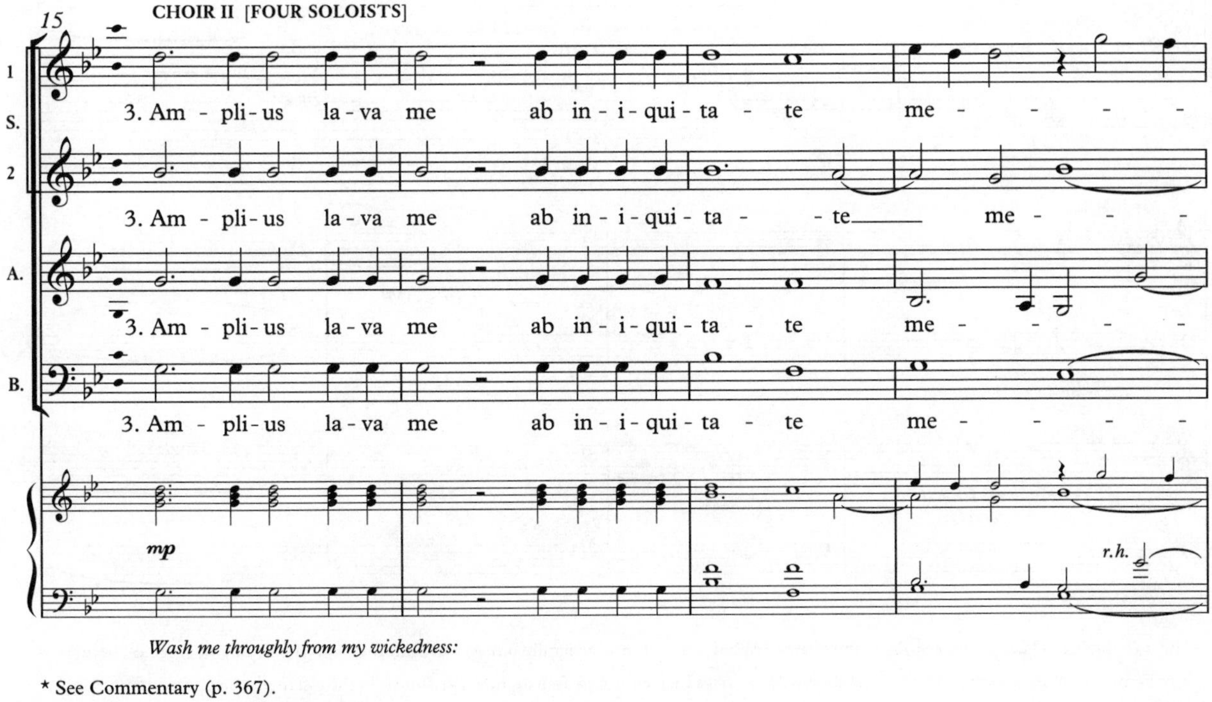

Wash me throughly from my wickedness:

* See Commentary (p. 367).

† Acute accents denote stressed syllables.

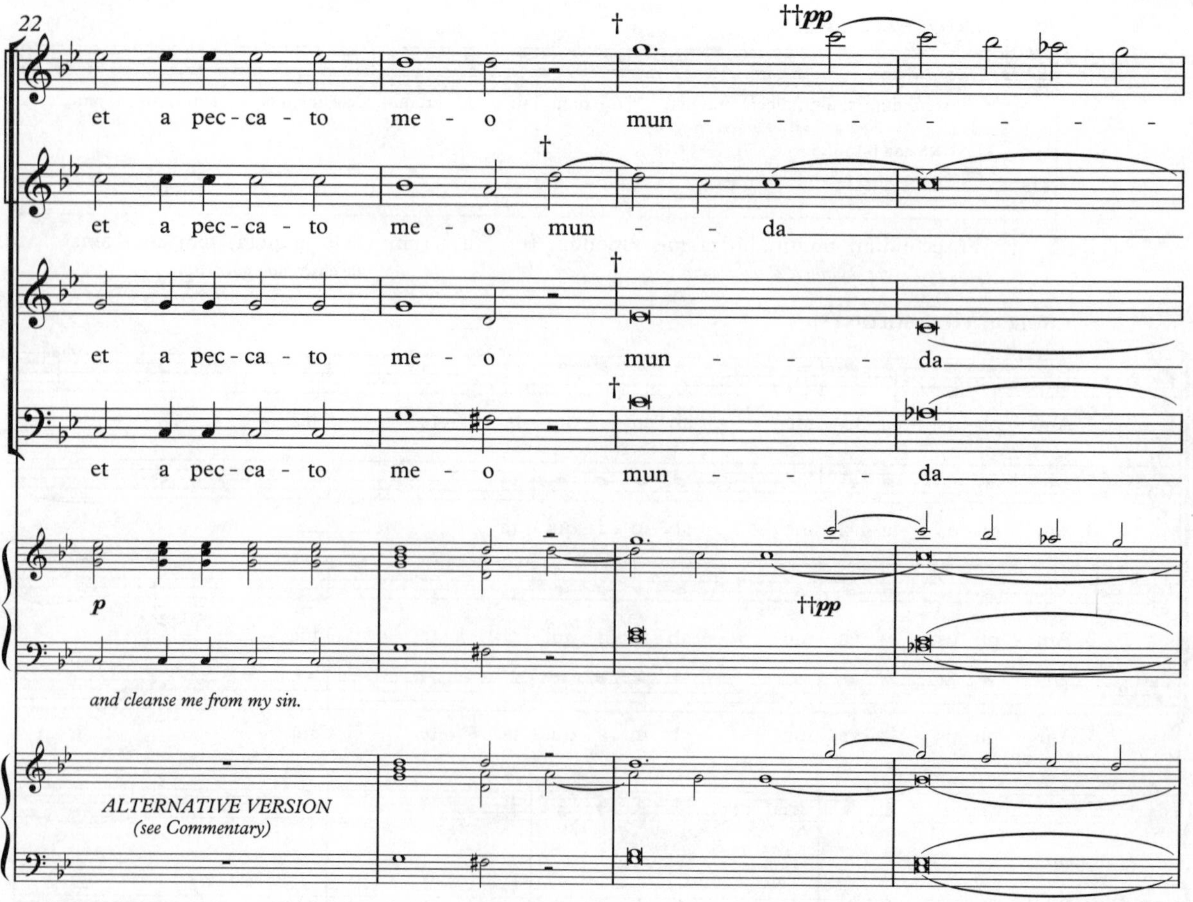

* This ♯ (applying to later verses also) is in the source (Alfieri, 1840) but is generally omitted in performance. If omitting it, sing o here.

† If preferred, from here to the end of all the four-voiced verses may be sung a fourth lower, as shown in the alternative keyboard reduction.

†† This ***pp*** is in the source (Mendelssohn, 1831).

* These accidentals (applying to later verses also) are in the source (Mendelssohn, 1831) but are generally omitted in performance.

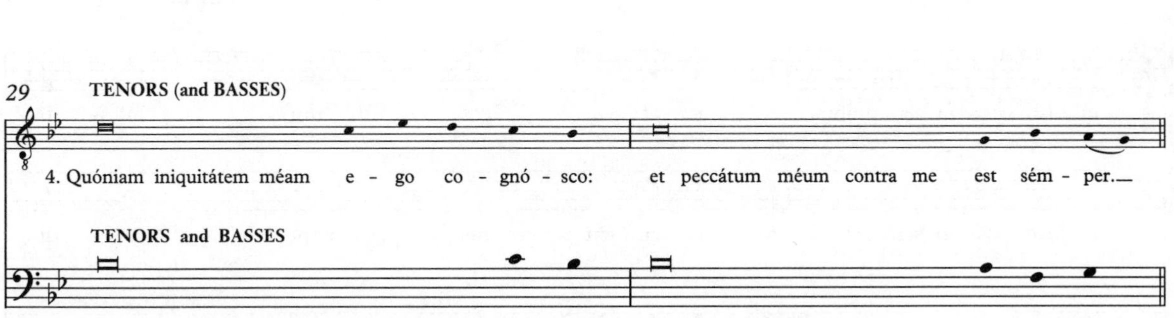

4. Quóniam iniquitátem méam ego co - gnó - sco: et peccátum méum contra me est sém - per.

For I acknowledge my faults: *and my sin is ever before me.*

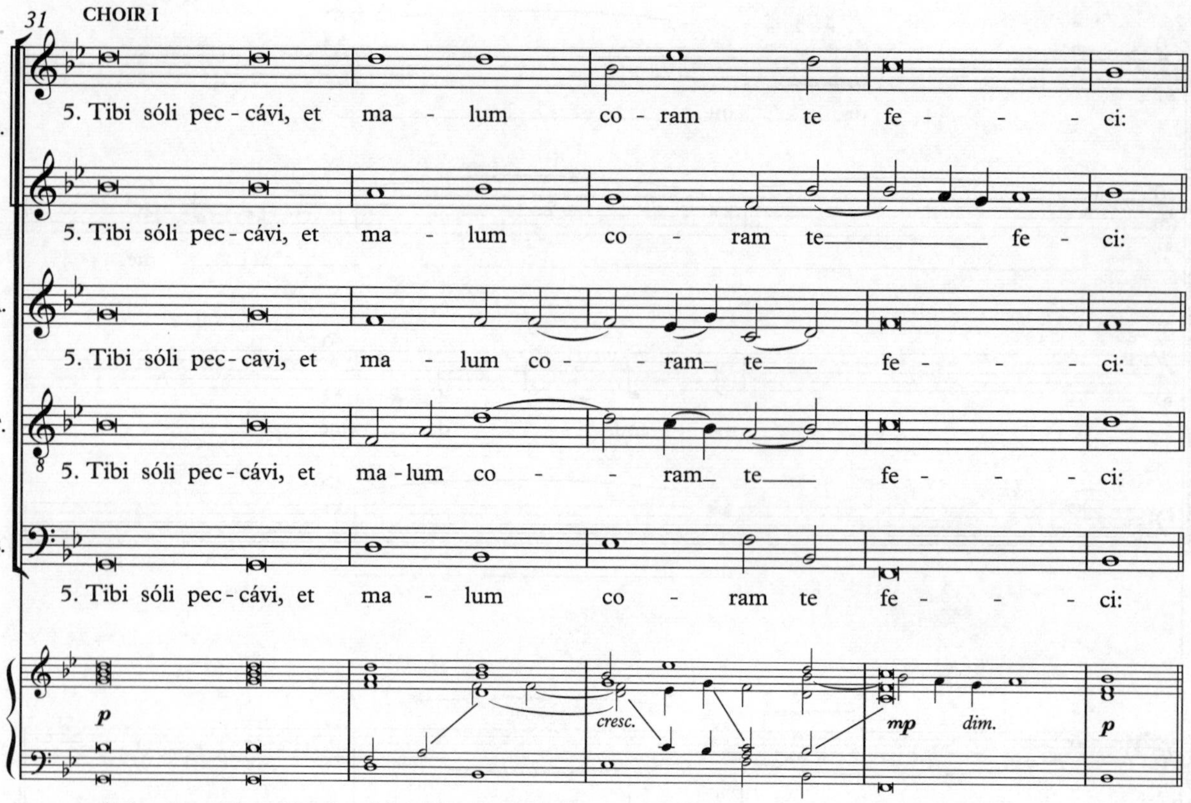

Against thee only have I sinned, and done this evil in thy sight:

that thou mightest be justified in thy saying, and clear when thou art judged.

But lo, thou requirest truth in the inward parts:

50
S.
A.
B.
- - - - - - sti: incérta et occúlta sapiéntiae tuae manife -
- (i) - - - - - - - sti: incérta et occúlta sapiéntiae tuae manife -
- - - - - - - sti: incérta et occúlta sapiéntiae tuae manife -
- - - - - - - sti: incérta et occúlta sapiéntiae tuae manife -

and shalt make me to understand wisdom secretly.

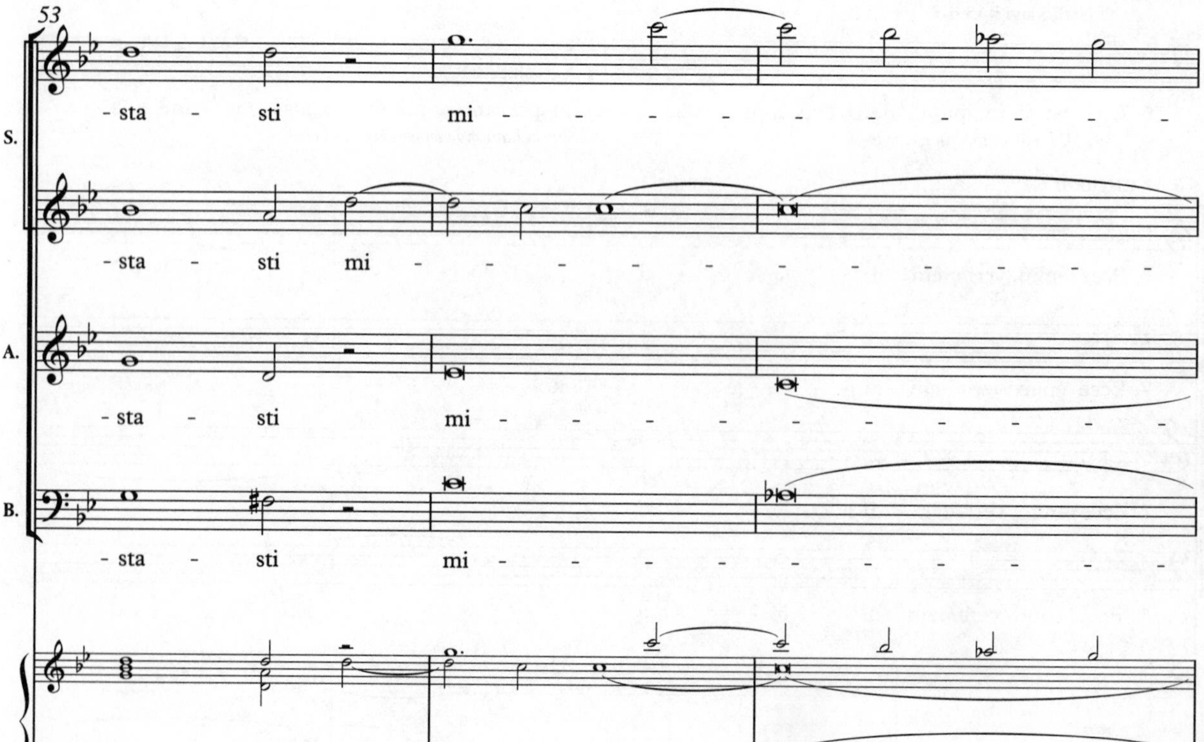
53
S.
A.
B.
- sta - sti mi - - - - - - - - - - - -
- sta - sti mi - - - - - - - - - - -
- sta - sti mi - - - - - - - - - - -
- sta - sti mi - - - - - - - - - - -

56
S.
A.
B.
hi.
hi.
hi.
hi.
59
TENORS (and BASSES)
8. Aspérges me hyssó - po, et mun - dá - bor: lavábis me, et super nivem de - al - bá - bor.
TENORS and BASSES
8. Aspérges me hyssópo, et mun - dá - bor: lavábis me, et super nivem de - al - bá - bor.
Thou shalt purge me with hyssop, and I shall be clean: thou shalt wash me, and I shall be whiter than snow.
61
CHOIR I
S.
A.
T.
B.
9. Audítui méo dábis gáudium et lae - ti - ti - am:
9. Audítui méo dábis gáudium et lae - ti - ti - am:
9. Audítui méo dábis gáudium et lae - ti - ti - am:
9. Audítui méo dábis gáudium et lae - ti - ti - am:
9. Audítui méo dábis gáudium et lae - ti - ti - am:
f
Thou shalt make me hear of joy and gladness:

that the bones which thou hast broken may rejoice.

75
TENORS (and BASSES)
10. Avérte fáciem túam a pec - cá - tis mé - is: et ómnes iniquitátes mé - as dé - le.
TENORS and BASSES
10. Avérte fáciem túam a peccátis mé - is: et ómnes iniquitátes mé - as dé - le.
Turn thy face from my sins: and put out all my misdeeds.
77
CHOIR II
S.
11. Cor múndum créa in me, De -
11. Cor múndum créa in me, De -
A.
11. Cor múndum créa in me, De -
B.
11. Cor múndum créa in me, De -
mf
r.h.
Make me a clean heart, O God:
82
S.
-us: et spíritum réctum ínnova in vi - sce - ri - bus me -
-us: et spíritum réctum ínnova in vi - sce - ri - bus me -
A.
-us: et spíritum réctum ínnova in vi - sce - ri - bus me -
B.
-us: et spíritum réctum ínnova in vi - sce - ri - bus me -
and renew a right spirit within me.

86
S.
is.
is.
A.
is.
B.
is.
90
TENORS (and BASSES)
12. Ne projícias me a fá - ci - e tú - a: et spíritum sánctum túum ne áu - fe - ras a me.
TENORS and BASSES
12. Ne projícias me a fácie tú - a: et spíritum sánctum túum ne áu - fe - ras a me.
Cast me not away from thy presence:
and take not thy holy Spirit from me.
92
CHOIR I
S.
13. Rédde mihi laetítiam salu - ta - ris tu - i:
13. Rédde mihi laetítiam salu - ta - ris tu - i:
A.
13. Rédde mihi laetítiam salu - ta - ris tu - i:
T.
13. Rédde mihi laetítiam salu - ta - ris tu - i:
B.
13. Rédde mihi laetítiam salu - ta - ris tu - i:
mp
cresc.
mf
mp
O give me the comfort of thy help again:

and stablish me with thy free Spirit.

106
TENORS (and BASSES)
14. Docébo iní - quos ví - as tú - as: et ímpii ad te con - ver - tén - tur.
TENORS and BASSES
14. Docébo iníquos vías tú - as: et ímpii ad te con - ver - tén - tur.
Then shall I teach thy ways unto the wicked:
and sinners shall be converted unto thee.
108
CHOIR II
S.
15. Líbera me de sanguínibus, Déus, Déus sa - lu - tis me - - - - -
15. Líbera me de sanguínibus, Déus, Déus sa - lu - - tis me - - - -
A.
15. Líbera me de sanguínibus, Déus, Déus sa - lu - tis me - - - - -
B.
15. Líbera me de sanguínibus, Déus, Déus sa - lu - tis me - - - -
mf
r.h.
Deliver me from blood-guiltiness, O God, thou that art the God of my health:
111
S.
- - - - - - - - - - - - - ae: et exsultábit língua mea ju -
- - - - - - - - - - - ae: et exsultábit língua mea ju -
A.
- - - - - - - - - - - ae: et exsultábit língua mea ju -
B.
- - - - - - - - - - - - - ae: et exsultábit língua mea ju -
and my tongue shall sing of thy righteousness.

115
S.
-sti - ti - am tu - - - - - - - - - - -
-sti - ti - am tu - - - - - - - - - - - -
A.
-sti - ti - am tu - - - - - - - - - - -
B.
-sti - ti - am tu - - - - - - - - - - -
118
S.
- - - - - - - - - - - - - - - am.
- - - - - - - - - - - - - - - - am.
A.
- - - - - - - - - - - - - - - - am.
B.
- - - - - - - - - - - - - - - - am.
121
TENORS (and BASSES)
16. Dómine, lábia mea a - pé - ri - es: et os méum annuntiábit láu - dem tú - am.
TENORS and BASSES
16. Dómine, lábia mea a - pé - ri - es: et os méum annuntiábit láu - dem tú - am.
Thou shalt open my lips, O Lord:
and my mouth shall shew thy praise.

For thou desirest no sacrifice, else would I give it thee:

but thou delightest not in burnt-offerings.

132
S.
- cta - - - - - - - - - - - - be - ris.
non de - le - cta - - - - - - - - - - - be - ris.
A.
- be - - ris, non de - le - - cta - - be - ris.
T.
— non de - le - - cta - - - - - - be - ris.
B.
non— de - - le - - cta - - - - - - be - ris.
dim.
p

136 TENORS (and BASSES)
18. Sacrifícium Deo spíritus con - tri - bu - lá - tus: cor contrítum et humiliátum, Déus, non de - spí - ci - es.—
TENORS and BASSES
18. Sacrifícium Deo spíritus contribu - lá - tus: cor contrítum et humiliátum, Déus, non de - spí - ci - es.

The sacrifice of God is a troubled spirit: *a broken and contrite heart, O God, shalt thou not despise.*

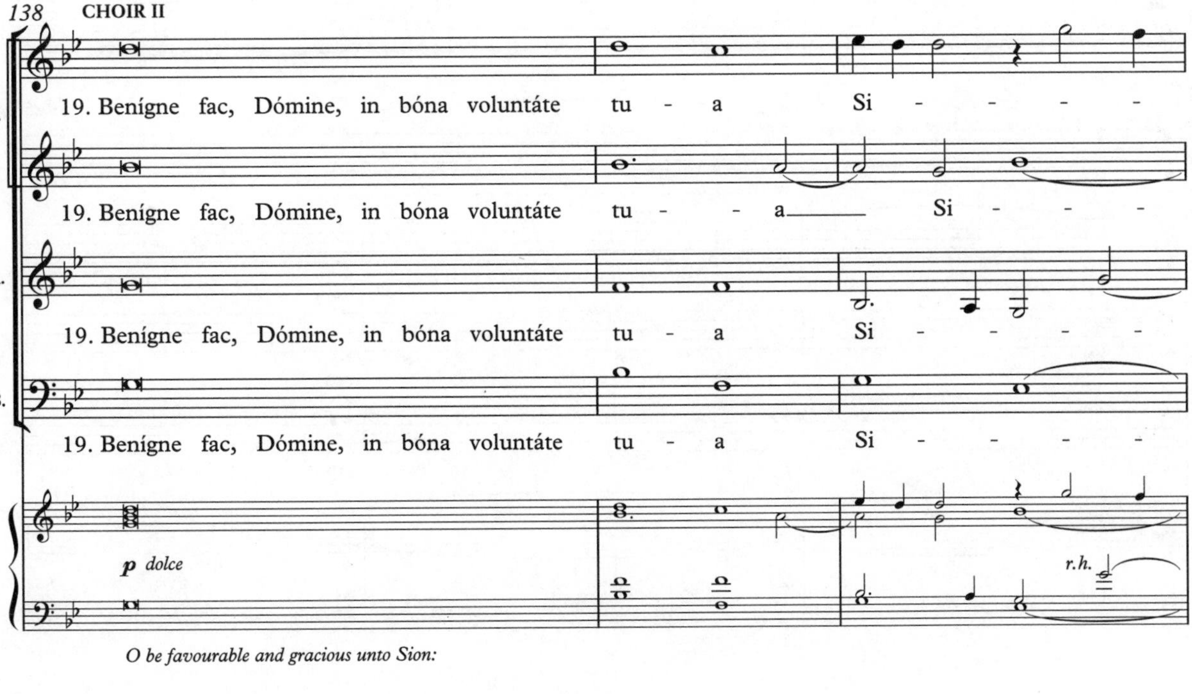
138 CHOIR II
S.
19. Benígne fac, Dómine, in bóna voluntáte tu - a Si - - - -
19. Benígne fac, Dómine, in bóna voluntáte tu - - a— Si - - - -
A.
19. Benígne fac, Dómine, in bóna voluntáte tu - a Si - - - -
B.
19. Benígne fac, Dómine, in bóna voluntáte tu - a Si - - - -
p dolce
r.h.

O be favourable and gracious unto Sion:

141
S.
on: ut aedificéntur
on: ut aedificéntur
A.
on: ut aedificéntur
B.
on: ut aedificéntur
build thou the walls of
145
mu - ri Je - - ru - - - -
mu - ri Je - - ru - - - -
mu - ri Je - - ru - - -
mu - ri Je - - ru - - -
Jerusalem.
148
sa - lem.
sa - lem.
sa - lem.
sa - lem.

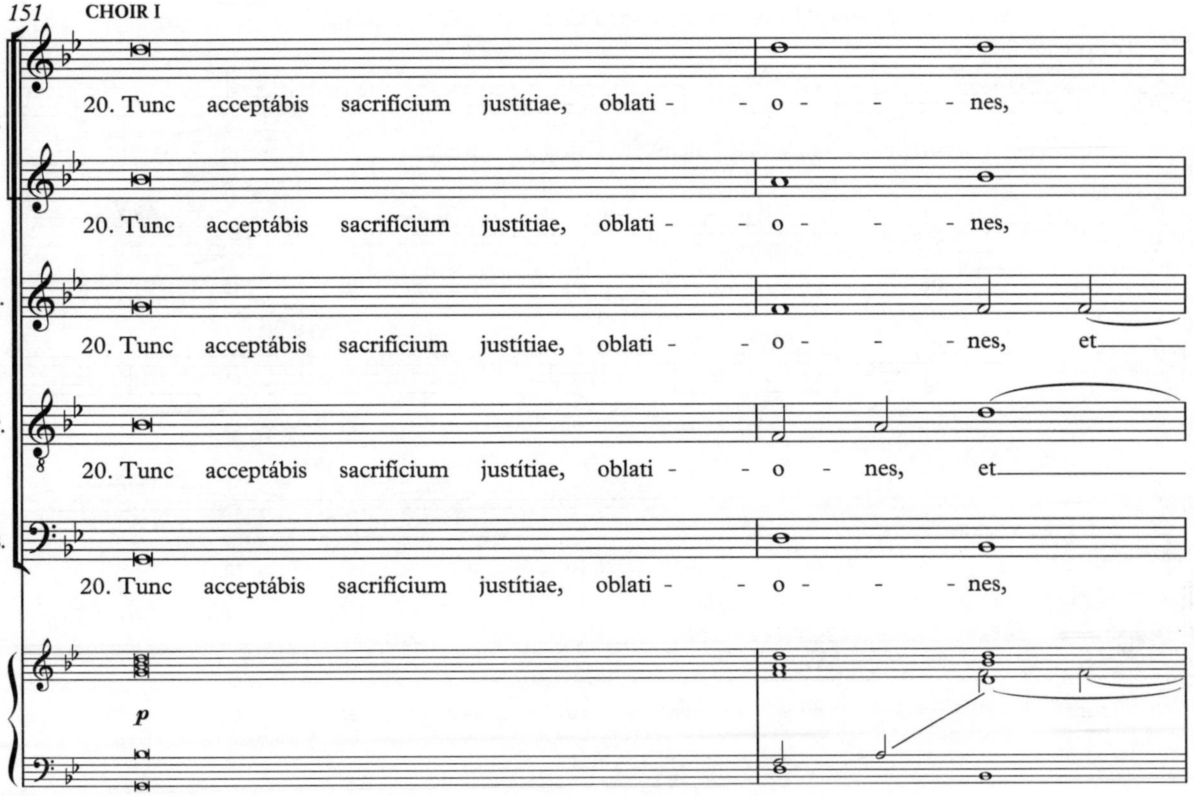

Then shalt thou be pleased with the sacrifice of righteousness, with the burnt-offerings and oblations:

**Questo ultimo Verso si canta Adagio, e Piano, smorzando a poco a poco l'Armonia.*

*'This final verse is sung slowly and softly, gradually reducing the sound.' [Instruction from Burney's edition, 1771]

159
S.
- re tu - - um vi - - - - tu - los.
- re tu - - um vi - - - - tu - los.
A.
- re tu - - um vi - - - - tu - los.
T.
- re tu - - um vi - - - - - - tu - los.
B.
- re tu - - um vi - - - - tu - los.
S.
- re tu - - um vi - - - - tu - los.
- re tu - - um vi - - - - - - tu - los.
A.
- re tu - - um vi - - - - - - tu - los.
B.
- re tu - - um vi - - - - tu - los.
ppp

2. Christus factus est

(*Jesus once for our salvation was crucified*)

Gradual for Maundy Thursday
English text by Paul England

FELICE ANERIO
(*c.*1560–1614)

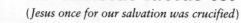

* 3/1 — o o in source

* This ♯ is in the source, but a C♮ may be thought preferable here.

† C in source

3. Otche nash

(*The Lord's Prayer*)

Old Slavonic text from the Divine Liturgy
English paraphrase by John Rutter

ANTONY ARENSKY (1861–1906)
Op. 40 no. 3

Note: See p. vii for pronunciation guide. The symbol ŏ indicates a sound closer to 'a' than to 'o'.

10
pp
ya-ko na nye-bye-ssi i na zyem-li. Khlyeb nash na-sushch-nyi dazhd nam dnyess, i ŏ-
as it is in thy hea-ven high a-bove. Give us this day our dai-ly bread, and let
ya-ko na nye-bye-ssi i na zyem-li. Khlyeb nash na-sushch-nyi dazhd nam dnyess, i ŏ-
as it is in thy hea-ven high a-bove. Give us this day our dai-ly bread, and let
ya-ko na nye-bye-ssi i na zyem-li. Khlyeb nash na-sushch-nyi dazhd nam dnyess, i ŏ-
as it is in thy hea-ven high a-bove. Give us this day our dai-ly bread, and let
ya-ko na nye-bye-ssi i na zyem-li. Khlyeb nash na-sushch-nyi dazhd nam dnyess, i ŏ-
as it is in thy hea-ven high a-bove. Give us this day our dai-ly bread, and let
14
-sta-vi nam dol-gi na-sha, ya-ko zhe i myi ŏ-sta-vlya-yem dol-zhni-kom na-shim;
all our debts be for-giv-en, as we grant for-give-ness to those whose debts are un-to us.
-sta-vi nam dol-gi na-sha, ya-ko zhe i myi ŏ-sta-vlya-yem dol-zhni-kom na-shim;
all our debts be for-giv-en, as we grant for-give-ness to those whose debts are un-to us.
-sta-vi nam dol-gi na-sha, ya-ko zhe i myi ŏ-sta-vlya-yem dol-zhni-kom na-shim;
all our debts be for-giv-en, as we grant for-give-ness to those whose debts are un-to us.
-sta-vi nam dol-gi na-sha, ya-ko zhe i myi ŏ-sta-vlya-yem dol-zhni-kom na-shim;
all our debts be for-giv-en, as we grant for-give-ness to those whose debts are un-to us.

* This bar may be omitted.

4. O Jesu Christ, meins Lebens Licht

(*Lord Jesu Christ, my life and light*)

Words by Martin Behm (1557–1622)
Translation by John Rutter

J. S. BACH (1685–1750)
BWV 118

* Transcribed from the instrumental accompaniment. Scores and instrumental parts are available on rental (see Index of Orchestrations).

* Voice parts tacent 2nd time (the ending of the motet).

27
Christ, meins Le - - bens Licht,
Christ, my life and light,
- - - - - bens Licht,
and light,
Licht, meins Le - bens Licht,
light, my life and light,
32
Mein Hort, mein
My strength, my
Mein Hort, mein
My strength, my
Mein Hort,
My strength,

37
Trost, mein Zu - - - ver - - - - -
stay, my day - - - star
Trost, mein Zu - - - ver - -
stay, my day - - - star
mein Trost, mein Hort, mein Trost,
my stay, my strength, my stay,
Mein Hort, mein Trost, mein Zu - ver - -
My strength, my stay, my day - star
sim.
41
-sicht,
bright,
-sicht, mein Hort, mein Trost, mein Zu - ver - sicht,
bright, my strength, my stay, my day - star bright,
mein Hort, mein Zu - ver - sicht,
my strength, my day - star bright,
-sicht, mein Hort, mein Trost, mein Zu - ver - sicht,
bright, my strength, my stay, my day - star bright,

46
Auf Er - den bin ich
On earth I have no
Auf Er - den bin ich nur ein
On earth I have no home or
51
Auf Er - - - den bin ich
On earth I have no
nur ein Gast, nur ein Gast, auf Er - - - den bin ich nur
home or rest, on earth I have no home or rest,
Gast, nur ein Gast, auf Er - - - - den bin ich
rest, home or rest, on earth I have no
Auf Er - den bin ich nur ein
On earth I have no home or

56
nur ein Gast
home or rest,
ein Gast, auf Er - den bin ich nur ein Gast, bin
no home or rest, on earth I have no home, have
nur ein Gast, ein Gast, auf Er - den bin ich, bin
home, no home, no home or rest, on earth I have
Gast, auf Er - den bin ich nur ein Gast, bin ich
rest, on earth I have no home or rest, have no
61
ich nur ein Gast
no home or rest,
ich nur ein Gast
no home or rest,
nur ein Gast
home or rest,

65
Und
By
70
Und
By
drückt mich sehr der Sün - den Last, der Sün -
all my grie - - - - vous sin op - pressed, by all
Und drückt mich sehr der Sün - den
By all my grie - - - - vous sin op -

75
drückt mich sehr der Sün - den
all my grie - - - - - - vous sin op - -
- - - den Last, und drückt mich sehr der Sün - - den
my sin, by all my grie - vous sin op -
Last, und drückt mich sehr der Sün - den
- pressed, by all my grie - vous sin op - -
sim.
79
Und drückt mich sehr
By all my grie - - - -
Last, und drückt mich sehr der
- pressed, by all my grie - - vous
Last, und drückt mich sehr der Sün - - - den Last,
- pressed, by all my grie - - vous sin op - pressed,
Last, und drückt mich sehr der Sün - - den
- pressed, by all my grie - vous sin op -

83
der Sün - - den Last.
- vous sin op - - - pressed.
Sün - den Last, und drückt mich sehr der
sin op - - pressed, by all my grie - vous
und drückt mich sehr der Sün - den Last,
by all my grie - - vous sin op - pressed,
Last, und drückt mich sehr der Sün - - - -
- pressed, by all my grie - vous sin
87
D.S. al Fine
(back to p. 28)
Sün - - den Last, der Sün - den Last.
sin op - pressed, by sin op - pressed.
der Sün - - - - - - - - - - - den Last.
by sin op - pressed.
- - den Last, der Sün - den Last.
op - pressed, by sin op - pressed.
D.S. al Fine
(back to p. 28)

5. Warum ist das Licht gegeben dem Mühseligen?

(Lord, why is the light vouchsafed?)

Words from the Bible and Martin Luther
Translation by John Rutter

JOHANNES BRAHMS (1833–97)
Op. 74 no. 1

* Job 3: 20–3

11
den be - trüb - ten Her - zen, den be - trüb - - ten Her - zen, und das
to the down - cast spi - rits, to the down - - cast spi - - rits, and life
Le - - ben den be - trüb - - - - - - - ten Her - zen, den be -
giv - - en to the down - - - - - - - cast spi - rits, to the
f
War - um ist das Licht ge - ge - ben dem Müh - se - li - gen, und das Le - -
Lord, why is the light vouch - safed to the wea - ry of soul, and life giv - -
f
War - um
Lord, why
f
f
15
f
Le - ben den be - trüb - - - ten Her - zen, war - um ist das
giv - en to the down - - - cast spi - rits, Lord, why is the
-trüb - ten Her - zen, den be - trüb - - - ten Her - - zen, und das Le - ben
down - cast spi - rits, to the down - - - cast spi - - rits, and life giv - en
- ben den be - trüb - - - - - - - ten Her - zen, den be - trüb - ten
- en to the down - - - - - - - cast spi - rits, to the down - cast
ist das Licht ge - ge - ben dem Müh - se - li - gen, und das Le - - ben
is the light vouch - safed to the wea - ry of soul, and life giv - - en
f

19
Licht ge - ge - ben, ge - ge - ben den be - trüb - - ten
light vouch - safed to the wea - ry, to the down - - cast
den be - trüb - ten Her - - - zen, den be - trüb - - ten Her -
to the down-cast spi - - - rits, to the down - - cast spi -
Her - zen, den be - trüb - ten, den be - trüb - - ten Her -
spi - rits, to the down - cast, to the down - - cast spi -
den be - trüb - ten Her - zen, den be - trüb - - ten, den be -
to the down - cast spi - rits, to the down - - cast, to the
dim.
23
p f
Her - - - - zen? War - um?
spi - - - - rits? Why, Lord?
- - - - - zen? War - um? War - um? Die des To -
- - - - - rits? Why, Lord? Why, Lord? Who for death
- - - - - zen? War - um? War - um? Die des To - -
- - - - - rits? Why, Lord? Why, Lord? Who for death
-trüb - ten Her - zen? War - um? War - um? Die
down - cast spi - rits? Why, Lord? Why, Lord? Who

30
p dolce
p
und kommt nicht, die des To - des war -
and death comes not, who for death are long -
dolce
p
- des war - - ten und kommt nicht, die des To - des war - -
are long - - ing, death comes not, who for death are long - -
dolce
p
- des war - ten und kommt nicht, die des To - des war -
are long - ing, and death comes not, who for death are long -
dolce
des To - des war - ten und kommt nicht,
for death are long - ing, and death comes not,
dolce

36
cresc.
f
- ten und kommt nicht, und kommt nicht, und grü - ben ihn
- ing, and death, and death comes not; they seek it like
cresc.
- ten und kommt nicht, kommt nicht, und grü - ben ihn
- ing, and death, and death comes not; they seek it like
cresc.
f
- ten und kommt, und kommt nicht, kommt nicht, und grü - ben ihn
- ing, and death, and death, death comes not; they seek it like
cresc.
f
und kommt nicht, und kommt nicht, und kommt nicht, und grü - ben ihn
and death comes not, comes not, and comes not; they seek it like
cresc.
f

41
dim. p espress.
wohl aus dem Ver - bor - ge - nen; die sich fast freu - en und sind
pre - cious trea - sure bu - ried deep; their hearts are glad, and they are
dim. p espress.
wohl aus dem Ver - bor - ge - nen; die sich fast freu - en und sind fröh - lich, sind
pre - cious trea - sure bu - ried deep; their hearts are glad, and they are joy - ful, are
dim. p espress.
wohl aus dem Ver - bor - ge - nen; die sich fast freu - en und sind
pre - cious trea - sure bu - ried deep; their hearts are glad, and they, they are
dim. p espress.
wohl aus dem Ver - bor - ge - nen; die sich fast freu - en und sind
pre - cious trea - sure bu - ried deep; their hearts are glad, and they are
dim. p espress.
46
p dolce f
fröh - lich, dass sie das Grab be - kom - men. War - um?
joy - ful, to find the grave a - waits them. Why, Lord?
p dolce f
fröh - lich, dass sie das Grab be - kom - men. War - um?
joy - ful, to find the grave a - waits them. Why, Lord?
p dolce f
fröh - lich, dass sie das Grab be - kom - men. War - um?
joy - ful, to find the grave a - waits them. Why, Lord?
p dolce f
fröh - lich, dass sie das Grab be - kom - men. War - um?
joy - ful, to find the grave a - waits them. Why, Lord?
p dolce f

53
pp
Und dem Man - ne, dess Weg ver - bor - gen ist, und Gott vor ihm den -
Why is light giv'n to him whose way is hid, and God him - self shows
p
pp
War - um? und Gott vor ihm den -
Why, Lord? and God him - self shows
p pp
War - um? Und dem Man - ne, dess Weg ver - bor - gen ist, und Gott vor ihm den -
Why, Lord? Why is light giv'n to him whose way is hid, and God him - self shows
p pp
War - um? und Gott vor ihm den -
Why, Lord? and God him - self shows
p pp

61
pp
-sel - ben be - de - - - cket,
not where his path lies,
pp
-sel - ben be - de - cket, und dem Man - ne, dess Weg ver - bor - gen ist,
not where his path lies, why is light giv'n to him whose way is hid,
pp p
-sel - ben be - de - - - cket, und
not where his path lies, and
pp p
-sel - ben be - de - cket, und dem Man - ne, dess Weg ver - bor - gen ist, und
not where his path lies, why is light giv'n to him whose way is hid, and
pp p

69
p
cresc.
cresc.
und Gott vor ihm den - sel - ben be - de - - - - -
and God him - self shows not where his path
und Gott vor ihm den - sel - ben be - de - - - - - - - - -
and God him - self shows not where his path
Gott vor ihm den - sel - - - ben be - de - - - - - - - - -
God him - self shows not where his path
Gott vor ihm den - sel - ben be - de - - - cket, be - de - - - - -
God him - self shows not where his path lies, his path
76
f
p
-cket. War - - um?
lies? Why, Lord?
- cket. War - - um? War - - - um?
lies? Why, Lord? Why, Lord?
- - cket. War - - um? War - - - um?
lies? Why, Lord? Why, Lord?
- cket. War - - um? War - - - um?
lies? Why, Lord? Why, Lord?

* Lamentations 3: 41

93
cresc.
las - set uns un - ser Herz samt den Hän-den auf - he - - ben, las - set
let us lift up our heart with our hands un - to God, let us lift
las - set uns un - ser Herz samt den Hän-den auf - he - ben,
let us lift up our heart with our hands un - to God, let
p cresc.
- mel, las - set uns un - ser Herz samt den
- vens, let us lift up our heart with our
p cresc.
Him - mel, las - set uns un - ser Herz
hea - vens, let us lift up our heart
1st BASSES
Las - set
Let us
cresc.
97
1 S. 2
uns, las - set uns un - ser Herz samt den Hän - den auf -
up, let us lift up our heart with our hands un - to
las - set, las - set uns un - ser Herz samt den
us lift, let us lift up our heart with our
A.
Hän - den auf - he - ben, las - set uns un - ser Herz
hands un - to God, let us lift up our heart
T.
samt den Hän - - den auf - he - ben, un - ser Herz samt den
with our hands un - to God, lift our heart with our
1 B. 2
uns un - ser Herz samt den Hän - den auf - he - ben zu Gott,
lift up our heart with our hands un - to God, un - to God,
2nd BASSES
Las - set uns un - ser Herz samt den Hän - den,
Let us lift up our heart with our hands,

100
rit.
-he - ben zu Gott, zu Gott im Him - - - mel.
God, un - to God, to God in the hea - - - vens.
Hän - den auf - he - ben zu Gott, zu Gott im Him - mel, Gott im Him - mel.
hands un - to God, un - to God, to God in the hea - vens, in the hea - vens.
samt den Hän-den auf - he - ben zu Gott im Him - mel.
with our hands un - to God, un - to God in the hea - vens.
Hän - den auf - he - ben zu Gott im Him - mel.
hands un - to God, to God in the hea - vens.
samt den Hän-den auf - he - ben zu Gott im Him - mel.
with our hands un - to God, un - to God in the hea - vens.
samt den Hän-den auf - he - ben zu Gott im Him - mel.
with our hands un - to God, un - to God in the hea - vens.
rit.

3. Langsam und sanft [**Slow and soft**]

* James 5: 11

108
f
-dul - det ha - ben, wir prei - sen se - lig, se - - -
-dure their tri - als, we count them bless - ed, bless - - -
f
er - dul - - - det ha - ben, wir_ prei - - sen_ se - - -
en - dure their tri - als, we_ count_ them bless - - -
f
-dul - det_ ha - ben, wir prei - sen, wir_ prei - sen se - - - lig, wir_
-dure_ their tri - als, we count them, we_ count them bless - - - ed, we_
f
-dul - - det, er - dul - - det ha - ben, wir prei - sen se -
-dure, en - dure their tri - als, we count_ them bless -
f
-dul - - - - det ha - ben, wir_ prei - sen se - - lig, wir_ prei - sen,
-dure their tri - als, we_ count them bless - - ed, we_ count_ them,
f
- det ha - ben, wir prei - sen, wir_ prei - sen se - - lig, wir prei - sen
their tri - als, we count_ them, we_ count them bless - ed, we count them
f

113
-lig, die er - dul - det ha - ben.
-ed who en - dure their tri - als.
-lig, die er - dul - det, er - dul - - - det ha - ben.
-ed who en - dure, who en - dure their tri - als.
prei - sen se - - - - lig, die er - dul-det ha - ben.
count them bless - - - ed who en - dure their tri - als.
-lig, se - - lig, die er - dul - - det ha - - ben.
-ed, bless - - ed who en - dure their tri - - als.
wir prei - sen se - lig, die er - dul - - det ha - - ben.
we count them bless - ed who en - dure their tri - - als.
se - lig, wir prei - sen se - lig, die er - dul - det ha - - ben.
bless - ed, we count them bless - ed who en - dure their tri - - als.

* In the tempo of no. 2 (bar 85)

125
p cresc.
denn der Herr ist barm-her - - zig___ und ein Er-bar - - mer, denn der
for___ the Lord God shows mer - - cy___ and has com-pas - - sion, for the
p cresc.
f
-se-hen; denn der Herr ist barm-her - zig___ und ein Er-bar - mer,
al-so, for___ the Lord God shows mer - cy___ and has com-pas - sion,
-se - - - hen; denn der Herr ist barm-her - - zig___ und
al - - - so, for___ the Lord God shows mer - - cy___ and
-se - hen, ge - se - hen, denn der Herr ist barm-her - zig
ye___ know it al - so, for___ the Lord God shows mer - cy
-hen, habt ihr ge - se - - hen, denn___ der
-so, ye know it al - - so, for___ the
habt___ ihr,___ habt ihr___ ge - se - - hen,
ye___ know, ye know___ it al - - so,
129
Herr,___ denn der Herr ist barm-her - - zig und ein Er-
Lord,___ for the Lord God shows mer - - cy and has com-
denn der Herr ist barm-her - - - - - zig und ein___ Er-
for the Lord God shows mer - - - - - cy and has___ com-
ein___ Er - bar - mer, denn___ der Herr ist barm-her - zig,
has___ com - pas - sion, for___ the Lord God shows mer - cy,
und ein Er - bar - - - - - - - - mer, denn der Herr___
and has com - pas - - - - - - - - sion, for the Lord___
Herr ist barm - her - - zig___ und ein___ Er - bar - - mer,
Lord God shows mer - - cy___ and has___ com - pas - - sion,
denn___ der Herr ist barm-her - zig, denn___ der Herr ist barm-
for___ the Lord God shows mer - cy, for___ the Lord God shows

4. Choral [Chorale]

* Martin Luther

140
-trost ist mir mein Herz und Sinn, Sanft und stil - - le.
heart and mind at last con - soled, Calm my spi - - rit.
-trost ist mir mein Herz und Sinn, Sanft und stil - - le.
heart and mind at last con - soled, Calm my spi - - rit.
-trost ist mir mein Herz und Sinn, Sanft und stil - - le.
heart and mind at last con - - soled, Calm my spi - - rit.
-trost ist mir mein Herz und Sinn, Sanft und still.
heart and mind at last con - soled, Calm spi - rit.
144
Adagio
Wie Gott mir ver - hei - ssen hat, Der Tod ist mir Schlaf wor - den.
God has made his pro - mise sure, In death we are but sleep - ing.
Wie Gott mir ver - hei - ssen hat, Der Tod ist mir Schlaf wor - den.
God has made his pro - mise sure, In death we are but sleep - ing.
Wie Gott mir ver - hei ssen hat, Der Tod ist mir Schlaf wor - den.
God has made his pro - mise sure, In death we are but sleep - ing.
Wie Gott mir ver - hei - ssen hat, Der Tod ist mir Schlaf wor - den.
God has made his pro - mise sure, In death we are but sleep - ing.
Adagio

6. Ach, arme Welt

(*Alas, vain world*)

Words of unknown authorship
Translation by John Rutter

JOHANNES BRAHMS (1833–97)
Op. 110 no. 2

Con moto
f
sf
S.
A.
1. Ach, ar - me Welt, du trü - gest mich, Ja, das be - kenn ich
1. A - las, vain world, I see your snares; With guile they take us
T.
B.
4
espress.
ei - gent - lich, Und kann dich doch nicht
un - a - wares, Yet in your power I
S. mei - - den,
A. *lan - - guish,*
T. mei - den, und kann dich
B. *lan - guish, yet in your*
7
und kann dich doch nicht mei - - - - den.
yet in your power I lan - - - - guish.
2. Du fal - sche Welt, du
2. In time, false world, your
doch, und kann dich doch nicht mei - den.
power, yet in your power I lan - guish.
11
bist nicht wahr, Dein Schein ver - geht, das weiss ich zwar, Mit Weh und gro - ssem
emp - ty show Will pass a - way, as well I know, In woe and bit - ter

15
S. Lei - - den, mit Weh und gro - ssem Lei - - - - -
A. an - - guish, in woe and bit - ter an - - - - -
T. Lei - den, mit Weh und gro - ssem Lei - den, und gro - ssem Lei - -
B. an - guish, in woe and bit - ter an - guish, and bit - ter an - -
18
f sempre
- den. 3. Dein Ehr, dein Gut, du ar - me Welt, Im Tod, in rech - ten
- guish. 3. Your pomp, your wealth last but a day; In death and need they
- den.
- guish.
f sempre
22
espress.
Nö - ten fehlt, Dein Schatz ist ei - tel fal - sches Geld, Dess hilf mir, Herr, zum
fade a - way, Your gold is naught but worth - less clay: God grant the peace I
espress.
26
rit.
dim.
p
S. Frie - den, dess hilf mir, Herr, zum Frie - - - - den.
A. cher - ish, God grant the peace I cher - - - - ish.
dim.
p
T. Frie - den, dess hilf mir, Herr, dess hilf mir, Herr, zum Frie - den.
B. cher - ish, God grant the peace, God grant the peace I cher - ish.

7. Geistliches Lied

(*Sacred song*)

Words by Paul Flemming (1609–40)
English version by John Rutter

JOHANNES BRAHMS (1833–97)
Op. 30

* Or piano, 3 or 4 hands [Brahms gives this as an alternative, but the pedal part should be played an octave lower if using only three hands.]

12
Trau - - ren, sei stil-le, wie Gott es
-tress thee; Fear no-thing, trust God's own
dau - ren mit Trau-ren, sei stil-le, wie Gott es
-press thee, dis - tress thee; Fear no-thing, trust God's own
mit Trau - - ren, sei stil-le, wie
dis - tress thee; Fear no-thing, trust
nichts nicht dau-ren mit Trau-ren, sei stil-le,
thought op - press thee, dis - tress thee, Fear no-thing,
16
fügt, so sei ver-gnügt mein Wil - le, mein Wil - - le!
will, and be thou still, my spi - rit, my spi - - rit.
fügt, so sei ver - gnügt mein Wil - - le!
will, and be thou still, my spi - - rit.
Gott es fügt, so sei ver-gnügt mein Wil - - le!
God's own will, and be thou still, my spi - - rit.
wie Gott es fügt, so sei ver - gnügt!
trust God's own will, and be thou still.

20
p
Was willst du heu - te
Heed not with care and
p
Was willst du
Heed not with
p
Was
Heed
24
f
sor - gen auf mor - gen, auf mor - gen? Der Ei - ne steht
sor - row the mor - row, the mor - row: our Fa - ther who
heu - te sor - gen auf mor - gen?
care and sor - row the mor - row:
cresc.
f
willst du heu - te sor - gen auf mor - gen, auf mor - gen? Der
not with care and sor - row the mor - row, the mor - row: our
p
cresc.
Was willst du heu - te sor - gen auf mor - gen?
Heed not with care and sor - row the mor - row:
[mf]

28
p
al - - lem für, der gibt auch dir,
all doth see shall give to thee,
f
p
steht al - lem für, der gibt auch dir,
who all doth see shall give to thee,
p
Ei - ne steht al - lem für, der gibt auch
Fa - ther who all doth see shall give to
f
p
p
steht al - lem für, der gibt
who all doth see shall give
[dim.]
[p]
32
p
der gibt auch dir das Dei - ne, das Dei - - -
shall give to thee thy por - tion, thy por - - -
p
der gibt auch dir das Dei - - -
shall give to thee thy por - - -
p
dir, der gibt auch dir das Dei - ne, das
thee, shall give to thee thy por - tion, thy
p
auch dir, der gibt auch dir das
to thee, shall give to thee thy

36
- ne.
- tion.
- ne.
- tion.
Dei - ne.
por - tion.
Dei - ne.
por - tion.
40
p
Sei nur in al - lem Han - del
From right - eous paths then range not,
p
Sei nur in
From right - eous
p
Sei nur in al - lem
From right - eous paths then

44
ohn' Wan - - - del, steh' fe - ste, was
and change not; be stead-fast, for
al - lem Han - del ohn' Wan - del, steh' fe - ste,
paths then range not, and change not; be stead-fast,
Han - del ohn' Wan - - - del,
range not, and change not:
p
Sei nur in al - lem Han - del ohn' Wan - del,
From right - eous paths then range not, and change not:
48
Gott be - - schleusst, das ist und heisst das Be - ste, das
God is just; give him thy trust for ev - er, for
was Gott be - schleusst, das ist und heisst das
for God is just; give him thy trust for
steh' fe - ste, was Gott be - schleusst, das ist und heisst das
be stead-fast, for God is just; give him thy trust for
steh' fe - ste, was Gott be - schleusst, das ist das
be stead-fast, for God is just; trust him for

52
Be - ste.
ev - er.
Be - ste.
ev - er.
Be - ste.
ev - er.
Be - ste.
ev - er.
p
A - - - - - - men,
p
A - - - -
56
molto cresc.
A - - - - - - -
molto cresc.
f
- - - men,
a - - - - - - - -
molto cresc.
A - - - - -
molto cresc.
a - - - - - - men,
[molto cresc.]
[f]

60
poco a poco dim.
-men, a - - - - - - - - - - - - - - - -
poco a poco dim.
-men, a - - - - - - - - - - - - - - -
f
poco a poco dim.
- - - - men, a - - - - - - - - -
f
poco a poco dim.
a - - - - - - - - - - - - - - - - -
[dim.]
64
p
p
- - men, a - - men.
p
p
- - men, a - - men.
p
p
-men, a - - men.
p
p
- - - - - - men, a - - men.
[p]

8. Ave Maria

(*Hail, Virgin Mary*)

The Angelic Salutation
English version by John Rutter

ANTON BRUCKNER
(1824–96)

* 'Very slow'. The German marking appears in the first edition but not in other early sources.

13
ff
Je - sus.
Je - sus.
p
ff
Je - sus, Je - sus.
Je - sus, Je - sus.
tu - - i, Je - sus, Je - sus, Je - sus.
bear - - est, Je - sus, Je - sus, Je - sus.
tu - - i, Je - sus, Je - sus.
bear - - est, Je - sus, Je - sus,
21
mf
San-cta Ma - ri - a, san-cta Ma - ri - a, san-cta Ma - ri - a,
O ho-ly Ma - ry, O ho-ly Ma - ry, O ho-ly Ma - ry,
San-cta Ma - ri - a, san-cta Ma - ri - a, ma -
O ho-ly Ma - ry, O ho-ly Ma - ry, God's
1st BASSES
2nd BASSES
Ped.
*

27
p
ma - ter De - - - - - i, o - ra pro no - - bis
God's pure Mo - - - - - ther, pray for us sin - - ners,
ma - ter De - - - - - i, o - ra pro no - - bis
God's pure Mo - - - - - ther, pray for us sin - - ners,
o - ra pro no - bis
pray for us sin - ners,
- ter De - - - - - i,
pure Mo - - - - - ther,
o - ra pro no - bis
pray for us sin - ners,
1
B.
2
- ter De - - - - - i, o - ra, o - ra pro no - - bis
pure Mo - - - - - ther, pray for us, pray for us, O
ma - ter De - - - - - i, o - ra, o - ra pro no - - bis
God's pure Mo - - - - - ther, pray for us, pray for us, O
33
dim.
S.
pec - ca - to - - - - ri - bus, nunc et in ho - ra
pray for sin - - - ners all, now and when earth - ly
A.
pec - ca - to - - - - ri - bus, nunc et in ho - ra
pray for sin - - - ners all, now and when earth - ly
unis.
T.
pec - ca - to - - - - ri - bus, nunc et in ho - ra
pray for sin - - - ners all, now and when earth - ly
unis.
B.
pec - ca - to - - - - ri - bus, nunc et in ho - ra
pray for sin - - - ners all, now and when earth - ly

39
mor - tis no - strae, mor - tis no - strae. San - cta Ma - ri - a,
life is end - ed, life is end - ed. O ho - ly Ma - ry,
mor - tis no - strae, mor - tis no - strae. San - cta Ma - ri - a,
life is end - ed, life is end - ed. O ho - ly Ma - ry,
unis.
mor - tis no - strae, mor - tis no - strae. San - cta Ma - ri - a,
life is end - ed, life is end - ed. O ho - ly Ma - ry,
mor - tis no - strae, mor - tis no - strae. San - cta Ma - ri - a,
life is end - ed, life is end - ed. O ho - ly Ma - ry,
45
o - ra pro_ no - - - - - - bis. A - - - men.
pray for us_ sin - - - - - - ners.
o - ra pro no - - - - - - bis. A - - - men.
pray for us sin - - - - - - ners.
unis.
o - ra pro_ no - - - - - - bis. A - - - men.
pray for us_ sin - - - - - - ners.
o - ra pro no - - - - - - bis. A - - - men.
pray for us sin - - - - - - ners.

9. Christus factus est

(*Christ became obedient unto death*)

Gradual for Maundy Thursday*
Translation by John Rutter

ANTON BRUCKNER
(1824–96)

* Philippians 2: 8, 9

11
pp
f
dim.
-ens u-sque ad mor - tem, mor-tem au - tem
-ent, o - be-dient un - to death, e - ven death up -
-ens u-sque ad mor - tem, mor-tem au - tem
-ent, o - be-dient un - to death, e - ven death up -
-ens u-sque ad mor - tem, mor-tem au - tem
-ent, o - be-dient un - to death, e - ven death up -
-ens u-sque ad mor - tem, mor - tem au - tem cru - - - - -
-ent, o - be-dient un - to death, e - ven death up - on
17
pp
p poco a poco cresc.
cru - - - - - cis. Pro - pter quod et De - us
-on the cross. Where - fore God hath cho - sen
cru - - - - - cis. Pro - pter quod et De - us
-on the cross. Where - fore God hath cho - sen
cru - - - - - cis. Pro - pter quod et De - us
-on the cross. Where - fore God hath cho - sen
- - - - - cis. Pro - pter quod et De - us
the cross. Where - fore God hath cho - sen

23
f
mf poco a poco cresc.
ex - al - ta - vit il - lum, pro - pter quod et De - - us
him to be ex - alt - ed, where - fore God hath cho - - sen
ex - al - ta - vit il - lum, pro - pter quod et De - - us
him to be ex - alt - ed, where - fore God hath cho - - sen
ex - al - ta - vit il - lum, pro - pter quod et De - - us
him to be ex - alt - ed, where - fore God hath cho - - sen
cresc.
ex - al - ta - vit il - lum, pro - pter quod et De - us
him to be ex - alt - ed, where - fore God hath cho - sen
27
ff
p
mf
ex - al - ta - vit il - lum et de - dit il - li no - men, et de - dit il - li
him to be ex - alt - ed; his Name is of the Fa - ther, his Name is of the
ex - al - ta - vit il - lum et de - dit il - li no - men, et de - dit il - li
him to be ex - alt - ed; his Name is of the Fa - ther, his Name is of the
ex - al - ta - vit il - lum et de - dit il - li no - men, et de - dit il - li
him to be ex alt - ed; his Name is of the Fa - ther, his Name is of the
ex - al - ta - vit il - lum et de - dit il - li no - men, et de - dit il - li
him to be ex - alt - ed; his Name is of the Fa - ther, his Name is of the

32
p poco a poco cresc.
no - men, quod est su - - per, su - - - - per,
Fa - ther, which is high - - er, high - - - - er,
p poco a poco cresc.
no - men, quod est su - - per, su - - - - per,
Fa - ther, which is high - - er, high - - - - er,
mf cresc.
no - men, quod est su - - - - per,
Fa - ther, which is high - - - - er,
p poco a poco cresc.
no - men, quod est su - - - - per, su - - - - per,
Fa - ther, which is high - - - - er, high - - - - er,
p poco a poco cresc. mf
37
ff ff p
su - per o - mne no - men, quod est su - per o - mne no - men,
high - er than all o - ther, which is high - er, high - er than all o - ther,
ff ff p pp
su - per o - mne no - men, quod est su - per o - mne, o - mne
high - er than all o - ther, which is high - er, high - er, high - er than all
ff ff p pp
su - per o - mne no - men, quod est su - per o - mne, o - mne
high - er than all o - ther, which is high - er, high - er, high - er than all
ff ff p
su - per o - mne no - men, quod est su - - per o - mne no - men,
high - er than all o - ther, which is high - - er, high - er than all o - ther,
ff ff p pp

43
mf
su - per, su - per, quod est su - - - - -
high - er, high - er, which is high - - - - -
no-men,
o - ther,
mf
quod est su - per,
which is high - er,
mf
no-men, quod est su - - - - - per, su - - - - -
o - ther, which is high - - - - - er, high - - - - -
mf
quod est su - - - - - per, su - - - - -
which is high - - - - - er, high - - - - -
mf
48
cresc. f p poco a poco cresc.
- - - - - - per o - mne nomen, su - - - - per,
- - - - - - er than all o - ther, high - - - - er,
cresc. f f
su - per o - mne no-men, quod est
high - er than all o - ther, which is
cresc. f p poco a poco cresc.
- - - per o - mne no-men, su - - - per,
- - - er than all o - ther, high - - - er,
cresc. f p poco a poco cresc.
- - - per o - - mne no-men, su - - - - per,
- - - er than all o - ther, high - - - - er,
cresc.
f
p poco a poco cresc.

53
f cresc.
ff
fff
su - per o - mne no - men, quod est su - per o - - - mne
high - er than all o - ther, high - er than all o - - - ther,
cresc.
su - per o - mne no - men, quod est su - per o - - - mne
high - er than all o - ther, high - er than all o - - - ther,
su - per o - mne no - men, quod est su - per o - - - mne
high - er than all o - ther, high - er than all o - - - ther,
su - per o - mne no - men, quod est su - per o - - - mne
high - er than all o - ther, high - er than all o - - - ther,
61
dim.
p
pp
no - men, o - mne no - men, quod est
high - er than all o - ther, which is
no - men, o - mne no - men, quod est su - - - -
high - er than all o - ther, which is high - - - -
no - men, o - mne no - men, quod est su - - -
high - er than all o - ther, which is high - - -
no - men, o - mne no - men, quod est su - - - - -
high - er than all o - ther, which is high - - - - -

69
dim.
ppp poco a poco cresc.
su - - per o - mne no - men, quod est
high - - er than all o - ther, which is
- - - per o - mne no - men, quod est su - per,
- - - er than all o - ther, which is high - er,
- - - - - per o - mne no-men, quod est su -
- - - - - er than all o - ther, which is high -
- - - - per o - mne no - men, quod est su - per o - mne
- - - - er than all o - ther, which is high - er than all
74
su - per o - mne, o - mne no - - - - - men.
high - er, high - er than all o - - - - - ther.
su - per o - - - - - mne no - - - - - men.
high - er than all o - - - - - ther.
- per, su - per o - mne, o - mne no - - - - - men.
- er, high - er, high - er than all o - - - - - ther.
no - men, o - mne, o - mne no - - - - - men.
o - ther, high - er than all o - - - - - ther.

10. Os justi

(The just man in his heart shall see wisdom)

Gradual at Mass of Doctors*
English version by John Rutter

ANTON BRUCKNER
(1824–96)

* Psalm 37: 31–2

13
dim.
sa - - - - - - pi - en - - ti - am,
wis - - - - - - dom from the Lord,
dim.
unis. p
sa - - - - - - pi - en - - ti - am, et lin - gua
wis - - - - - - dom from the Lord, his tongue will
unis.
dim.
- - - - - - - pi - en - - ti - am,
- - - - - - - dom from the Lord,
dim.
- - - - - - - pi - en - - ti - am,
- - - - - - - dom from the Lord,
dim.
p
18
p
cresc.
et lin - - gua e - jus lo - - que - tur ju -
his tongue will ev - er speak judge - ment and
cresc.
e - jus lo - - que - tur ju - di - ci - um, ju - di - ci - um, ju -
ev - er speak judge - ment and right - eous - ness, speak judge - ment and
p
poco a poco cresc.
et lin - - gua
his tongue will
poco a poco cresc.

22
mf
- di - - - - - - - - ci - um, ju - - - -
right - - - - - - - - eous - ness, and
f
- di - - - - - - ci - um, et
right - - - - - eous - ness, his
mf
et lin - - - - gua e - jus lo - -
his tongue will ev - er speak
cresc. sempre
e - jus lo - - - que - - - tur ju - di - ci - um, lo - -
ev - er speak judge - - ment and right - eous - ness, speak
mf
cresc. sempre

25
f
- di - ci - um, et lin - - - gua
right - eous - ness, his tongue will
lin - - - - gua e - jus lo - - - que - - - - tur ju -
tongue will ev - er speak judge - - - ment and
f
- que - tur, et lin - - - - gua e - - jus lo -
judge - ment, his tongue will ev - - er speak
f
- que - - tur ju - di - - ci - um, et
judge - - ment and right - eous - ness, his
f

28
dim.
p
dim.
e - - - jus, et lin - - gua e - jus lo - que - tur ju -
ev - - - er, his tongue will ev - er speak judge - ment and
p
dim.
- di - ci - um, et lin - gua e - jus lo - que - tur ju -
right - eous - ness, his tongue will ev - er speak judge - ment and
dim.
p
dim.
- que - - tur ju - di - ci - um, et lin - gua e - jus lo - que - tur ju -
judge - - ment and right - eous - ness, his tongue will ev - er speak judge - ment and
dim.
p
lin - - gua e - jus,
tongue will ev - er,
dim.
p
dim.
32
pp
mf
- di - ci - um, et lin - gua e - jus, et
right - eous - ness, his tongue will ev - er, his
pp
cresc. sempre
- di - ci - um, et lin - gua e - jus lo - que - tur ju -
right - eous - ness, his tongue will ev - er speak judge - ment and
pp
cresc.
- di - ci - um, et lin - gua e - jus lo - que - tur ju - di - ci -
right - eous - ness, his tongue will ev - er speak judge - ment and right - eous -
pp
cresc.
et lin - gua e - jus lo - que - tur ju - di - ci -
his tongue will ev - er speak judge - ment and right - eous -
pp
cresc.
mf

37
cresc.
ff
lin - - gua e - jus lo - - que - - - - - tur ju -
tongue will ev - er speak judge - - - - - ment and
mf
cresc.
ff
-di - ci - um, lo - - que - - - - - tur ju -
right - eous - ness, speak judge - - - - - ment and
mf
cresc.
ff
-um, et lin - gua e - - jus lo - que - - - - - tur ju -
-ness, his tongue will ev - - er speak judge - - - - - ment and
mf
cresc.
ff
-um, et lin - gua e - jus lo - - que - - - - - tur ju -
-ness, his tongue will ev - er speak judge - - - - - ment and
cresc.
ff
41
p
dim.
-di - - ci - um. Lex De - i e - jus in cor - de ip - si -
right - eous - ness. God's sta - tutes rule in his heart as a just
p
dim.
-di - - ci - um. Lex De - i e - jus in cor - de ip - si -
right - eous - ness. God's sta - tutes rule in his heart as a just
p
dim.
-di - - ci - um. Lex De - i e - jus in cor - de ip - si -
right - eous - ness. God's sta - tutes rule in his heart as a just
p
dim.
-di - - ci - um. Lex De - i e - jus in cor - de ip - si -
right - eous - ness. God's sta - tutes rule in his heart as a just
p
dim.

49
p cresc. ff poco a poco dim.
-us, lex De - i, lex De - - - - i e - jus in
law, God's sta - tutes, God's sta - - - - tutes rule in his
-us, lex De - i, lex De - - - - i e - jus in
law, God's sta - tutes, God's sta - - - - tutes rule in his
pp mf cresc. ff poco a poco dim.
-us, lex De - i, lex De - i, lex De - i e - jus in
law, God's sta - tutes, God's sta - tutes, God's sta - tutes rule in his
-us, lex De - i, lex De - i, lex De - i e - jus in
law, God's sta - tutes, God's sta - tutes, God's sta - tutes rule in his
pp p cresc. mf cresc. ff poco a poco dim.
56
p dim.
cor - de ip - si - us, in cor - de, cor - de, in cor - de,
heart as a just law, rule in his heart, his heart,
cor - de ip - si - us, in cor - de, cor - de, in cor - de, cor - de,
heart as a just law, rule in his heart, rule in his heart,
cor - de ip - si - us, in cor - de, cor - de, in cor - de, in cor - de,
heart as a just law, rule in his heart, his heart, his heart,
cor - de ip - si - us, in cor - de, in cor - de, in
heart as a just law, in his heart, rule in his
p dim.

★ It is recommended that the Alleluia should not be sung (see Commentary, p. 369).

11. Locus iste

(*This is God's house*)

Gradual at Mass for the dedication of a church
Translation by John Rutter

ANTON BRUCKNER
(1824–96)

23
cresc.
p
-si - bi-lis est, ir - re - pre - hen - si - bi-lis est, ir - re -
glo - ri-ous Name, wor - thy of his glo - ri-ous Name, wor - - thy
cresc.
p
ir - re - pre - hen - si - bi-lis est, ir - re - pre - hen - si - bi - lis est,
wor - thy of his glo - ri-ous Name, wor - thy of his glo - ri - ous Name,
27
mf
p
-pre - - hen - si - bi - lis est.
Lo - cus i - ste
of his glo - ri - ous Name.
This is God's house,
mf
TENORS
BASSES
p
ir - re - pre - hen - si - bi - lis est. Lo - cus i - ste a
wor - thy of his glo - ri - ous Name. This is God's house, a
32
mf
f
a De - o fa - ctus est, lo - cus i - ste a De - o
a tem - ple he has made, this is God's house, a tem - ple
mf
f
De - o fa - ctus est, lo - cus i - ste a De - o
tem - ple he has made, this is God's house, a tem - ple
37
p
cresc.
f
fa - ctus est, a De - o, De - o, De -
he has made, a tem - ple God the Lord,
p
cresc.
f
fa - ctus est, a De - o, De - o, De -
he has made, a tem - ple God the Lord,
42
pp
- o, a De - o, De - o fa - ctus est.
a tem - ple God the Lord has made.
- o,
pp

12. Magnificat

Canticle of the BVM
(Luke 1: 46–55)

attributed to
DIETRICH BUXTEHUDE (1637–1707)

†*My soul doth magnify the Lord:*

* Transcribed from the original accompaniment for strings and continuo
** Solo and tutti markings are only editorial suggestions.
† Translation from the 1662 Book of Common Prayer

and my spirit hath rejoiced in God my Saviour.

For he hath regarded the lowliness of his hand-maiden.

44
-lae su - ae: ec - ce e - nim ex hoc, ex hoc be -
TENOR [Solo]
TENOR and BASS [Soli]
ec - ce e - nim, ec - ce e - nim ex hoc be -
For behold, from henceforth
50
SOPRANOS [Tutti]
om - nes, om - nes ge - ne - ra - ti -
[Tutti]
-a - tam me di - cent om - nes, om - nes ge - ne - ra - ti -
[Tutti]
-a - tam me di - cent om - nes, om - nes ge - ne - ra - ti -
f
all generations shall call me blessed.
57
- o - nes, om - nes, om - nes ge - ne - ra - ti - o - nes.
- o - nes, om - nes, om - nes ge - ne - ra - ti - o - nes.
- o - nes, om - nes, om - nes ge - ne - ra - ti - o - nes.

65
SOPRANOS 1 and 2 [Soli]
Qui - a fe - cit mi - hi ma - gna qui po - tens est: et san - ctum
mf
For he that is mighty hath magnified me:
6 7 6♯
and holy is his Name.
71
no - - - - - - - - - - - - men e - jus,
[♯] 6 6 4 ♯ [♯]
77
et san - ctum no - - - - - - - - - - - - -
[♯] 6 4♯ [♯]
82
- - men e - - jus.
ALTO [Solo]
Et mi - - se - ri -
TENOR [Solo]
Et mi - se - ri -
BASS [Solo]
Et mi - se - ri-, mi - se - ri -
6 4 ♯ [6] 6
And his mercy is on them that fear him throughout all generations.

88
A.
-cor - di - a e - jus a— pro - ge - ni - e in pro -
T.
-cor - di - a e - jus a— pro - ge - ni - e
B.
-cor - di - a e - jus a— pro -
7 6♯ [6]
93
-ge - ni - es, in pro - ge - ni - es ti - men - - ti -
in pro - ge - - - - ni - es ti - men - - ti -
-ge - ni - e in pro - ge - ni - es ti - men - - -
[6 5] 6 4 ♯ 6
98
-bus e - - um, ti - men - - ti - bus e - - um.
-bus e - - um, ti - men - - ti - bus e - - um.
- ti - bus e - um, ti - men - ti - bus, ti - men - - - ti - bus e - - um.
6 5 4 ♯ 6 6 6 5 4 ♯

He hath shewed strength with his arm:

130
-o su - o: di - sper - sit su - per - bos, di - sper - sit su -
he hath scattered the proud in the imagination of their hearts.
136
-per - bos men - te cor - dis su - i, men - te cor - dis su - i.
143
ALTO [Solo]
De - po - su - it po - ten - tes de se - de, et ex - al -
TENOR [Solo]
mp
He hath put down the mighty from their seat: and hath exalted the humble and meek.

149
-ta - vit humi-les, et ex-al-ta - vit hu-mi-les.
-ta - vit hu-mi-les, et ex-al-ta - vit hu-mi-les.
6 4 ♯ 5 6 4 [6] 6 5 4 ♯
156 BASS [Solo]
E-su-ri-en-tes im-ple - vit bo-nis: et di-vi-tes di-
mf dolce
6 6
He hath filled the hungry with good things: and the rich he hath sent empty away.
161
-mi-sit, et di-vi-tes di-mi-sit, et di-vi-tes di-mi-sit in-
166
-a - - - - nes,
6 6 [6] [4 ♯]
171
in-a - - - -
6 ♯ 6

176
SOPRANOS 1 and 2
[Soli]
Su - sce - - - - - pit Is - ra - el
- - - nes.
He remembering his mercy hath holpen his servant Israel:
181
pu - e - rum su - um, re - cor - da - - - - - - tus, re - cor -
186
- da - - - - - - tus, re - cor - da - - - - - tus mi - se - ri -
190
- cor - di - ae su - ae, mi - se - ri - cor - di - ae su - - ae.

196
[Tutti]
S.
A.
T.
B.
Si - cut lo - cu - tus est ad pa - tres no - stros, A - bra - ham, A - bra - ham et
f
As he promised to our forefathers, Abraham and his seed, for ever.
202
se - mi - ni e - jus in sae - cu - la, A - bra - ham, A - bra - ham et
A - bra - ham, A - bra - ham et
se - mi - ni e - jus in sae - cu - la, A - bra - ham et
208
Ritornello
se - mi - ni e - jus in sae - cu - la.

Glory be to the Father,

and to the Son:

254
BASS [Solo]
glo - - - - ri - a, glo - - - - ri - a et Spi -
mf
and to the Holy Ghost;
259
-ri - tu - i San - cto, et Spi - ri - tu - i San -
264
-cto, et Spi - ri - tu - i San - - - - - - - - -
268
- - - - - - - - - - - - - - - - - cto,

* Slurs in these two bars are as given in the source.

284
S.1 [Solo]
et in saecula,
S.2 [Solo]
et in saecula,
S.
A.
et nunc, et semper,
T.
B.
et nunc, et semper,
6♯ 4 ♯
is now, and ever shall be: world without end. Amen.
289
[Tutti]
et in saecula saeculorum. Amen,
[Tutti]
saeculorum. Amen,
[Tutti]
saeculorum. Amen,
f
♯ 6 6 5 4 ♯
293
[Soli]
p
saeculorum. Amen.
[Solo]
p
saeculorum. Amen.
[Soli]
p
saeculorum. Amen.
p
6 6 5 4 ♯

13. O vos omnes

(*O ye people*)

Antiphon at 3rd Nocturn for Holy Saturday*
English version by Kenneth Sterne

PABLO CASALS
(1876–1973)

* Lamentations 1: 12

11
O vos o - mnes, qui tran - si - tis, qui tran - si - tis per vi - am, at -
O ye peo - ple that are pass - ing, pass - ing by me and see me, be -
unis.
-am, O vos o - mnes, qui tran - si - tis, qui tran - si - tis per vi - am, at -
-ing, O ye peo - ple that are pass - ing, pass - ing by me and see me, be -
16
-ten - di - te, at - ten - di - te,
-hold and see, be - hold and see,
at - ten - di - te, et vi -
be - hold and see and con -
-ten - di - te, at - ten - di - te, at - ten - di - te, et vi - de - te, at - ten - di - te, et vi -
-hold and see, be - hold and see, be - hold and see and con - sid - er, be - hold and see and con -

21
molto espr.
unis.
mp
-de - te: si est do - lor si - cut do - lor me - us,
- sid - er an - y sor - row, an - y sor - row as mine,
p molto espr.
unis.
mf
-de - te: si est do - lor, si est do - lor si - cut do - lor me - us, si est
- sid - er if there can be an - y sor - row, an - y sor - row as mine, if there
p molto espr.
unis.
mf
-de - te: si est do - lor, si est do - lor si - cut do - lor me - us, si est
- sid - er if there can be an - y sor - row, an - y sor - row as mine, if there
p molto espr.
unis.
mf
-de - te: si est do - lor, si est do - lor si - cut do - lor, do - lor me - us, si est
- sid - er if there can be an - y sor - row, an - y sor - row, an - y sor - row, if there
(mp)
p molto espr.
mf
26
mf
si est do - lor si - cut do - lor me - us, si - cut do - lor me -
an - y sor - row, an - y sor - row as mine, an - y sor - row as
do - lor, si est do - lor si - cut do - lor me - us, si - cut do - lor me -
can be an - y sor - row, an - y sor - row as mine, an - y sor - row as
do - lor, si est do - lor si - cut do - lor me - us, si - cut do - lor me -
can be an - y sor - row, an - y sor - row as mine, an - y sor - row as
do - lor, si est do - lor si - cut do - lor me - us, si - cut do - lor me -
can be an - y sor - row, an - y sor - row as mine, an - y sor - row as

31
-us, si est do - lor, si est do - - lor si - cut do - lor me - us.
mine, an - y sor - row, an - y sor - row like un - to my sor - row?
-us, si - - cut do - - lor me - - us.
mine, an - - y sor - - row as mine?
unis.
-us, si - cut do - lor me - us.
mine, an - y sor - row as mine?
-us, si - cut do - lor me - us.
mine, an - y sor - row as mine?
37
O vos o - mnes, o vos o - mnes, qui tran - si - tis per vi - - am.
O ye peo - ple, is it no - thing, is it no - thing to you, to you?
O vos o - mnes, o vos o - mnes, qui tran - si - tis per vi - - am.
O ye peo - ple, is it no - thing, is it no - thing to you, to you?
unis.
O vos o - mnes, o vos o - mnes, qui tran - si - tis per vi - - am.
O ye peo - ple, is it no - thing, is it no - thing to you?
O vos o - mnes, o vos o - mnes, qui tran - si - tis per vi - - am.
O ye peo - ple, is it no - thing, is it no - thing to you?

à M. César Franck

14. Cantique de Jean Racine

(Canticle of Jean Racine)

Words by Jean Racine (1639–99)
Translation by John Rutter

GABRIEL FAURÉ (1845–1924)
Op. 11

The accompaniment has been transcribed for strings and harp (see Index of Orchestrations).

A
13
TENORS pp
T.
No -
Our
BASSES pp
B.
Verbe é - gal au Très-Haut, no -
O di-vine Word a - bove, our
pp
16
-tre u - ni - que es - pé - ran - ce, Jour é - ter -
hope and con - so - la - tion, E - ter - nal
-tre u - ni - que es - pé - ran - ce, Jour é - ter -
hope and con - so - la - tion, E - ter - nal
19
SOPRANOS pp
S.
Nous
Our
ALTOS pp
A.
De la pai - si - ble nuit nous
The peace - ful night is past; our
-nel de la ter - re et des cieux, nous
light of the heav'ns and the earth: our
-nel de la ter - re et des cieux, nous
light of the heav'ns and the earth: our

22
S.
A.
T.
B.
rom - pons le si - len - - ce, Di - vin Sau - -
voi - ces greet the morn - - ing; Look down, O
- veur, jet - te sur nous les yeux,
Lord, and hear thy peo - ple's prayer,
25
cresc.
- veur, jet - te sur nous les yeux, Di -
Lord, and hear thy peo - - ple's prayer, Look
cresc.
cresc.
B
28
f
diminuendo
p
- vin Sau - - veur, jet - te sur nous les
down, O Lord, and hear thy peo - - ple's
f
diminuendo
p
B
f
diminuendo
p

31
yeux!
prayer!
il canto marcato
33
36
pp
39
dolce
C
Ré - pands sur nous le feu de ta
In - spire us, Lord, we pray, With the
dolce
C

42
cresc.
grâ - - ce puis - san - - te, que tout l'en - -
pow'r of thy Spi - - rit, That hell may
cresc.
[cresc.]
45
f
p subito
- fer, que tout l'en - fer fuie au son de ta voix, Dis -
flee, that hell may flee be - fore thy migh - ty word. From
f
f
p subito
48
- si - - pe le som - meil d'une â - me lan - guis -
slum - - ber wa - ken us, our wea - ry souls re -
p
Dis - si - pe le som - meil lan - - guis -
From slum - ber wa - ken us, our souls re -

51
D
S.
A.
T.
B.
mf
-san - - te, qui la con -
-vi - - ving, That we may
-san - - te, qui la con -
-vi - - ving, That we may
-san - - te, qui la con - duit à l'ou -
-vi - - ving, That we may ne - - ver for -
-san - - te, qui la con - - duit à l'ou -
-vi - - ving, That we may ne - - ver for -
54
f
-duit à l'ou - bli de tes lois,
ne - ver for - get thy laws!
-duit à l'ou - bli de tes lois, qui
ne - ver for - get thy laws! That
-bli de tes lois, qui la con -
-get all thy laws! That we may
-bli de tes lois, qui la con - -
-get all thy laws! That we may

57
f
qui la con - duit à l'ou - bli de tes lois!
That we may ne - ver for - get thy laws!
la con - duit à l'ou - bli de tes lois!
we may ne - ver for - get thy laws!
- duit à l'ou - bli de tes lois!
ne - - ver for - get all thy laws!
p
- duit à l'ou - bli de tes lois! Ô
ne - - ver for - get all thy laws! Lord
dim.
p
60
E
p
à ce peu - - ple fi -
on thy faith - ful con - gre -
Christ, sois fa - vo - ra - - ble à ce peu - - ple fi -
Je - sus Christ, have mer - - cy on thy con - gre -
E
sempre legato

63
p
Re -
Re -
-dè - - le pour te bé - - nir main - te -
-ga - - tion Now ga - - thered here in the
-dè - - le pour te bé - - nir main - te -
-ga - - tion Now ga - - thered here in the
66
p
Re - çois les chants qu'il
Re - ceive the hymns they
-çois les chants qu'il of - - fre à ta
-ceive the hymns they of - - fer to thy
-nant ras - sem - blé, à ta
sight of thy throne; to thy
-nant ras - sem - blé, Re - çois les chants qu'il
sight of thy throne; Re - ceive the hymns they

69
cresc.
of - - fre à ta gloi - re im - mor - tel - - le, Et
of - - fer to thy e - ter - nal glo - - ry; Re -
gloi - - re im - - - mor - tel - - le, Et
glo - - ry, to thy glo - - ry; Re -
gloi - - re im - mor - - tel - - le, Et
glo - - ry, to thy glo - - ry; Re -
of - fre à ta gloi - re im - - mor - - tel - - le, Et
of - fer to thy end - - less glo - - ry; Re -
72
F
f sempre
de tes dons qu'il re - tour - - ne com -
- newed by thy gifts may they go forth in

75
pp subito
-blé, Et de tes dons qu'il re -
peace, Re - newed by thy gifts may they
pp subito
-blé, Et de tes dons qu'il re -
peace, Re - - newed by thy gifts may they
pp subito
-blé, Et de tes dons qu'il re -
peace, Re - - newed by thy gifts may they
pp subito
-blé, Et de tes dons qu'il re -
peace, Re - - newed by thy gifts may they
pp subito
78
pp
-tour - - ne com - blé!
go forth in peace.
pp
-tour - - ne com - blé!
go forth in peace.
pp
-tour - - ne com - blé!
go forth in peace.
pp
-tour - - ne com - blé!
go forth in peace.
dolce

81
pp
Et de tes dons
Re - newed by thy gifts
pp
sempre dolce
84
ppp
poco rall.
qu'il re - tour - - - - -
may they go
ppp
poco rall.
pp
ppp
87
-ne com - blé!
forth in peace.

15. Panis angelicus

Words by St Thomas Aquinas (1225–74)
English text by John Rutter

(*Bread of the angel host*)

CESAR FRANCK (1822–90)
transcribed by John Rutter

*Transcribed from the original accompaniment for cello, harp and organ.

20
-num: O res mi - ra - bi - lis! man - du - cat
love: O gift most won - der - ful! Christ as our
ser - vus, et hu - mi-
all share his sa - cred
24
cresc.
f
Do - mi - num Pau - per, pau - per, ser - vus, et
sa - cra - ment: Hum - ble, low - ly, all share his
cresc.
f
cresc.
f
28
- lis,
feast;
p
cresc.
f
hu - mi - lis, pau - per, pau - per, ser - vus, et hu - mi - lis.
sa - cred feast; hum - ble, low - ly, all share his sa - cred feast.
p
cresc.
f
dim.
p
cresc.
f
33
(Ch.)
mf
Ch.
dim.
Man.

37
S. and A. unis. p cantabile
cresc.
Pa - nis an - ge - li - cus fit pa - nis
Bread of the an - gel host sent down from
T. and B. unis.
[mp]
Pa - nis an - ge - li - cus fit pa - nis ho - mi - num;
Bread of the an - gel host sent down from God a - bove;
p
Sw.
cresc.
Ped.
41
f
dim.
ho - mi - num; Dat pa - nis cae - li - cus fi - gu - ris ter - mi -
God a - bove; Bo - dy of Christ our Lord in to - ken of his
f
dim.
Dat pa - nis cae - li - cus fi - gu - ris ter - mi - num:
Bo - dy of Christ our Lord in to - ken of his love:
f
dim.
45
cresc.
-num: O res mi - ra - bi - lis! man - du - cat
love: O gift most won - der - ful! Christ as our
cresc.
O res mi - ra - bi - lis! man - du - cat Do - mi - num:
O gift most won - der - ful! Christ as our sa - cra - ment:
cresc.

S. Pau - - per et hu - - - mi - lis,
All share his sa - - - cred feast,
Do - mi - num:
sa - cra - ment:
A. Pau - per et hu - - - mi - lis,
All share his sa - - - cred feast,
Pau - - - per, pau - per, ser - - vus, et hu - mi - lis,
Hum - - - ble, low - ly, all share his sa - cred feast,
pau - - per, pau - per, ser - - vus, ser - vus, et hu - - mi-
hum - - ble, low - ly, share his sa - cred, his sa - - cred
pau - per, pau - per, ser - vus, et hu - - mi-
hum - ble, low - ly, all share his sa - - cred
- lis.
feast.
f
dim.
cresc.
Solo
rall.
ff
Sw.
a tempo
[p]
(Sw.)
pp

16. Jubilate Deo

Words from the Psalms

GIOVANNI GABRIELI
(1557–1612)

Jubilate Deo omnis terra, (*Ps. 100: 1*)
quia sic benedicetur homo
qui timet Dominum. (*Ps. 128: 5*)
Jubilate Deo omnis terra.
Deus Israel conjungat vos
et ipse sit vobiscum. (*Tobit 7: 15*)
Mittat vobis auxilium de sancto,
et de Sion tueatur vos. (*Ps. 20: 2*)
Jubilate Deo omnis terra.
Benedicat vobis Dominus ex Sion,
qui fecit caelum et terram. (*Ps. 134: 4*)
Jubilate Deo omnis terra.
Servite Domino in laetitia. (*Ps. 100: 1*)

O be joyful in the Lord, all ye lands,
for thus shall the man be blessed
that feareth the Lord.
O be joyful in the Lord, all ye lands.
May the God of Israel unite you
and himself be with you.
May he send thee help from the sanctuary,
and strengthen thee out of Sion.
O be joyful in the Lord, all ye lands.
The Lord that made heaven and earth
give thee blessing out of Sion.
O be joyful in the Lord, all ye lands.
Serve the Lord with gladness.

* The bass is original; figuring and realization are editorial (see Commentary, p. 370). Instrumental parts for this motet, doubling vocal parts, are available on rental (see Index of Orchestrations, p. 378).

7
S.
- - - ra,
- - - ra,
A.
ter - - - ra,
ter - - - ra, qui - a sic be - ne - di - ce - tur ho - mo, sic be -
T.
- - - - ra, qui - a sic be - ne - di - ce - tur ho - mo, be - ne - di - ce - tur
- - - ra, qui - a sic be - ne - di - ce - - tur ho -
B.
ter - - - ra, qui - a sic be - ne - di - ce - tur ho -
ter - - - ra, qui - a sic be - ne - di - ce - tur ho - mo
mf
4 3♮ 6 4 3 6 5 6 7 6 6 5 7 6
13
S.
Ju - bi - la - te
A.
Ju - bi -
- ne - di - ce - tur ho - mo qui ti - met Do - mi - num. Ju - bi - la - te
T.
ho - - - - mo qui ti - met Do - mi - num, Do - - mi - num.
- mo qui ti - met Do - mi - num, qui ti - met Do - mi - num.
B.
- mo qui ti - met Do - mi - num, qui ti - met Do - mi - num.
qui ti - met Do - mi - num, qui ti - met Do - mi - num. Ju - bi - la - te
f
6 5 6 5 6 5 6 6 6 6 5 4 3

19
S.
Ju - bi - la - te De - o om - - - - - - - - nis ter - -
De - o om - - - - - - - - - nis ter - -
A.
- la - te De - o om - - - - - - - - nis ter - - - - - - - - - -
De - o om - - - - - - nis ter - - - - - - - - - - -
T.
Ju - bi - la - te De - o om - - - - - - nis ter - - - - - - -
Ju - bi - la - te De - o om - - - - nis, om - - - - nis ter - -
B.
Ju - bi - la - te De - o om - - - - - - nis ter - -
De - o om - - - - - - nis, om - nis ter - -
cresc.
ff
6 5 6 4 3
25
S.
- ra. De - us, De - us Is - ra - el con - jun - gat,
- ra. De - us, De - us Is - ra - el con - jun - gat,
A.
- ra. De - us con - jun - gat, con -
- ra. De - us, De - us Is - ra - el con - jun - gat,
T.
- ra. De - us, De - us Is - ra - el con - jun - gat, con -
- ra. De - us, De - us Is - ra - el con - jun - gat,
B.
- ra. De - us, De - us Is - ra - el con - jun - gat, con -
- ra. De - us con - jun - gat, con -
mf
6 5 6 5

33
S.
con-jun-gat, con - jun - gat vos, et ip - se
con-jun-gat, con - jun - - gat vos, et ip - se, et ip - se
A.
-jun-gat, con - jun - - - gat vos, et ip - se sit vo-
con-jun-gat, con - jun - gat vos, et ip - se, et ip - se
T.
-jun-gat, con - jun - - gat vos, et ip - se
con-jun-gat, con - jun - - gat vos, et ip - se, et ip - se
B.
-jun-gat, con - jun - - - gat vos, et ip - se, et ip - se
-jun-gat, con - jun - - - gat vos, et ip - se
40
S.
sit vo-bis - cum, vo - bis - cum, sit vo-bis - cum, sit vo-bis -
sit vo-bis - cum, vo - bis - cum, sit vo-bis - cum.
A.
-bis - cum, sit vo-bis - cum, et ip-se sit vo-bis -
sit vo - bis - cum, et ip-se sit vo-bis - cum.
T.
sit vo-bis - cum, sit vo-bis - cum, et ip - se sit vo-bis -
sit vo-bis - cum, et ip - se sit vo - bis -
B.
sit vo-bis - cum, sit vo-bis - cum, sit vo-bis -
sit vo-bis - cum, sit vo-bis - cum, sit vo-bis - cum.
cresc.
f

46
S.
-cum. Mit - - - - - - - - - tat vo - - - - bis
Mit - - - - - - - - - - - tat vo - - - bis au - xi - li -
A.
-cum.
Mit - tat vo - - - - bis
Mit - - - - - - - - tat vo - - - - - bis au - xi - li -
T.
-cum.
Mit - - - - - - - tat vo - bis au - xi - li -
-cum.
Mit - - tat vo - bis au - xi - li -
B.
-cum.
Mit - - - - - - - tat vo - - - bis au - xi - li -
Mit - - - - - - - tat vo - - - - - bis
mf
6 6 4 4 3♯ ♮ ♭ 6 5
54
S.
au - xi - li - um de san - cto:
-um de san - cto: et de Si - on tu - e - a - tur
A.
au - xi - li - um de san - cto:
-um de san - cto; et de Si - on tu - e - a - tur
T.
-um de san - cto: et de Si - on tu - e - a - tur
-um de san - cto, de san - cto:
B.
-um de san - cto: et de Si - on tu - e - a - tur
au - xi - li - um de san - cto:
6 6 5 ♯ 6 5 5

62
S.
tu - e - a - tur vos, et de Si - on
vos, et de Si - on tu - e - a - tur
A.
tu - e - a - tur vos, et de Si - on, et de Si - on
vos, tu - e - a - tur vos, et de Si - on tu - e - a - tur
T.
vos, et de Si - on, et de Si - on tu - e - a - tur
tu - e - a - tur vos, et de Si - on tu - e - a - tur
B.
vos, et de Si - on
tu - e - a - tur vos, et de Si - on tu - e - a - tur
70
S.
tu - e - a - tur vos, tu - e - a - tur vos. Ju - bi - la - te De -
vos, tu - e - a - tur vos. Ju - bi - la - te De -
A.
tu - e - a - tur vos. Ju - bi - la - te De - o om -
vos, tu - e - a - tur vos, tu - e - a - tur vos. Ju - bi -
T.
vos, tu - e - a - tur vos. Ju - bi - la - te De - o om -
vos, tu - e - a - tur vos. Ju - bi - la - te De - o om -
B.
tu - e - a - tur vos. Ju - bi - la - te De - o om -
vos. Ju - bi - la - te De - o, ju - bi - la - te De -
cresc.
f

77
S.
- o om - - - - - - - - - nis ter - - - - ra.
- o om - - - - - - nis ter - ra.
A.
- nis ter - - - - - - - - - - ra. Be - ne-
- la - te De - o om - - - nis ter - - - ra. Be - ne-di -
T.
- - - - - nis ter - - - - - - - - - ra. Be - ne-
- - - nis ter - - - - - - - - ra.
B.
- - nis, om - - - nis ter - - - ra.
- o om - - - - - nis ter - - - ra. Be - ne-
mp
4 3♮
83
S.
Be - ne - di - cat vo - bis Do - - - mi -
Be - ne - di - cat vo - - bis Do - mi -
A.
-di - cat vo - bis Do - mi - nus ex Si - - - - - -
- cat vo-bis Do - - - mi - nus
T.
-di - cat vo - bis Do - mi - nus
Be - ne - di - cat vo - bis Do - -
B.
-di - cat vo - bis Do - mi - nus
6 5 7 6 ♯ 6 6 4 7 6

* Conductors may wish to shorten this, and the asterisked notes in bars 105 and 106, to ♩s.

101
S.
qui fe - cit cae - lum et ter - ram, qui fe - cit
- lum et ter - ram, qui fe - cit cae - lum,
A.
ter - - - ram, qui fe - cit cae - lum et ter - ram,
qui fe - cit cae - lum et ter - ram, qui
T.
cae - lum et ter - ram, qui fe - cit cae - lum,
qui fe - cit cae - lum, qui fe - cit
B.
qui fe - cit cae - lum, qui fe - cit cae - lum et ter - ram.
cae - lum et ter - ram, qui fe - cit
f
6 6 7 6
106
S.
cae - lum et ter - ram. Ju - bi - la - te De - o om -
qui fe - cit cae - lum et ter - ram. Ju - bi - la - te De - o om -
A.
qui fe - cit cae - lum et ter - ram. Ju - bi - la - te De - o
fe - cit cae - - lum et ter - ram. Ju - bi - la - te De - o
T.
qui fe - cit cae - lum et ter - ram. Ju - bi - la - te De - o
cae - lum. Ju - bi - la - te De - o, ju - bi - la - te
B.
Ju - bi - la - te De - o
cae - lum, qui fe - cit cae - lum et ter - ram. Ju - bi - la - te De -
7 6 5

112
S.
- - - - nis, om - - - nis ter - ra. Ser -
- - - - - - - - nis, om - nis ter - - - - - - ra. Ser -
A.
om - - - - nis ter - - - - ra. Ser -
om - - - - - - - nis ter - ra. Ser -
T.
om - - nis, om - - - nis ter - ra. Ser - vi -
De - o om - - - nis, om - nis ter - ra.
B.
om - - - - - - nis ter - - - - - - - - ra. Ser -
- o om - - - - - - nis ter - - - - - - - ra.
mf
6 6 4 3
119
S.
- vi - te Do - mi - no, ser - vi - te Do - mi - no
- vi - te Do - mi - no, ser - vi - - - te Do - - mi - no
A.
- vi - te Do - mi - no, ser - vi - te Do - mi - no
- vi - te Do - mi - no, ser - - vi - - te Do - mi - no
T.
- te Do - mi - no, ser - vi - - - te Do - mi - no
Ser - vi - - - te Do - mi - no
B.
- vi - te Do - mi - no, ser - vi - te Do - mi - no
Ser - vi - - - te Do - mi - no
cresc.
f
♮ 4 3♮ ♮ ♮ 4 3♯ ♮

* $\frac{3}{1}$ in source. Note values have been quartered from here to bar 131, in bars 138–42, and in bars 149–152.

139
S.
-ti - ti - a, in lae - ti - ti - a, ser - vi - te,
in lae - ti - ti - a, ser - vi - te,
A.
in lae - ti - - ti - a, lae - ti - ti - a, ser - vi -
-ti - ti - a, lae - ti - ti - a, ser - vi -
T.
-ti - ti - a, in lae - ti - - ti - a, ser - vi -
in lae - ti - ti - a, ser - vi- - te,
B.
-ti - - ti - a, in lae-ti-ti - a,
in lae - ti - - ti - a, in lae-ti-ti -
145
S.
ser - vi - te, ser - vi - te Do - - mi - no in lae - ti - ti -
ser - vi - te, ser - vi - te Do - mi - no
A.
- te, ser - vi - te Do - - mi - no in lae -
-te, ser - vi - te Do - - mi - no in lae - ti - ti -
T.
- - te, ser - vi - te, ser - vi - te Do - mi - no
ser - vi - te Do - mi-no in lae - ti - ti -
B.
in lae- ti - ti - a, ser - vi - te Do - mi - no in lae - ti - - ti-
-a, ser - vi - te Do - - mi - no

151
S.
-a, in lae - ti - ti - a, in lae - ti - ti - a,
in lae - ti - - ti - a, in lae - ti - ti - a, in lae -
A.
- ti - - ti - a, ser - vi - te, ser - vi - te
- a, in lae - ti - ti - a, ser - vi - te, ser - vi - te, ser -
T.
in lae - ti - - ti - a, in lae - ti - ti - a, ser - vi - te
- a, lae - ti - - ti - a, in lae - ti - ti - a, ser - vi - te Do - mi - no
B.
- a, in lae - ti - ti - a, ser - vi - te, ser -
in lae - ti - - ti - a, ser - vi - te, ser - vi - te Do - mi -
ff
6
9 8 4 3 9 8 4 3
157
S.
in lae - ti - - - - - - - - ti - a.
- ti - ti - a, in lae - ti - - - - ti - a.
A.
Do - mi - no in lae - ti - - - - - - - ti - a.
- vi - te Do - mi - no in lae - ti - - - - - - ti - a.
T.
in lae - ti - - - - - - - - ti - a.
in lae - ti - - - - - ti - a.
B.
- vi - te Do - mi - no in lae - ti - ti - a.
- no in lae - ti - - - - - ti - a.
9 8 4 3

17. O vos omnes

(*Hearken, O ye people*)

Responsory at Matins for Holy Saturday*
English version by John Rutter

CARLO GESUALDO
(*c.*1561–1613)

* Lamentations 1: 12

Note: Bars in this edition are of either four or six beats' length.

11
S.
- de - te si est do - lor, si est do -
- on me: is there sor - row, is there sor -
A.
- - - te si est do - - - lor, si est
me: is there sor - - - row, is there
T.
- te si est do - lor, si est
me: is there sor - row, is there
- de - te si est do - - lor, do - lor,
- on me: is there sor - - row, sor - row,
B.
- te si est do - - - - lor,
me: is there sor - - - - row,
p
poco a poco cresc.
16
S.
- lor, si est do - lor, si est do - lor si -
- row, is there sor - row, is there sor - row like
A.
do - - - - - lor, si est do - lor si -
sor - - - - - row, is there sor - row like
T.
do - - - - - - - lor, si est do - lor si -
sor - - - - - - - row, is there sor - row like
si est, si est do - lor si -
is there, is there sor - row like
B.
si est do - lor
is there sor - row
f
poco a poco dim.

FINE
21
2nd time: [𝄐]
S.
-cut do - lor me - us, si - cut do - lor me - us. At -
un - to my sor - row, like un - to my sor - row? Be -
A.
-cut do - lor me - us, si - cut do - lor me - - - - us. At -
un - to my sor - row, like un - to my sor - - - - row? Be -
T.
- cut do - lor me - us, si - cut do - lor me - us. At -
un - to my sor - row, like un - - to my sor - row? Be -
-cut do - lor me - us, si - cut do - lor, do - lor me - us. At -
un - to my sor - row, like un - to my sor - row, sor - row? Be -
B.
si - cut do - lor me - us. At -
like un - to my sor - row? Be -
2nd time: [𝄐] FINE
p
f
26
'Si est dolor'
D. S. al Fine
S.
- ten - - di - te, et vi - de - te
- hold and see, look up - on me:
A.
- ten - di - te, et vi - de - - - - - - - - - te
- hold and see, look up - on me:
T.
- ten - - di - te et vi - de - - - te
- hold and see, look up - on me:
- ten - di - te, at - ten - di - te, et vi - de - - - te
- hold and see, be - hold and see, look up - on me:
B.
- ten - - di - te, et vi - de - - te
- hold and see, look up - on me:
'Si est dolor'
D. S. al Fine
mf cresc.
f

18. The Cherubic Hymn

(*Izhe kheruvimyi*)

Words from the Orthodox Liturgy
English version by John Rutter

MIKHAIL GLINKA
(1804–57)

Note: See p. vii for pronunciation guide. The symbol ŏ indicates a sound closer to 'a' than to 'o'.

rit.
tai - no, tai - no ŏb - ra - zu - yu - shchye,
Ho - ly, Ho - ly, Ho - ly Lord of hosts.
tai - no, tai - no ŏb - ra - zu - yu - shchye,
Ho - ly, Ho - ly, Ho - ly Lord of hosts.
tai - no ŏb - ra - zu - yu - shchye, ŏb - ra - zu - yu - shchye,
Ho - ly, Ho - ly, Ho - ly Lord, Ho - ly Lord of hosts.
tai - no, tai - no ŏb - ra - zu - yu - shchye, ŏb - ra - zu - yu - shchye,
Ho - ly, Ho - ly, Ho - ly Lord of hosts, Ho - ly Lord of hosts.
tai - no ŏb - ra - zu - yu - shchye,
Ho - ly, Ho - ly Lord of hosts.
tai - no, tai - no ŏb - ra - zu - yu - shchye,
Ho - ly, Ho - ly, Ho - ly Lord of hosts.
cresc.
mf dim.
rit.
a tempo
i zhi - vŏ - tvŏ - rya - shchei Troi -
Bless - ed Trin - i - ty, we praise
i zhi - vŏ - tvŏ - rya - shchei Troi -
Bless - ed Trin - i - ty, we praise
i zhi - vŏ - tvŏ - rya - shchei Troi -
Bless - ed Trin - i - ty, we praise
i zhi - vŏ - tvŏ - rya - shchei Troi -
Bless - ed Trin - i - ty, we praise
i zhi - vŏ - tvŏ - rya - shchei Troi -
Bless - ed Trin - i - ty, we praise
i zhi - vŏ - tvŏ - rya - shchei Troi -
Bless - ed Trin - i - ty, we praise
a tempo

22
S.
-tsye tri - ssvya - tu - yu pyessn pri - pye -
thee, as we sing our thrice - ho - ly
A.
-tsye tri - ssvya - tu - yu pyessn pri - pye - va -
thee, as we sing our thrice - ho - ly hymn
T.
-tsye tri - ssvya - tu - yu pyessn pri - pye - va -
thee, as we sing our thrice - ho - ly hymn
-tsye tri - ssvya - tu - yu pyessn, tri - ssvya - tu - yu pyessn pri - pye -
thee, as we sing our thrice - ho - ly hymn, our thrice - ho - ly
B.
-tsye tri - ssvya - tu - yu pyessn pri - pye -
thee, as we sing our thrice - ho - ly
-tsye tri - ssvya - tu - yu pyessn pri - pye - va - yu -
thee, as we sing our thrice - ho - ly hymn to
(p) cresc.
mf
29
rit.
a tempo
S.
-va - yu - shchye, vsya - ko - ye nyi - nye zhi -
hymn to thee. Now as we draw near thy
A.
- yu - shchye, vsya - ko - ye nyi - nye zhi -
to thee. Now as we draw near thy
T.
- yu - shchye, vsya - ko - ye nyi - nye zhi -
to thee. Now as we draw near thy
-va - yu - shchye, vsya - ko - ye nyi - nye zhi -
hymn to thee. Now as we draw near thy
B.
-va - yu - shchye, vsya - ko - ye nyi -
hymn to thee. Now as we draw
-shchye, vsya - ko - ye
thee. Now as we
rit.
a tempo

* In Russian liturgical use, a solo male voice here intones on C♯ as follows: 'Vlasti vsyekh pravoslavnykh Khristian, da pŏ mnye ŏt Gospod Bogu o Tsarstvii svŏyem, vsyegda amin i prissnŏ, i vŏ vyeki vyekov.' *(By the authority of all Orthodox Christians, granted to me from the Lord God with his kingdom, so be it always and for ever, and from age unto age.')*

48
Allegro moderato
ALTOS
TENORS 1 and 2
A.
T.
Ya - ko da Tsa - rya vsyekh pŏ -
Glo - ry be to God in the
Ya - ko da Tsa - rya vsyekh pŏ - dyi - myem, ya - - - - - ko
Glo - ry be to God in the high - est, glo - - - - - ry
54
SOPRANOS
S.
A.
T.
B.
Ya - ko da Tsa - rya vsyekh pŏ - dyi - myem, da
Glo - ry be to God in the high - est, to
-dyi - myem, ya - ko da Tsa - rya vsyekh
high - est, glo - ry be to God in
da Tsa - rya vsyekh pŏ - dyi - myem, ya - ko
be to God in the high - est, glo - ry
BASSES 1 and 2
Ya - ko da Tsa -
Glo - ry be to
60
Tsa - rya vsyekh pŏ - dyi - myem, an - gyel - ski - mi nye -
God in the high - est: with the an - ge - lic
pŏ - dyi - myem, vsyekh pŏ - dyi - myem, an - gyel - ski - mi nye -
the high - est, in the high - est: with the an - ge - lic
da Tsa - rya vsyekh pŏ - dyi - myem,
be to God in the high - est:
-rya vsyekh pŏ - dyi - myem, vsyekh pŏ - dyi - myem,
God in the high - est, in the high - est:
pp

* If the English text is being used, sing normal 'alleluya'.

19. Ave maris stella

(*Hail, bright star of heaven*)

Vesper hymn, *c.* 9th century
English version by John Rutter

EDVARD GRIEG
(1843–1907)

12
cresc. molto
f
re - is: Pro - fer lu - men cae - cis, Ma - la no - stra pel - le, Bo -
bind us, Purge the sins that blind us; From all e - vil guard us, Pray
re - is: Pro - fer lu - men cae - cis, Ma - la no - stra pel - le, Bo - na
bind us, Purge the sins that blind us; From all e - vil guard us, Pray God's
re - is: Pro - fer lu - men cae - cis, Ma - la no - stra pel - le, Bo - na
bind us, Purge the sins that blind us; From all e - vil guard us, Pray God's
re - is: Pro - fer lu - men cae - cis, Ma - la no - stra pel - le, Bo - na
bind us, Purge the sins that blind us, From all e - vil guard us, Pray God's
cresc. molto
f
17
poco rit.
a tempo
dim.
p
pp
- na cun - cta pos - ce, cun - cta pos - ce. Vi - tam prae - sta
God's gifts re - ward us, God's gifts re - ward us. Make us, pure and
cun - cta pos - ce, cun - cta pos - ce. Vi - tam prae - sta
gifts re - ward us, God's gifts re - ward us. Make us, pure and
cun - cta pos - ce. Vi - tam prae - sta
gifts re - ward us. Make us, pure and
cun - cta pos - ce. Vi -
gifts re - ward us. Make
poco rit.
a tempo
dim.
p
pp
p

poco animato
23
mf cresc.
pu - ram, I - ter pa - ra tu - tum, Ut, vi - den - tes Je - sum, Sem - per
low - ly, Fol - low thee, all - ho - ly; Crown our souls' en - dea - vour, Joy with
- tam prae - sta pu - ram, Ut, vi - den - tes Je - sum, Sem - per
us pure and ho - ly; Crown our souls' en - dea - vour, Joy with
tranquillo
28
f
pp dolce
col - lae - te - mur. Sit laus De - o Pa - tri,
Christ for ev - er. Praise to God, and bless - ing,
col - lae - te - mur, col - lae - te - mur. Sit laus De - o Pa - tri,
Christ for ev - er, joy for ev - er. Praise to God, and bless - ing,

34
cresc. molto
f
dim.
Sum - mo Chri - sto de - cus, Spi - ri - tu - i San - cto; Tri - bus ho - nor
Christ our Lord con - fess - ing, With the Ho - ly Spi - rit One with thee in
Sum - mo Chri - sto de - cus, Spi - ri - tu - i San - cto; Tri - bus ho - nor
Christ our Lord con - fess - ing, With the Ho - ly Spi - rit One with thee in
cresc. molto
39
p
poco rit.
pp
più lento
u - nus, ho - nor u - nus. A - men.
me - rit, one in me - rit.
u - nus. A - men.
me - rit.

20. Ave Virgo sanctissima

(*Hail, most holy and blessed maid*)

Text of unknown authorship
Translation by John Rutter

FRANCISCO GUERRERO
(1528–99)

11
S.
- ter pi - is - - si - ma, ma - ris stel -
-ther of Christ our Lord, our gui - ding
De - i Ma - ter pi - is - - si - ma,
gen - tle Mo - ther of Christ our Lord,
A.
- - - ter pi - is - - si - ma, pi - - is - si - ma,
- - - ther of Christ our Lord, of Christ our Lord,
T.
- i Ma - - ter, De - i Ma - ter pi - is - si - ma, ma -
gen - tle Mo - - ther, gen - tle Mo - ther of Christ our Lord, our
B.
- ma, De - i Ma - - - ter pi - is - si - ma, ma -
maid, gen - tle Mo - - - ther of Christ our Lord, our
cresc.
16
S.
- la, ma - ris stel - la cla - ris - - si - ma.
star, our gui - ding star in splen - - dour bright.
ma - ris stel - la, ma - ris stel - la cla -
our gui - ding star, our gui - ding star in
A.
ma - ris stel - la cla - ris - si - ma, ma - ris stel - la cla - ris - si - ma,
our gui - ding star in splen - dour bright, our gui - ding star in splen - dour bright,
T.
- ris stel - - la cla - ris - si - ma, cla - ris - - si - ma, ma -
gui - - ding star in splen - dour bright, in splen - - dour bright, our
B.
- ris stel - la, ma - ris stel - la cla - ris - si - ma.
gui - ding star, our gui - - ding star in splen - dour bright.
mf

21
S.
Sal - - - - - - ve,
Hail thou,
-ris - si - ma. Sal - - -
splen - dour bright. Hail
A.
— cla - ris - - - - - - - si - ma. Sal - - - - -
— in splen - - - - - - - dour bright. Hail
T.
-ris stel - la cla - ris - si - ma. Sal - - - - - ve, sal - ve sem -
gui - ding star in splen - dour bright. Hail thou, hail thou Vir -
B.
— Sal - - - - - - - - - ve, sal - - ve,
— Hail thou, hail thou,
dim.
mp
27
S.
sal - - - - ve, sal - - -
hail thou, hail
- - ve, sal - - - - ve,
thou, hail thou,
A.
- ve, sal - - - ve, sal - - - - - - ve, sal-
— thou, hail thou, hail thou, hail
T.
- per glo - ri - o - - sa, sal - - - ve, sal - - - - -
- gin ev - er glo - - rious, hail thou, hail
B.
sal - - ve, sal - - - - ve, sal - ve sem - per glo - ri - o -
hail thou, hail thou, hail thou Vir - gin ev - er glo -
cresc.
mf
cresc.
f

33
S.
- ve sem - per glo - ri - o - - - sa,
thou Vir - gin ev - er glo - - - rious,
sal - - - - ve sem - per glo - ri - o - - - sa,
hail thou Vir - gin ev - er glo - - - rious,
A.
- - ve sem - per glo - - - ri - o - - - sa, mar - ga -
thou Vir - gin ev - - - er glo - - - rious, like a
T.
- ve, sal - ve sem - per glo - ri - o - - sa, sal - ve sem - per glo - ri - o - sa,
thou, hail thou Vir - gin ev - er glo - - rious, hail thou Vir - gin ev - er glo - rious,
B.
- sa, glo - ri - o - sa, sal - ve sem - per glo - ri - o - sa,
- rious, ev - er glo - rious, hail thou Vir - gin ev - er glo - rious,
dim.
mf
espress.

39
S.
mar - ga - ri - ta pre - ti - o - sa, pre - ti - o -
like a pre - cious pearl thou shi - nest, thou shi - -
mar - ga - ri - ta pre - ti -
like a pre - cious pearl thou
A.
- ri - ta pre - ti - o - - - sa, pre - ti - - - - - - o - -
pre - cious pearl thou shi - - - nest, thou shi - - - - - - -
T.
mar - ga - ri - ta pre - - - ti - o - - - sa, pre - ti -
like a pre - cious pearl thou shi - - - nest, thou shi -
B.
mar - ga - ri - ta pre - ti - o - sa, mar - ga - ri - ta pre - ti - o - -
like a pre - cious pearl thou shi - nest, like a pre - cious pearl thou shi -

44
S.
A.
T.
B.
- - sa, mar - - ga - ri - ta pre - ti - o - sa,
- - nest, like a pre-cious pearl thou shi - nest,
-o - sa, pre - ti - o - - sa, mar - - ga -
shi - nest, thou shi - - - - nest, like a
- - sa, mar - ga - ri - ta pre - ti - o - sa, mar - ga - ri - ta pre - ti -
- - nest, like a pre - cious pearl thou shi - nest, like a pre- cious pearl thou
- o - sa, pre - ti - o - - - - sa, mar - ga - ri - ta pre - ti - o -
- - nest, thou shi - - - - - nest, like a pre - cious pearl thou shi -
- - sa,
- - nest,
dim.
mp
49
si - - cut li - li - um for - mo - - sa,
fair - er than the li - ly art thou,
-ri - ta pre - ti - o - sa, si - - cut li - li -
pre-cious pearl thou shin - est, fair - er than the
- o - sa, mar - ga - ri - ta pre - - ti - - o - sa,
shi - nest, a pre - cious pearl thou shi - - nest,
-sa, pre - ti - o - - - sa, si - cut li - - li - -
-nest, thou shi - - - nest, fair - er than the li - -
mar - ga-ri - ta pre - ti - o - sa, si - cut li - li - um for-mo -
like a pre-cious pearl thou shi - nest, fair - er than the li - - ly art

54
S.
si - cut li - li - um for - mo - sa, ni - tens,
fair - er than the li - ly art thou, love - ly
- um for - mo - - sa, si - - cut li - li - um for - mo - sa,
li - ly art thou, fair - - er than the li - ly art thou,
A.
si - cut li - - li - um for - - mo - - sa, ni -
fair - er than the li - ly art thou, art thou, love -
T.
-um for - mo - sa, ni - tens, o - lens ve -
- ly, fair - er art thou, love - ly as a rose
B.
- - sa, si - cut li - - li - um for - mo - sa, ni -
thou, fair - er than the li - ly art thou, love -
cresc.
mf
59
S.
o - lens ve - lut ro - - - - - - - sa, ni - tens, o - lens
as a rose in fra - - - - - grant bloom, love - - ly as a
ni - tens, o - lens ve - lut ro - - - - - -
love - ly as a rose in fra - - - - - grant
A.
-tens, o - lens ve - lut ro - sa, ve - lut ro - - - sa, ni -
- ly as a rose in bloom, love - ly as a rose, love -
T.
- lut ro - - sa, ve - lut ro - sa, ni - tens, o - lens ve - lut
in fra - grant bloom, fra - grant bloom, love - ly as a rose in
B.
- tens, o - lens ve - lut ro - - - sa, ve - - - - - lut ro -
- ly as a rose in fra - - grant, fra - - - - grant
cresc.
f dolce
dim.

64
S.
ve - lut ro - - - - - - - - sa, ni - tens, o - lens ve -
rose in fra - - - - - - grant bloom, love - ly as a rose in
- sa, ni - - tens, o - lens ve - lut ro - - - - - - - - - sa,
bloom, love - ly as a rose in fra - - - - - - - grant bloom,
A.
- tens, o - lens ve - lut ro - - - - sa, ni - tens, o - lens ve - lut ro -
- ly as a rose in fra - - grant bloom, love - ly as a rose in fra - grant
T.
ro - sa, ve - lut ro - - - sa, ni - tens, o - lens ve - lut ro -
bloom, a rose in fra - - grant bloom, love - ly as a rose in fra -
B.
- sa, ni - tens ve - lut ro - sa, ni -
bloom, love - ly as a rose in bloom, love -
mf
dim.
69
S.
- lut ro - sa, ve - lut ro - sa.
fra - - grant bloom, in fra - grant bloom.
ni - tens, o - lens ve - - lut ro - sa.
love - ly as a rose in fra - - grant bloom.
A.
- sa, ni - tens, o - lens ve - lut ro - - - sa.
bloom, love - ly as a rose in fra - - grant bloom.
T.
- - sa, ve - - - lut ro - sa.
- grant bloom, a rose in fra - grant bloom.
B.
- - tens ve - lut ro - - - sa, ve - lut ro - - sa.
- ly as a rose in fra - - grant bloom, in fra - - grant bloom.
mp
dim.
p

21. Pater noster

(The Lord's Prayer)

Matthew 6: 9–13

JACOB HANDL (Gallus)
(1550–91)

Our Father, which art in heaven,

Note: In view of Handl's explicit division of the eight voices into two choirs, antiphonal layout (SSAA – TTBB) is recommended.

Hallowed be thy Name.

18
S.
A.
T.
B.
san-cti-fi-ce-tur no-men tu-um;
ad-
ad-ve-ni-at re-gnum tu-um;
Thy kingdom come.
25
-ve-ni-at re-gnum tu-um;
fi-at vo-lun-tas tu-a,
si-
Thy will be done, in earth as it is in heaven.

Give us this day our daily bread.

And forgive us our trespasses (debts), *as we forgive them that trespass against us.*

And lead us not into temptation;

69
S.
in ten-ta - ti - o - nem; sed li - be - ra nos a ma - - lo.
in ten-ta - ti - o - - nem, sed li - be - ra nos a ma - - lo.
A.
in ten - ta - ti-o - - nem; sed li - be - ra nos a ma - - lo.
in ten-ta - ti-o-nem; sed li - be - ra nos a ma - lo.
T.
-du-cas in ten - ta - ti - o - nem; sed li - be-
-du-cas in ten - ta - ti - o - nem; sed li - be-
B.
-du-cas in ten - ta - ti - o - nem; sed li - be-
-du-cas in ten - ta - ti - o - nem; sed li - be-
dim.
But deliver us from evil.
75
S.
A - - - - men, a - - men, a -
A - - - - - - - men, a - - men,
A.
A - men, a - -
A - - men, a - - men,
T.
-ra nos a ma - lo. A - - - - - men, a -
-ra nos a ma - lo. A - - - men, a -
B.
-ra nos a ma - lo. A - - men,
-ra nos a ma - lo. A - - men,
p e dolce
cresc.
mp

80
S.
-men, a - - - - - - - - - men, a - men,
a - men, a - - - - - - men, a - - men, a -
A.
-men, a - men, a - - men,
a - men, a - men, a - men,
a - - men,
a - -
T.
- men, a - - - men, a -
- - men, a - - - men, a -
B.
a - - men, a - - men,
a - - men, a - - men,
cresc.

85
S.
a - - - - - men, a - - - men, a - - men.
-men, a - - - - - men, a - - - - - men.
A.
a - - - - men, a - - - - - - - - men.
-men, a - - - - - - - men, a - men.
T.
- - men, a - - - - - - men.
- men, a - - men, a - - - men.
B.
a - - men, a - - - - - men, a - - men.
a - - men, a - - - - men, a - - - - men.
mf

22. Dixit Maria

(*Thus answered Mary*)

Luke 1: 38
Translation by John Rutter

HANS LEO HASSLER
(*c.* 1564–1612)

10
-lum, di - xit Ma - ri - a ad an - - - - ge - lum, di -
word, thus an-swered Ma - ry the an - - - - gel's word, thus
- ge - lum, di - xit Ma - ri - - a ad an - ge - lum, di - xit
- gel's word, thus an-swered Ma - - ry the an - gel's word, thus an -
an - ge - lum, di - xit Ma - ri - - a ad an - - - - ge - lum, ad an - ge -
an - gel's word, thus an-swered Ma - ry the an - - - - gel's word, the an - gel's
- ge - lum, di - xit Ma - ri - a ad an -
- gel's word, thus an-swered Ma - ry the an -
15
-xit Ma - ri - a ad an - - - ge - lum, ad an - - - ge -
an-swered Ma - ry the an - - - gel's word, thus an - - - swered
Ma - ri - a ad an - ge - lum, di - xit Ma - ri -
- swered Ma - ry, thus an - swered she, thus an - - swered Ma -
-lum, di - xit Ma - ri - a ad an - - - - ge -
word, thus an-swered Ma - ry the an - - - - gel's
- - ge - lum, di - xit Ma - ri -
- - gel's word, thus an - swered Ma -

20
-lum, ad an - - - - - ge - lum: Ec - ce an - cil - la Do -
she the an - - - - - gel's word: Be - hold the hand-maid of
- a ad an - ge - lum, ad an - ge-lum: Ec - ce an - cil - la Do -
- ry the an - gel's word, the an - gel's word: Be - hold the hand-maid of
- lum, ad an - - ge - lum: Ec - ce an-cil - la Do - -
word, the an - - gel's word: Be - hold the hand - maid of
- a ad an - - - ge - lum: Ec - ce an - cil - la Do -
- ry the an - - - gel's word: Be - hold the hand-maid of
p dolce
25
- mi - ni, ec - - ce an - cil - la Do - - mi - ni, fi - -
the Lord, be - - hold the hand-maid of the Lord; if
- mi - ni, ec - - ce an - cil - la Do - - mi - ni, fi - - at
the Lord, be - - hold the hand-maid of the Lord; if God
- mi - ni, ec - ce an - cil - la Do - - mi - ni, fi - - -
the Lord, be - hold the hand - maid of the Lord; if
- mi - ni, ec - ce an - cil - la Do - - mi - ni,
the Lord, be - hold the hand-maid of the Lord,
mp
cresc.

31
-at mi- - - hi se-cun-dum ver-bum tu-
God wills it, so be it as thou say-
mi- - hi, fi- at mi- hi se-cun- dum ver-bum tu- -
wills it, if God wills it, so be it as thou say - -
-at mi- - - - - hi se-cun- dum ver- bum tu-
God wills it, so be it as thou say-
fi- - at mi- hi
if God wills it,
mf
35
-um, se-
-est, so
-um, se-cun-dum ver- bum tu- - um, se-cun-dum ver-bum tu- -
-est, so be it as thou say- - est, so be it as thou say- -
-um, se- cun- dum ver-bum tu- - - um, ver - bum tu - um, se-
-est, so be it as thou say- - - est, as thou say - est, so
se-cun-dum ver- bum tu- - um, se-cun-dum ver-bum tu- -
so be it as thou say- - est, so be it as thou say- -
p subito

D. S. (back to p. 161)
39
1st time
-cun - dum ver - bum tu - um, se - cun - dum ver - bum tu - - um.
be it as thou say - est, so be it as thou say - - est.
- - - - - um, se - cun - dum ver - - bum tu - - - um.
- - - - - est, so be it as thou say - - - est.
-cun - dum ver - bum tu - um, se - cun - dum ver - bum tu - - - um.
be it as thou say - est, so be it as thou say - - - est.
- - um, se - cun - dum ver - - bum tu - um.
- - est, so be it as thou say - est.
D. S. (back to p. 161)
1st time
cresc.
mf
42b
2nd time
tu - - um, se - cun - dum ver - bum tu - um.
say - - est, so be it as thou say - est.
tu - um, se - cun - dum ver - - bum tu - - um.
say - est, so be it as thou say - - est.
tu - - - um, se - cun - dum ver - bum tu - um.
say - - - est, so be it as thou say - est.
- bum tu - um, se - cun - dum ver - - - - - bum tu - um.
thou say - est, so be it as thou say - est.
2nd time
poco f

23. Crux fidelis

(*Cross most faithful*)

Words attributed to Venantius Fortunatus (*c.* 530–609)
Translation by John Rutter

JOHN IV, King of Portugal
(1604–56)

11
sil - va ta - lem pro - fert, Fron - de, flo - re,
grew there one so bless - ed, Branch - es, blos - soms
sil - va ta - lem pro - fert, Fron - de, flo - re
grew there one so bless - ed, Branch - es, blos - soms
sil - va ta - lem pro - fert, Fron - de, flo - re,
grew there one so bless - ed, Branch - es, blos - soms
sil - va ta - lem pro - fert, Fron - de, flo - re,
grew there one so bless - ed, Branch - es, blos - soms
cresc.
mp
p
16
ger - mi - ne: Dul - ce lig - num,
green and fair: Sweet - est wood,
ger - mi - ne: Dul - ce lig - num,
green and fair: Sweet - est wood,
ger - mi - ne: Dul - ce lig - num,
green and fair: Sweet - est wood,
ger - mi - ne: Dul - ce lig - num,
green and fair: Sweet - est wood,
mp
p

21
dul - ces cla - vos, Dul - ce
sweet - est nails, Sweet - est
dul - ces cla - vos, Dul - ce
sweet - est nails, Sweet - est
dul - ces cla - vos, Dul - ce
sweet - est nails, Sweet - est
dul - ces cla - vos, Dul - ce
sweet - est nails, Sweet - est
p
26
pon - dus su - sti - net. A - men.
bur - den thou dost bear.
pon - dus su - sti - net. A - men.
bur - den thou dost bear.
pon - dus su - sti - net. A - men.
bur - den thou dost bear.
pon - dus su - sti - net. A - men.
bur - den thou dost bear.
cresc.
mp
p
pp

24. Ave Maria

Words of unknown authorship

JOSQUIN DESPREZ
(*c.*1440–1521)

* The alto and tenor parts being similar in range, conductors may wish to consider assigning both of them to a mixture of altos and tenors.

12
Vir - go se - re - na, se - re-na.
Vir - go se - re - na.
cum, Vir - go se - re - na.
mi-nus te - cum, Vir - go se - re -
cresc.
mf
dim.
fair virgin.
16
A-ve cu-jus con-cep - ti-o, So -
A-ve cu-jus con-cep - ti - o, cu-jus con - cep-ti-o, So -
A-ve cu-jus con-cep - ti-o, So -
na. A-ve cu-jus con-cep - ti - o, So -
mp
mf
Hail to you whose conception,
full
21
le-mni ple - na gau-di-o, Cae - le - sti - a, ter - re - stri - a, No -
le-mni ple - na gau-di-o, Cae-le-sti-a, ter - re-stri-
le-mni ple - na gau-di-o, Cae-le - sti - a, ter - re - stri - a, No - va
le-mni ple - na gau-di-o, Cae-le - sti - a, ter-re - stri - a, No -
cresc.
of holy joy,
fills heaven and earth with new rejoicing.

25
-va re - plet lae - - ti - - ti - a. A - ve cu-jus na -
- a, No-va re - - plet lae - - ti - ti - a, lae-ti - ti - a. A - ve cu-jus
re - plet lae - - ti - - - ti - a.
-va re - plet lae - ti - - - - ti - a.
f
dim.
mp
Hail to you whose birth we celebrated,
29
- ti - vi-tas, na-ti - - vi-tas Ut lu-ci-fer lux
na-ti - - - - vi - tas Ut
No - stra fu - it so-le-mni-tas, so-le - mni-tas,
No-stra fu-it so-le - - - - mni - tas,
mf
più marcato
like the day-star rising,
34
o-ri - ens Ve - rum so - lem prae-ve - - -
lu - ci - fer lux o-ri - ens Ve-rum so - lem prae - ve - - - - ni -
Ut lu - ci - fer lux o-ri - ens Ve - rum so - lem prae - ve - -
Ut lu - ci - fer lux o - ri - - ens Ve - rum so -
cresc.
f
foretelling the true Sun.

38
- - - - ni-ens. A-ve pi-a hu-mi - li - tas,
-ens. A-ve pi-a hu-mi - - li-tas,
- - - - ni - ens. Si-ne vi-ro fe-cun-
-lem prae - ve - ni - ens. Si-ne vi-ro fe-cun-
dim.
mp legato
Hail, holy and humble one,
fruitful without a man,
42
Cu - jus an-nun-ci-a - ti - o
Cu - jus an-nun-ci-a - ti-o
- di - tas, No - stra fu - it sal -
- - di-tas, No - stra fu - it sal-
you whose annunciation was our salvation.
46
[𝅗𝅥. = 𝅗𝅥 of preceding]
A-ve ve-ra vir - gi - ni-tas, Im-ma-cu -
A-ve ve-ra vir - gi - ni-tas, Im-ma-cu -
-va - - - ti-o. A-ve ve-ra vir-gi - ni-tas, Im-ma -
- va - - ti - o. A-ve ve-ra vir - gi - ni-tas, Im-ma-cu -
poco cresc.
mf
mp
Hail, true virginity, spotless chastity,

★ Some sources have a ♩ rest after this note (making a 3/4 bar).

53
-la - ta ca - sti - tas, Cu - jus pu - ri - fi - ca - ti - o No - stra fu - it pur -
-la - ta ca - sti - tas, Cu - jus pu - ri - fi - ca - ti - o No - stra fu - it pur-ga -
-cu-la - ta ca - sti-tas, Cu-jus pu-ri - fi-ca - ti - o No-stra fu-it pur -
-la - ta ca - sti - tas, Cu - jus pu - ri - fi - ca - ti - o No - stra fu - it pur -
mp
cresc.
mf
whose purification cleansed us also.
62
-ga - ti - o. A - ve prae - cla - ra om - ni - bus
- ti - o, pur - ga - ti - o. A - ve prae - cla - ra om - ni -
-ga - ti - o. A - ve prae - cla -
-ga - ti - o. A - ve prae - cla - ra
dim.
mp
mf
Hail to you who excel in all the angelic virtues,
67
An - ge - li - cis vir - tu - ti - bus,
-bus An - ge - li - cis vir - tu - ti -
- ra om - ni - bus An - ge - li - cis
om - ni - bus An - ge - li - cis vir -

71
Cu - jus fu - it as - sum - pti - o
-bus, Cu - jus fu - it as - sum - - - -
vir - tu - ti - bus, Cu - jus fu - it as - sum - pti -
-tu - - - ti - bus, Cu - jus fu - it as - sum - pti -
you whose assumption glorified us also.
75
No - stra glo - ri - fi - ca - ti - o.
-pti - o No - stra glo - ri - fi - ca - ti - o, glo - ri - fi - ca - ti -
-o No - stra glo - ri - fi - ca - ti -
-o No - stra glo - ri - fi - ca - ti -
79
O Ma - ter De - i, Me - men - to me - i. A - men.
-o. O Ma - ter De - i, Me - men - to me - i. A - men.
-o. O Ma - ter De - i, Me - men - to me - i. A - men.
-o. O Ma - ter De - i, Me - men - to me - i. A - men.
mp
p
O Mother of God, remember me.

25. Adoramus te, Christe

(Jesu, Saviour, we adore thee)

Antiphon at Feasts of the Holy Cross
Translation by John Rutter

ORLANDE DE LASSUS
(1532–94)

Note: The original clef combination suggests performance by SSAT, at a higher pitch than given here.

10
- bi, qui - - a per tu - am san -
- ways, for thou, who death's dark tor - -
- bi, qui - a per tu - am san - - ctam, per
- ways, for thou, who death's dark tor - - ment, who
- bi, qui - a per tu - am san - ctam cru -
- ways, for thou, who death's dark tor - ment suf - -
qui - - a per tu - am san - ctam cru -
for thou, who death's dark tor - ment suf - -
mp
cresc.
mf
15
- ctam cru - - - cem re - de - mi - - sti mun -
- ment suf - - - fered, by thy cross re - deemed
tu - am san - ctam, per tu - am san - ctam cru - cem re - - de - mi - sti
death's dark tor - ment, who death's dark tor - ment suf - fered, by thy cross re -
- cem, per tu - am san - ctam cru - cem re - de - mi - sti mun -
- fered, who death's dark tor - ment suf - fered, by thy cross re - deemed
- cem, per tu - am san - ctam cru - cem re - de - mi - sti
- fered, who death's dark tor - ment suf - fered, by thy cross re -
cresc.
poco f
mf

20
- dum. Do - mi - ne, mi - se - re - re no - - - -
us. Lord, we pray, have mer - cy up - on
mun - dum. Do - - mi - ne, mi - se - re - re no -
-deemed us. Lord, we pray, have mer - cy up - - - - on
- - dum. Do - - mi - ne, mi - se-re-re no - - -
us. Lord, we pray, Lord, we pray, have mer - - -
mun - dum. Do - - mi - ne, mi - se - re - re no - - -
-deemed us. Lord, we pray, have mer - cy up - on
mp
25
-bis, mi - se - re - re no - - - bis, mi - se - re-re no - bis.
us, have mer - cy up - on us: Lord, have mer-cy on us.
-bis, mi - se - re - re no-bis, mi - se-re - re no - bis.
us, have mer - cy up - - - on us: Lord, have mer - cy on us.
-bis, mi - se-re-re no - - - bis, mi - se - re-re no - bis.
-cy, Lord, we pray, have mer - - - cy: Lord, have mer-cy on us.
-bis, mi - se - re - re no - - bis, mi - se - re-re no - bis.
us, have mer - cy up - on us: Lord, have mer-cy on us.
più f
mf
mp
p

26. Ave verum Corpus

(*Hail, true Body*)

14th-century Eucharistic hymn
English version by John Rutter

ORLANDE DE LASSUS
(1532–94)

6
S.
de Ma - - ri - - a Vir - - gi - ne:
Born of Ma - - - - ry, Vir - - gin maid,
de Ma - ri - - - - a Vir - - gi - ne:
Born of Ma - - - - ry, Vir - - gin maid,
A.
de Ma - ri - - - - a Vir - - gi - ne: Ve -
Born of Ma - - - ry, Vir - - gin maid, Who
T.
de Ma - ri - - - - a Vir - gi - ne: Ve -
Born of Ma - - - ry, Vir - gin maid, Who
De Ma - ri - - a, de Ma - ri - a Vir - - gi - ne: Ve - re
Born of Ma - ry, of Ma - ry, blest Vir - - gin maid, Who the
B.
De Ma - ri - - - a Vir - - gi - ne: Ve -
Born of Ma - - - ry, Vir - - gin maid, Who
p
mp
cresc.
mf
mp
11
in cru - ce pro
By thy cross for
in cru - ce
By thy cross
- re pas - sum, im - mo - la - - - - tum in cru - ce
the price of our sal - va - - - - tion By thy cross
- re pas - - sum, im - - mo - la - - tum:
the price of our sal - va - - tion
pas - - sum, im - mo - la - - - - tum:
price of our sal - va - - - - - tion
- re pas - sum im - mo - la - - - - tum:
the price of our sal - va - - - - tion
(mp)

16
S.
ho - - - - - mi - ne:
us hast paid:
pro ho - - mi - ne:
for us hast paid:
A.
pro ho - - - - - - mi - ne:
for us hast paid:
T.
Cu - jus la - tus per - - -
From whose bo - dy, pierced
Cu - jus la - tus per - fo -
From whose bo - dy, pierced
B.
Cu - jus la - tus per - -
From whose bo - - dy, pierced
20
S.
un - - da flu - - - xit san - gui - ne, san -
Flowed the wa - - ter and the blood, and
un - - da flu - - - xit, un - - da
Flowed the wa - - - ter, flowed, flowed
A.
un - - da flu - xit san - - gui - ne, un - da
Flowed the wa - ter and the blood, flowed the
T.
- fo - ra - - tum un - - - da flu - - - xit san -
and bro - - ken Flowed the wa - - - ter and
- ra - - - - tum un - - da flu - xit
and bro - - - - ken Flowed the wa - ter
B.
- fo - ra - - tum un - - - da flu - - - - xit
and bro - - ken Flowed the wa - - - - ter
legato e dolce
cresc.
mf

24
S.
- - gui - ne. E - sto no - - bis prae - gu - sta -
the blood. Through thy trial and bit - ter an -
flu - xit san - gui - ne. E - sto no - bis prae - gu - sta -
wa - ter and the blood. Through thy trial and bit - ter an -
A.
flu - xit san - gui - ne. E - sto no - bis prae - gu - sta -
wa - ter and the blood. Through thy trial and bit - ter an -
T.
- gui - ne.
the blood.
san - gui - ne. E - sto no - bis prae - gu -
and the blood. Through thy trial and bit - ter
B.
san - gui - ne.
and the blood.
mp
29
S.
- - - - tum. O
- - - - guish Most
- - - - tum.
- - - - guish
A.
- - - - tum in mor - tis ex - a - mi -
- - - - guish, In death's hour be thou our
T.
In mor - tis ex - a - mi - ne.
In death's hour be thou our food.
- sta - - - tum in mor - tis ex - a - mi - ne.
an - - - guish In death's hour be thou our food.
B.
In mor - tis ex - a - mi - ne.
In death's hour be thou our food.
dim.
p

34
S.
dul - - - - - - - - cis, O pi - - - - - - -
gra - - - - - - - - cious, most ho - - - - - - -
O dul - - - - - - - - - cis, O pi - - - -
Most gra - - - - - - - - cious, most ho - - - -
A.
-ne. O pi - - - - - - - e,
food. Most gra - - - - - - cious,
T.
B.
39
- - e, O Je - - - su, O
- - ly, O Sa - - - viour, O
- - e, O Je - - su, Fi - li
- - ly, O Sa - - viour Christ, Son
O Je - su, O Je - su, Fi - li Ma - ri - -
O Sa - viour, O Sa - viour Christ, Son of Ma - -
O Je - - - - su, Fi - -
O Sa - - - - viour Christ,
O Je - - - - su, O Je - su,
O Sa - - - viour, O Sa - viour
O Je - - - - su, Fi - li
O Sa - - - - viour Christ, Son
cresc.
mp

43
S.
Je - su, Fi - li Ma - ri - ae: mi - se - re - re
Sa - viour Christ, Son of Ma - ry: Look on me in
Ma - ri - ae: mi - se - re - re
of Ma - ry: Look on me in
A.
- ae, Fi - li Ma - ri - ae: mi - se - re - re
- ry, O Son of Ma - ry: Look on me in
T.
- li Ma - ri - ae: mi - se - re - re
Son of Ma - ry: Look on me in
Fi - li Ma - ri - ae:
Christ, Son of Ma - ry:
B.
Ma - ri - ae:
of Ma - ry:
47
S.
me - i, mi - se - re - re me - i. A - men.
mer - cy, look on me in mer - cy.
me - i, mi - se-re - re me - i. A - men.
mer - cy, look on me in mer - cy.
A.
me - i, mi - se - re - re me - i. A - men.
mer - cy, look on me in mer - cy.
T.
me - i, mi - se - re - re me - i. A - men.
mer - cy, look on me in mer - cy.
mi - se - re - re me - i. A - men.
look on me in mer - cy.
B.
mi - se - re - re me - i. A - men.
look on me in mer - cy.

27. Timor et tremor

(*Fearful and trembling, my spirit is troubled*)

Words from the Psalms
Translation by John Rutter

ORLANDE DE LASSUS
(1532–94)

Timor et tremor venerunt super me,
et caligo cecidit super me. (*Ps. 55: 5*)
Miserere mei Domine, miserere,
quoniam in te confidit anima mea. (*Ps. 57: 1*)
Exaudi Deus deprecationem meam, (*Ps. 61: 1*)
quia refugium meum es tu, (*Ps. 71: 2*)
et adjutor fortis. (*Ps. 71: 6*)
Domine invocavi te, non confundar. (*Ps. 31: 19*)

7
S.
tre - mor ve - ne - runt su - per me, ve - ne - runt su - per
trem - bling, my spi - rit is trou - bled, my spi - rit is trou -
A.
- mor ve - ne - runt su - per me, ve - ne - runt su - per
trem - bling, my spi - rit is trou - bled, my spi - rit is trou-
tre - mor ve - ne - runt su - per me, ve - ne - runt su -
trem - bling, my spi - rit is trou - bled, my spi - rit is
T.
tre - mor ve - ne - runt su - per
trem - bling, my spi - rit is trou -
tre - mor ve - ne - runt, ve - ne - runt su - per me,
trem - bling, my spi - rit, my spi - rit is trou - bled,
B.
tre - mor ve - ne - runt su - per me, ve -
trem - bling, my spi - rit is trou - bled, my
13
S.
me, ve - ne - runt su - per me, et ca - li - go
- bled, my spi - rit is trou - bled, yea, and dark - ness
A.
me, ve - ne - runt su - per me, et ca - li -
- bled, my spi - rit is trou - bled, yea, and dark -
- per me, ve - ne - runt su - per me, et ca - li - go ce - ci-
trou - bled, my spi - rit is trou - bled: yea, and dark - ness com - eth
T.
me, ve - ne - runt su - per me, et ca - li - go
- bled, my spi - rit is trou - bled, yea, and dark - ness
ve - ne - runt su - per me, ve - ne - runt su - per me, ce - ci-
my spi - rit is trou - bled, my spi - rit is trou - bled, dark - ness
B.
- ne - runt su - per me, et ca - li - go ce -
spi - rit is trou - bled: yea, and dark - ness com -
mp
dim.
p

* If this E is too low, omit it and sing the preceding B as a ♩

31
S.
- i, quo - ni - am in te con - fi - dit
- cy: for my soul hath trust - - ed in thee,
A.
- i, quo - ni - am in te con - fi - - - -
- cy: for my soul hath trust - ed in
- i, quo - ni - am in te con - fi - dit
- cy: for my soul hath trust - ed, hath trust - ed
T.
quo - ni - am in te con - fi - dit
for my soul hath trust - ed in thee,
- i, quo - ni - am in te con - fi - dit
- cy: for my soul hath trust - ed in thee,
B.
- i, quo - ni - am in te con - fi - dit
- cy: for my soul trust - ed in thee,
mf
più marcato
f
36
S.
a - ni - ma me - a, a - ni - ma me - a.
hath trust - ed in thee, trust - ed in thee, in thee.
A.
- dit a - ni - ma me - a, a - ni - ma me - a.
thee, hath trust - ed in thee, hath trust - ed in thee.
a - ni - ma me - a, a - ni - ma me - a, a - ni - ma me - a.
in thee, hath trust - ed, hath trust - ed in thee, hath trust - ed in thee.
T.
a - ni - ma me - a, a - ni - ma me - a.
my soul hath trust - ed, hath trust - ed in thee.
a - ni - ma me - a, a - ni - ma me - a, a - ni - ma me - a.
trust - ed in thee, for my soul hath trust - ed, hath trust - ed in thee.
B.
a - ni - ma me - a, a - ni - ma me - a.
trust - ed in thee, trust - ed in thee.
mf

Secunda Pars

54
S.
qui - a re - fu - gi - um me - um es tu,
For thou, Lord, art my re - fuge and strong - hold:
A.
-um me - um es tu, qui - a re - fu - gi - um me - um es tu,
re - fuge and strong - hold, for thou, Lord, art my re - fuge and strong - hold:
-um me - um es tu, re - fu - gi - um me - um es tu, et
re - fuge and strong - hold, thou art my re - fuge and strong - hold: and
T.
-um me - um es tu, et ad - ju -
re - fuge and strong - hold: and thou art
qui - a re - fu - gi - um me - um es tu, et ad - ju -
for thou, Lord, art my re - fuge and strong - hold: thou art ev -
B.
-um me - um es tu, et ad - ju -
re - fuge and strong - hold: and thou art
cresc.
60
S.
et ad - ju - tor for - tis. Do - mi - ne
thou art ev - er with me. Lord, my strength,
A.
et ad - ju - tor for - tis. Do - mi - ne
thou art ev - er with me. Lord, my strength,
ad - ju - tor for - tis. Do - mi - ne,
thou art ev - er with me. Lord, my strength,
T.
-tor for - tis. Do - mi - ne, Do -
ev - er with me. Lord, my strength, Lord,
- tor for - tis. Do - mi - ne
- er with me. Lord, my strength,
B.
- tor for - tis. Do - mi - ne, Do -
ev - er with me. Lord, my strength, Lord,
mf cresc.
f

65
S.
in - vo - ca - vi te, in - vo - ca - - vi te, non con-fun -
un - to thee I cry, un - to thee I cry: hear me, I
A.
in - vo - - ca - vi te, in - vo - - ca - vi te, non con-fun -
un - to thee I cry, un - to thee I cry: hear me, I
Do - mi - ne in - vo - - ca - vi te, non con - fun - dar, non con - fun -
Lord, my strength, un - to thee I cry: hear me, I pray, hear me, I
T.
- mi - ne in - vo - ca - - vi te, in - vo - ca - vi te, non con - fun -
my strength, un - to thee I cry, un - to thee I cry: hear me, I
in - vo - ca - vi te, in - vo - ca - vi te,
un - to thee I cry, un - to thee I cry:
B.
- mi - ne in - vo - ca - - vi te, in - vo - ca - vi te,
my strength, un - to thee I cry, un - to thee I cry:
mf
70
S.
- dar, non con - fun - dar, non con - fun - dar, non con -
pray, hear me, I pray, con - found me not, con - found
A.
- dar, non con - fun - dar, non con - fun - dar, non con - fun - dar, non con - fun - dar, non con -
pray, hear me, I pray, hear me, I pray, hear me, I pray, hear me, I pray, con - found
- dar, non con - fun - dar, non con - fun - dar, non con - fun - dar, non con - fun -
pray, hear me, I pray, hear me, I pray, hear me, I pray, hear me, I
T.
- dar, non con - fun - dar, non con - fun - dar, non con -
pray, hear me, I pray, con - found me not, con - found
non con - fun - dar, non con - fun - dar, non con - fun - dar, non
hear me, hear me, hear me, I pray, con - found me, con - found
B.
non con - fun - dar, non con - fun - dar, non con - fun - dar, non
hear me, I pray, hear me, I pray, con - found me not, con -
cresc.
f
il basso marcato

75
S.
-fun - dar, non con - fun - dar, non con - fun - dar, non con - fun - dar, non con-
me not, con - found me not, con - found me not, Lord, con - found me not, con-
A.
-fun - dar, non con - fun - - dar, non con -
me not, con - found me not, con - found
-dar, non con - fun - dar, non con - fun - dar, non con - fun - dar, non con -
pray, con - found me, con - found me not, Lord, con - found me, con - found
T.
-fun - dar, non con - fun - dar, non con - fun - dar, non con - fun -
me, con - found me not, Lord, con - found me not, con - found me
con - fun - dar, non con - fun - dar, non con - fun - dar,
me not, con - found me not, Lord, con - found me not,
B.
con - fun - dar, non con - fun - dar, non con - fun - dar, non con - fun - dar, non
-found me not, con - found me not, con - found me not, con - found me not, con -
79
S.
- fun - dar, non con - fun - dar.
- found me not, con - found me not.
A.
-fun - dar, non con - fun - dar, non con - fun - dar.
me not, con - found me not, con - found me not.
-fun - dar, non con - fun - dar.
me not, Lord, con - found me not.
T.
-dar, non con - fun - dar.
not, Lord, con - found me not.
non con - fun - dar, non con - fun - dar.
con - found me not, con - found me not.
B.
con - fun - dar, non con - fun - dar, non con - fun - dar.
-found me not, con - found me not, yea, con - found me not.
(f)

28. Crucifixus a 8

(*Christ was crucified*)

Words from the Nicene Creed
English version by John Rutter

ANTONIO LOTTI
(*c.*1667–1740)

6
S.
Cru - ci - fi - - - - - - xus,
Christ was cru - - - - - ci - fied,
Cru - ci - fi - - - - - - - - - xus,
Christ was cru - - - - - - - - - ci - fied,
A.
Cru - ci - fi - - - xus, cru - ci - fi - - - - xus,
Christ was cru - - ci - fied, cru - - - - - - ci - fied,
- fi - - - - - xus, cru - - - ci - fi - - - - xus,
cru - - - - - ci - fied, was cru - ci - - - fied,
T.
- xus, cru - - - - - ci - fi - - - - - xus,
- ci - fied, was cru - - ci - - - fied,
- - - - xus, cru - ci - - - fi - xus,
- - - ci - fied, Christ was cru - - ci - fied,
B.
- ci - - - - - fi - xus, cru - ci - fi - - - - xus,
- - - - - - - ci - fied, cru - - - ci - - - fied,
cru - - - ci - - - fi - - - - - - - - - - xus,
- fied, Christ was cru - - - ci - fied,
cresc.
mp cresc.
f

12
S.
cru - ci - fi - xus e - ti - am pro no - bis,
cru - ci - fied for us and our sal - va - tion,
cru - ci - fi - xus e - ti - am pro no - bis, cru - ci - fi - xus
cru - ci - fied for us and our sal - va - tion, cru - ci - fied for
A.
cru - ci - fi - xus e - ti - am pro no - - bis,
cru - ci - fied for us and our sal - va - - tion,
cru - ci - fi - xus e - ti - am pro no - bis,
cru - ci - fied for us and our sal - va - tion,
T.
cru - ci - fi - xus e - ti - am pro no - - - - - bis,
cru - ci - fied for us and our sal - va - - - - - tion,
cru - ci - fi - xus e - ti - am pro no - - bis, cru - ci - fi - xus
cru - ci - fied for us and our sal - va - - tion, cru - ci - fied for
B.
cru - ci - fi - xus e - ti - am pro no - bis,
cru - ci - fied for us and our sal - va - tion,
cru - ci - fi - xus e - ti - am pro no - bis, cru - - ci - - fi - xus,
cru - ci - fied for us and our sal - va - tion, cru - - ci - - fied, was
mp
cresc.
mf
[3♮] 7 6 [4 3♮] 7 6

15
S.
cru - ci - fi - xus e - ti - am pro no - - bis
cru - ci - fied for us and our sal - va - - tion,
e - ti - am pro no - bis, pro no - - - - - - bis:
us and our sal - va - tion, sal - va - - - - - - tion,
A.
e - ti - am pro no - - - bis
cru - ci - fied for our sal - va - tion,
e - ti - am pro no - - - - - bis sub Pon - ti - o Pi -
cru - ci - fied for our sal - va - tion, He suf - fered un - der
T.
cru - ci - fi - xus e - ti - am pro no - - - - bis sub Pon - ti - o Pi -
cru - ci - fied for us and our sal - va - - - - tion, He suf - fered un - der
e - ti - am pro no - - - - - - - bis
us and our sal - va - - - - - - - tion,
B.
cru - ci - fi - xus e - ti - am pro no - - - - bis sub Pon - ti - o Pi -
cru - ci - fied for us and our sal - va - - - - tion, He suf - fered un - der
cru - ci - fi - xus e - ti - am pro no - - - - bis
cru - ci - fied for us and our sal - va - - - - tion,
cresc.
f
p
7 6♭ 4 3 9 5 8 6 4 5 3 (6) 4 2 6

19
S.
sub Pon-ti-o Pi-la - to:
He suf-fered un-der Pi - late:
pas- - - - -
Ah!
A.
sub Pon-ti-o Pi-la - to:
He suf-fered un-der Pi - late:
-la - to, sub Pon-ti-o Pi-la - - to:
Pi - late, he suf-fered un-der Pi - - late:
T.
-la - to, sub Pon-ti-o Pi-la - - - to, sub
Pi - late, he suf-fered un-der Pi - - - late, he
sub Pon-ti-o Pi-la - to, sub Pon-ti-o Pi-la-to,
He suf-fered un-der Pi - late, he suf-fered un-der Pi - late,
B.
-la - to, sub Pon-ti-o Pi-la-to,
Pi - late, he suf-fered un-der Pi - late,
sub Pon-ti-o Pi-la - - to, sub
He suf-fered un-der Pi - - late, he
cresc.
mp

22
S.
pas - - - - - - - - - - - -
Ah! how
- - sus,
how long
sub Pon-ti - o Pi-la - to:
he suf-fered un-der Pi-late:
A.
pas - - - - sus,
Ah! how long
sub Pon-ti - o Pi-la - to:
he suf-fered un-der Pi-late:
pas - - - - - - sus,
Ah! how long
sub
he
T.
Pon-ti - o Pi-la - to, sub Pon-ti - o Pi-la - to,
suf-fered un-der Pi-late, he suf-fered un-der Pi-late,
sub Pon-ti - o Pi-la - to:
he suf-fered un-der Pi-late:
sub Pon-ti - o Pi-la - to,
he suf-fered un-der Pi-late,
sub
he
B.
sub Pon-ti - o Pi-la - to:
he suf-fered un-der Pi-late:
pas - - - -
Ah!
Pon-ti - o Pi-la - to,
suf-fered un-der Pi-late,
sub Pon-ti - o Pi-la - to:
he suf-fered un-der Pi-late:
cresc.
mf

* Some editions give A♭ here, but the source has A♮ .

30
S.
A.
T.
B.
- sus, et se - pul - - tus est, pas - sus, et se - pul - -
bit - ter the pains he bore; he gave up his spi - -
- sus, et se - pul - - tus est, pas - sus, et se - pul - -
the bit - ter pains he bore; he gave up his spi - -
- sus, et se - pul - - tus est, pas - sus, et se - pul - -
bit - ter the pains he bore; he gave up his spi - -
- sus, et se - pul - tus est, pas - sus, et se - pul - -
bit - ter the pains he bore; he gave up his spi - -
se - - pul - - tus est, pas - sus et se - pul - tus, et se -
bit - ter pains he bore; he gave up his spi - rit, he gave
- sus, et se - pul - tus est, pas - sus, et se - pul - -
the bit - - ter pains he bore; he gave up his spi - -
- sus, et se - pul - - tus est, pas - sus, et se - pul - -
bit - ter the pains he bore; he gave up his spi - -
- sus, et se - pul - - tus est, pas - sus, et se - pul - -
bit - ter the pains he bore; he gave up his spi - -
dim.
mf

35
S.
- - - - - - tus, et se - pul - - tus est.
- - - - - - rit, and was laid to rest.
- - - - - - tus, et se - pul - - tus est.
- - - - - - rit, and was laid to rest.
A.
- - - - - - tus, et se - pul - - tus est.
- - - - - - rit, and was laid to rest.
- - - - - - tus, et se - pul - - - tus est.
- - - - - - rit, and was laid to rest.
T.
- pul - - - - - tus, et se - pul - - tus est.
up his spi - rit, and was laid to rest.
- - - - - - tus, et se - pul - - - - tus est.
- - - - - - rit, and was laid to rest.
B.
- - - - - - tus, et se - pul - - - tus est.
- - - - - - rit, and was laid to rest.
- - - - - - tus, et se - pul - - - tus est.
- - - - - - rit, and was laid to rest.
mp dim.
p
4 3♭ 7 5 9 4 8 3♭ 7 5 [3♮] ♮ [6] 4 4 3♮ [♮]

29. Psalm 43

(*Richte mich, Gott*)

English version 19th cent.

F. MENDELSSOHN (1809–47)
Op. 78 no. 2

12
p
Wa - rum
Where - fore
p
Wa - rum
Where - fore
p
Gott, du bist der Gott mei - ner Stär - ke; wa - rum ver - stös - sest du mich?
God, thou art the God of my strength; O why dost thou cast me from thee?
p
Gott, du bist der Gott mei - ner Stär - ke; wa - rum ver - stös - sest du mich?
God, thou art the God of my strength; O why dost thou cast me from thee?
p
17
läs - sest du mich so trau - rig geh'n, wenn mein Feind mich drängt?
mourn I be - cause the e - ne - my sore - ly op - press - eth me?
läs - sest du mich so trau - rig geh'n, wenn mein Feind mich drängt?
mourn I be - cause the e - ne - my sore - ly op - press - eth me?
f
Sen - de dein
Send out thy
f
Sen - de dein
Send out thy
f

22
f
S.
1
2
A.
1
2
T.
1
2
B.
1
2
Sen - de dein Licht und dei - ne Wahr - heit, dass sie mich lei - ten zu dei - nem
Send out thy light, thy light and truth, Lord; O let them lead me, and bring me
Sen - de dein Licht und dei - ne Wahr - heit, dass sie mich lei - ten zu dei - nem
Send out thy light, thy light and truth, Lord; O let them lead me, and bring me
Sen - de dein Licht und dei - ne Wahr - heit, dass sie mich lei - ten zu dei - nem
Send out thy light, thy light and truth, Lord; O let them lead_ me, and bring me
Sen - de dein Licht und dei - ne Wahr - heit, dass sie mich lei - ten zu dei - nem
Send out thy light, thy light and truth, Lord; O let them lead_ me, and bring me
Licht und dei - ne Wahr - heit, dass sie mich lei - ten zu dei - nem
light, thy light and truth, Lord; O let them lead me, and bring me
Licht und dei - ne Wahr - heit, dass sie mich lei - ten zu dei - nem
light, thy light and truth, Lord; O let them lead me, and bring me
Licht und dei - ne Wahr - heit, dass sie mich lei - ten zu dei - nem
light, thy light and truth, Lord; O let them lead me, and bring me
Licht und dei - ne Wahr - heit, dass sie mich lei - ten zu dei - nem
light, thy light and truth, Lord; O let them lead me, and bring me

28
hei-li-gen Ber - ge, und zu dei - ner Woh-nung, und zu dei-ner Woh - nung.
un-to thy ho-ly hill and__ to___ thy dwell-ing place, and to thy dwell-ing place.
hei-li-gen Ber - ge, und zu dei - ner Woh-nung, und zu dei-ner Woh - nung.
un-to thy ho-ly hill and__ to___ thy dwell-ing place, and to thy dwell-ing place.
hei-li-gen Ber - ge, und zu dei - ner Woh-nung, und zu dei-ner Woh - nung.
un-to thy ho-ly hill and__ to__ thy dwell-ing place, and to thy dwell-ing place.
hei-li-gen Ber - ge, und zu dei - ner Woh-nung, und zu dei-ner Woh - nung.
un-to thy ho-ly hill and__ to__ thy dwell-ing place, and to thy dwell-ing place.
mf
hei-li-gen Ber - ge, und zu_ dei - ner Woh-nung, und zu dei-ner Woh - nung. Dass
un-to thy ho-ly hill and___ to__ thy dwell-ing place, and to thy dwell-ing place. And
mf
hei-li-gen Ber - ge, und zu dei - ner Woh-nung, und zu dei-ner Woh - nung. Dass
un-to thy ho-ly hill and__ to___ thy dwell-ing place, and to thy dwell-ing place. And
mf
hei-li-gen Ber - ge, und zu dei - ner Woh-nung, und zu dei-ner Woh - nung. Dass
un-to thy ho-ly hill and__ to___ thy dwell-ing place, and to thy dwell-ing place. And
mf
hei-li-gen Ber - ge, und zu dei - ner Woh-nung, und zu dei-ner Woh - nung. Dass
un-to thy ho-ly hill and__ to___ thy dwell-ing place, and to thy dwell-ing place. And
mf

34
Andante
S.
A.
T.
B.
mf
Dass ich hin - ein ge - he zum
And then will I go to the
ich hin - ein ge - he zum Al - tar Got - tes, zu dem Gott,
then will I go to the al - tar of God, the God of my joy,
Andante
mf

42
cresc.
Al - tar Got - tes, zu dem Gott,
al - tar of God, the God of my joy,
der mei - ne
to God, the
sf
der mei - ne Freu - de und Won - ne ist,
to God, the God of my glad - ness and joy:
sf
cresc.

51
f
Freu-de und Won - ne ist,
God of my glad-ness and joy:
und dir, Gott, auf der
I will praise thee up-
Freu-de und Won - ne ist,
God of my glad-ness and joy:
und dir, Gott, auf der
I will praise thee up-
und dir, Gott, auf der Har - fe dan-ke, mein Gott,
I will praise thee up - on the harp, O my God,
und dir, Gott, auf der Har - fe dan-ke, mein Gott,
I will praise thee up - on the harp, O my God,
59
p
Har - fe dan - ke, mein Gott, dir dan - ke, mein Gott, dir,
- on the harp, O my God, praise thee, O my God, will
Har - fe dan - ke, mein Gott, dir dan - ke, mein Gott, dir,
- on the harp, O my God, praise thee, O my God, will
und dir, Gott, auf der Har - fe dan - ke, dir,
I will praise thee, will praise thee, O God, will
dir dan - ke, mein Gott, dir,
praise thee, O my God, will

66
dim.
ritard.
Gott, auf der Har - fe dan - ke, mein Gott, dir, Gott, auf der Har - fe dan - ke, mein
praise thee up - on the harp, O my God, will praise thee up - on the harp, O my
dim.
Gott, auf der Har - fe dan - ke, mein Gott, dir, Gott, auf der Har - fe dan - ke, mein
praise thee up - on the harp, O my God, will praise thee up - on the harp, O my
dim.
Gott, auf der Har - fe dan - ke, mein Gott, dir, Gott, auf der Har - fe dan - ke, mein
praise thee up - on the harp, O my God, will praise thee up - on the harp, O my
dim.
Gott, auf der Har - fe dan - ke, mein Gott, dir, Gott, auf der Har - fe dan - ke, mein
praise thee up - on the harp, O my God, will praise thee up - on the harp, O my
ritard.
dim.
73
Allegro moderato
S.
Gott. Was be - trübst du dich, mei - ne See - le, und bist so un -
God. O my soul, why art thou cast down - ward, and why art thou dis -
A.
Gott. Was be - trübst du dich, mei - ne See - le, und bist so un -
God. O my soul, why art thou cast down - ward, and why art thou dis -
1
T.
Gott, mein Gott,
God, my God,
2
Gott, mein Gott,
God, my God,
1
B.
Gott, mein Gott,
God, my God, my God,
2
Gott, mein Gott, mein
God, my God, my
Allegro moderato

78
S.
-ru - hig in mir? Har - re auf Gott! Har - re auf Gott!
-qui - et - ed with - in me? Hope in the Lord, hope in the Lord,
A.
-ru - hig in mir? Har - re auf Gott! Har - re auf Gott!
-qui - et - ed with - in me? Hope in the Lord, hope in the Lord,
T.
mein Gott. Har - re auf Gott! Har - re auf Gott! denn ich
my God. Hope in the Lord, hope in the Lord, O my
mein Gott. Har - re auf Gott! Har - re auf Gott! denn ich
my God. Hope in the Lord, hope in the Lord, O my
B.
mein Gott. Har - re auf Gott! Har - re auf Gott! denn ich
my God. Hope in the Lord, hope in the Lord, O my
Gott. Har - re auf Gott! Har - re auf Gott! denn ich
God. Hope in the Lord, hope in the Lord, O my
85
Har - re auf Gott! Har - re auf Gott!
Hope in the Lord, hope in the Lord,
T.1 dan - ken.
praise him.
wer - de ihm noch dan - ken. Har - re auf Gott! Har - re auf Gott!
soul, for I will praise him. Hope in the Lord, hope in the Lord,

92
denn ich wer - de ihm noch dan - ken, dass er mei - - nes
O my soul, for I will praise him who is the health of my
denn ich wer - de ihm noch dan - ken, dass er mei - nes
O my soul, for I will praise him who is the health of my
denn ich wer - de ihm noch dan - ken, dass er mei - - nes
O my soul, for I will praise him who is the health of my
denn ich wer - de ihm noch dan - ken, dass er mei - - nes
O my soul, for I will praise him who is the health of my

98
An - ge - sichts Hil - fe, und mein Gott ist.
coun - te - nance, and my gra - cious Lord and God.
An - ge - sichts Hil - fe, und mein Gott ist.
coun - te - nance, and my gra - cious Lord and God.
An - ge - sichts Hil - fe, und mein Gott ist.
coun - te - nance, and my gra - cious Lord and God.
An - ge - sichts Hil - fe, und mein Gott ist.
coun - te - nance, and my gra - cious Lord and God.

30. Verleih uns Frieden

(*Lord, in thy mercy grant us peace*)

Words by Martin Luther (1483–1546)
English version by John Rutter

FELIX MENDELSSOHN
(1809–47)

* Transcribed from the original orchestral accompaniment. Score and parts are available on rental (see Index of Orchestrations, p. 378).

26
B
kein An - drer nicht, Der für uns könn - te strei - - -
our sword and shield, Lord who dost guide the na - - - -
cresc.
dim.
p
(Ped.)
31
cresc.
p
-ten, Denn du, un - ser Gott al -
- tions. De - fend us, O God, we
dim.
cresc.
sf
p
36
-lei - - ne.
pray thee.
dim.
p
C ALTOS
42
p e dolce
Ver-leih uns Frie - den gnä - dig - lich, Herr Gott, zu
Lord, in thy mer - cy grant us peace Through - out all
BASSES [p e dolce]
Ver - leih uns Frie - - - den, Herr
Lord, in thy mer - - - cy grant
C
(+ 4′)

47
[cresc.]
un - sern Zei - - ten! Es ist doch ja kein An - drer
ge - ne - ra - - tions; Thou art a - lone our sword and
[cresc.]
Gott, Herr Gott! Er ist doch ja kein An - drer nicht,
us thy peace; Thou art a - lone our sword and shield,
cresc.
53
D
[dim.]
nicht, Der für uns könn - te strei - - ten, Denn
shield, Lord who dost guide the na - - tions. De -
[p]
kein An - drer nicht, Der für uns könn - te strei - ten,
our sword and shield, Lord who dost guide the na - tions.
D
cresc.
dim.
p
dim.
59
cresc.
dim.
du, un - ser Gott al - lei - ne.
-fend us, O God, we pray thee.
cresc.
dim.
Denn du, un - ser Gott al - lei - ne.
De - fend us, O God, we pray thee.
cresc.
sf
p

65
cresc.
f
E
70
mf
[dim.]
S.
A.
Ver - leih uns Frie - den gnä - dig - lich, Herr Gott, zu un - sern
Lord, in thy mer - cy grant us peace Through - out all ge - ne -
T.
B.
mf
[dim.]
E
mf
dim.
76
p
cresc.
Zei - ten! Es ist doch ja kein An - drer nicht,
- ra - tions; Thou art a - lone our sword and shield,
p
cresc.
p
cresc.

82
S.
A.
T.
B.
Der für uns könn - te strei - - - ten,
Lord who dost guide the na - - - tions.
Der für uns könn - te, der für uns könn - - te strei - ten,
Lord who dost guide the na - tions, dost guide the na - tions.
Denn
De -
dim.
87
F
cresc.
Denn du, du, un - ser
De - fend us, O
Denn du, un - ser Gott, un - ser
De - fend us, O God, O
Denn du, du, un - ser Gott, un - ser
De - fend us, de - fend us, O
du, un - ser Gott, denn du, denn du, un - ser
-fend us, O God, de - fend, de - fend us, O
Man.
sf
Ped.

92
p
dim.
Gott, denn du al - lei - - -
God, de - fend us, we pray
Gott, denn du, du al - lei - - -
God, de - fend us, we pray
Gott, denn du, denn du al -
God, de - fend us, we pray, we
Gott, denn du, denn du al -
God, de - fend us, we pray, we
97
-ne!
thee.
-ne!
thee.
- lei - - - ne!
pray thee.
- lei - - - ne!
pray thee.
pp

31. Beatus vir

Psalm 112

CLAUDIO MONTEVERDI
(1567–1643)

Blessed is the man that feareth the Lord:

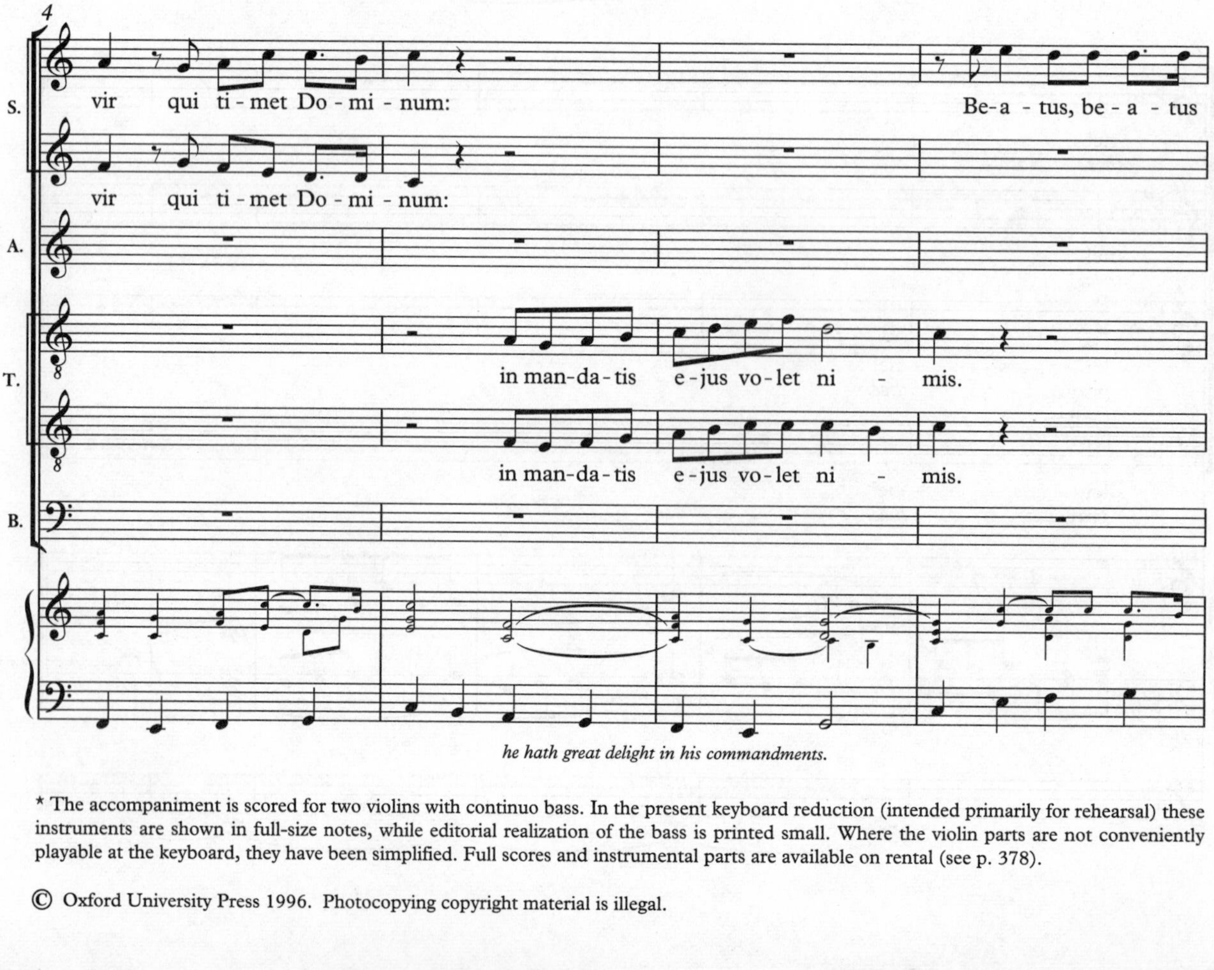

he hath great delight in his commandments.

* The accompaniment is scored for two violins with continuo bass. In the present keyboard reduction (intended primarily for rehearsal) these instruments are shown in full-size notes, while editorial realization of the bass is printed small. Where the violin parts are not conveniently playable at the keyboard, they have been simplified. Full scores and instrumental parts are available on rental (see p. 378).

His seed shall be mighty upon earth:

the generation of the

faithful shall be blessed. *Blessed is the man.*

Riches and plenteousness shall be in his house:

and his righteousness endureth for ever.

38
S.
be - a - tus, be - a - tus vir, be - a - tus, be - a - tus vir, be - a -
be - a - tus, be - a - tus vir, be - a -
A.
Be - a - tus, be - a - tus vir.
T.
sae-cu-lum sae - cu - li. Be - a - tus, be - a - tus vir.
sae-cu-lum sae - cu - li. Be - a - tus, be - a - tus vir.
B.
sae-cu-lum sae-cu - li. Be - a - tus, be - a - tus vir.
mf
p

43
C
S.
- - - - tus.
- - - - tus.
A.
T.
B.
C
mf
mf

Unto the godly there ariseth up light in the darkness:

he is merciful, loving, and righteous.

* $\Phi\,\frac{3}{1}$ in source. Note values have been quartered in this section.

and will guide his words with discretion.

88
S.
in ju - di - ci - o: qui - - a in ae - - ter - -
in ju - di - ci - o:
T.
qui - a in ae - ter - num non com - mo -
qui - a in ae - ter - num non com - mo - ve - bi -
BASSES
B.
qui - a in ae - ter - num, qui - a in ae - ter - num non
cresc.
For he shall never be moved:
95
(1st SOPS.)
E
-num non com - mo - ve - bi - tur.
- ve - bi - tur, non com - mo - ve - bi - tur.
- tur, non com - mo - ve - bi - tur.
com - mo - ve - - bi - - tur.
f
mf
102
1st SOPRANOS
In me - mo - ri - a ae -
2nd SOPRANOS
In me - mo - ri - a ae -
and the righteous shall be had in everlasting remembrance.

109
S.
-ter - na,
-ter - na,
1st TENORS
T.
ab au - di - ti -
BASSES
B.
e - rit ju - stus, e - rit ju - stus:
ab au -
He will not be afraid of any evil tidings:
116
T.
-o - ne ma - la non ti - me - bit, non ti - me - - bit.
ab au - di - ti - o - ne ma - la non ti - me - - bit.
B.
-di - ti - o - ne ma - la, ma - la non ti - me - - bit.
123
1st SOPRANOS
S.
Pa - ra - tum, pa - ra - tum, pa - ra - tum cor
2nd SOPRANOS
Pa - ra - tum, pa - ra - tum, pa - ra - tum cor
for his heart standeth fast,

130 (1st and 2nd SOPS.)
S.
e - jus, con - fir - ma - tum
T.
spe - ra - re, spe - ra - re, spe - ra - re in Do - mi-no,
spe - ra - re, spe - ra - re, spe - ra - re in Do - mi-no,
and believeth in the Lord.
His heart is established,
138
F
unis.
S.
est, non com - mo - ve -
T.
cor e - jus: non com - mo - ve - bi - tur
cor e - jus: non com - mo - ve - bi - tur do - nec de -
B.
non com - mo - ve - bi - tur do - nec de - spi - ci - at
F
f
and will not shrink:
until he see his desire upon his enemies.
146
S.
- bi - tur,
T.
do - nec de - spi - ci - at in - i - mi - cos su - os.
- spi - ci - at in - i - mi - cos su - os.
B.
in - i - mi - cos, in - i - mi - cos su - os.
mf

154
1st and 2nd SOPRANOS
S.
Di - sper-sit, di - sper - sit,
He hath dispersed abroad,
162
G
S.
de-dit,
T.
de-dit, de-dit pau - pe - ri - bus: ju-sti-ti-a e - jus ma - net,
de-dit, de-dit pau - pe - ri - bus: ju-sti-ti-a e - jus ma - net,
B.
ju-sti-ti-a e - jus ma - net,
G
and given to the poor:
and his righteousness remaineth for ever;
171
S.
cor - nu e-jus,
T.
ma-net in sae-cu-lum sae - cu - li: cor-nu
ma-net in sae-cu-lum sae - cu - li: cor-nu
B.
ma-net in sae-cu-lum sae - cu - li:
his horn shall be exalted with honour.

* Conductors may wish to consider assigning this section (up to bar 197) to soloists.

189
S.
glo - - - - - ri - a.
glo - - - - - ri - a.
T.
ex - al - ta - bi - tur in glo - - - - - - - - -
ex - al - ta - bi - tur in glo - - - - - - - - - -
B.
glo - - ri - a,
cresc.
193
S.
T.
- - - - - - - - - - - - - - - - - ri -
- - - - - - - - - - - - - - - - - - ri -
B.
in glo - ri -
f

The ungodly shall see it, and it shall grieve him:

he shall gnash with his teeth, and consume away;

the desire of the ungodly shall perish.

217
S.
-to-rum, de-si-de-ri-um pec-ca-to-rum pe-ri-bit, pe-ri-bit.
-to-rum, de-si-de-ri-um pec-ca-to-rum pe-ri-bit, pe-ri-bit.
A.
-to-rum, de-si-de-ri-um pec-ca-to-rum pe-ri-bit, pe-
-to-rum, de-si-de-ri-um pec-ca-to-rum pe-ri-bit, pe-
T.
-to-rum pe-ri-bit, pe-ri-bit, de-si-de-ri-um pec-ca-to-rum
B.
-to-rum pe-ri-bit, pe-ri-bit, de-si-de-ri-um pec-ca-to-rum
p
f
p

221
S.
Be-a-tus vir qui ti-met Do-mi-num.
Be-a-tus vir qui ti-met Do-mi-num.
A.
-ri-bit. Be-a-tus vir qui ti-met Do-mi-num.
-ri-bit, pe-ri-bit, pe-ri-bit. Be-a-tus vir qui ti-met Do-mi-num.
T.
pe-ri-bit, pe-ri-bit. Be-a-tus vir qui ti-met Do-mi-num.
B.
pe-ri-bit, pe-ri-bit. Be-a-tus vir qui ti-met Do-mi-num.
pp
f

228
J
S.
Glo - ri - a Pa - tri, glo - ri - a, et Spi - ri - tu - i San - cto,
glo - ri - a, et Spi - ri - tu - i San - cto,
A.
Glo - ri - a Pa - tri, glo - ri - a, et Fi - li - o, glo - ri - a, et Spi - ri - tu - i San - cto,
T.
Glo - ri - a Pa - tri, glo - ri - a, et Fi - li - o,
Glo - ri - a Pa - tri, glo - ri - a, et Fi - li - o, glo - ri - a, et Spi - ri - tu - i San - cto,
B.
glo - ri - a, et Fi - li - o,
J
mf
f
Glory be to the Father,
and to the Son:
and to the Holy Ghost;
234
S.
glo - ri - a, et nunc et sem - per,
glo - ri - a, et nunc et sem - per,
A.
glo - ri - a, Si - cut e - rat in prin - ci - pi - o, glo - ri - a, et nunc et sem - per,
T.
glo - ri - a, Si - cut e - rat in prin - ci - pi - o,
glo - ri - a, Si - cut e - rat in prin - ci - pi - o, glo - ri - a, et nunc et sem - per,
B.
glo - ri - a, Si - cut e - rat in prin - ci - pi - o,
mf
f
As it was in the beginning,
is now, and ever shall be:

238
S.
glo - ri - a, glo - ri - a,
glo - ri - a, glo - ri - a,
A.
glo - ri - a, et in sae - cu - la sae - cu - lo - - - - rum,
T.
glo - ri - a, et in sae - cu - la sae - cu - lo - - - - rum,
glo - ri - a, et in sae - cu - la sae - cu -
B.
glo - ri - a, et in sae - cu - la sae - cu - lo - - rum,
world without end.
240
S.
glo - ri - a, glo - ri - a,
glo - ri - a, glo - ri - a,
A.
glo - ri - a, et in sae - cu - la sae - cu - lo - - rum, glo - ri - a, glo - ri - a,
T.
glo - ri - a, et in sae - cu - la sae - cu - lo - - - - rum,
-lo - rum, glo - ri - a, glo - ri - a, glo - ri - a, glo - ri - a,
B.
glo - ri - a, et in sae - cu - la sae - cu - lo - - - - - rum,

242
S.
glo - ri - a, glo - ri - a,
glo - ri - a, glo - ri - a,
A.
glo - ri - a, et in sae - cu - la sae - cu - lo - - rum,
T.
glo - ri - a, et in sae - cu - la sae - cu - lo - - - - rum,
glo - ri - a, et in sae - cu - la sae - cu -
B.
glo - ri - a, et in sae - cu - la sae - cu - lo - - - - rum,
244
S.
glo - ri - a, glo - ri - a,
glo - ri - a, glo - ri - a,
A.
glo - ri - a, et in sae - cu - la sae - cu - lo - - rum, glo - ri - a, glo - ri - a,
T.
glo - ri - a, et in sae - cu - la sae - cu - lo - - - - rum,
- lo - - rum, glo - ri - a, glo - ri - a, glo - ri - a, glo - ri - a,
B.
glo - ri - a, et in sae - cu - la sae - cu - lo - - - - rum,

246
S.
glo-ri-a, et in sae-cu-la sae-cu - lo - rum, glo-ri-a, glo-ri-a, glo-ri-a, et in sae-cu-la sae-cu-
glo-ri-a, et in sae-cu-la sae-cu - lo - rum, glo-ri-a, glo-ri-a, glo-ri-a, et in sae-cu-la sae-cu-
A.
glo-ri-a, et in sae-cu-la sae-cu - lo - rum.
T.
glo-ri-a, et in sae-cu-la sae-cu - lo - rum.
glo-ri-a, et in sae-cu-la sae-cu - lo - rum, glo-ri-a, glo-ri-a, glo-ri-a, et in sae-cu-la sae-cu-
B.
glo-ri-a, et in sae-cu-la sae-cu - lo - rum, glo-ri-a, glo-ri-a, glo-ri-a, et in sae-cu-la sae-cu-
249
S.
-lo - rum. A - men.
-lo - rum. A - men.
A.
A - men, a - men.
T.
A - men.
-lo - rum. A - men.
B.
-lo - rum. A - men.
ff

32. Cantate Domino

(*Sing unto God the Lord*)

Words from Psalms 96 and 98
Translation by John Rutter

CLAUDIO MONTEVERDI
(1567–1643)

* May alternatively be sung by baritones, with all tenors singing Tenor 1 part.

8
S.
-ta - te et be - ne - di - ci - te no - mi - ni e - jus. Can - ta - te Do - mi - no
God the Lord, sing and bless ye his Name, bless ye his Name. Sing un - to God the Lord,
-ta - te et be - ne - di - ci - te no - mi - ni e - jus. Can - ta - te Do - mi - no
God the Lord, sing and bless ye his Name, bless ye his Name. Sing un - to God the Lord,
A.
-ta - te et be - ne - di - ci - te no - mi - ni e - jus. Can - ta - te Do - mi - no
God the Lord, sing and bless ye his Name, bless ye his Name. Sing un - to God the Lord,
T.
-ta - te et be - ne - di - ci - te no - mi - ni e - jus. Can - ta - te Do - mi - no
God the Lord, sing and bless ye his Name, bless ye his Name. Sing un - to God the Lord,
Can - ta - te Do - mi - no
Sing un - to God the Lord,
B.
Can - ta - te Do - mi - no
Sing un - to God the Lord,
f
16
S.
can - ti - cum no - - vum: can - ta - te, can - ta - te, can - ta - te et be - ne -
sing ye a new song, O sing ye, O sing ye to God the Lord, sing and
can - ti - cum no - - vum: can - ta - te, can - ta - te, can - ta - te et be - ne -
sing ye a new song, O sing ye, O sing ye to God the Lord, sing and
A.
can - ti - cum no - - vum: can - ta - te, can - ta - te, can - ta - te et be - ne -
sing ye a new song, O sing ye, O sing ye to God the Lord, sing and
T.
can - ti - cum no - - vum: can - ta - te, can - ta - te, can - ta - te et be - ne -
sing ye a new song, O sing ye, O sing ye to God the Lord, sing and
can - ti - cum no - - vum: can - ta - te, can - ta - te et be - ne -
sing ye a new song, O sing ye to God the Lord, sing and
B.
can - ti - cum no - - vum: can - ta - te, can - ta - te, can - ta - te et be - ne -
sing ye a new song, O sing ye, O sing ye to God the Lord, sing and

* Time signature and note values in this section are unaltered.

37
S.
Can - ta - - - - - te et ex - sul -
O sing ye with ex - ul -
Can - ta - - - - - te et ex - sul -
O sing ye with ex - ul -
A.
- te et ex - sul - ta - - - - - - - te,
ye with ex - ul - ta - - - - - - - tion,
T.
- te et ex - sul - ta - - - - - - - te,
ye with ex - ul - ta - - - - - - - tion,
ex - - sul - ta - - - - te,
ex - - ul - ta - - - - tion,
B.
Can - ta - te et ex - sul -
O sing ye with ex - ul -
42
S.
- ta - - te,
- ta - - tion,
- ta - - te,
- ta - - tion,
can - ta - - -
O sing
A.
can - ta - - -
O sing
T.
can - ta - - - - - te et ex - sul - ta - - te
O sing ye with ex - ul - ta - - tion
can - ta - - - - - te et ex - sul - ta - - te et
O sing ye with ex - ul - ta - - tion and
B.
- ta - te, can - ta - te et ex - sul - ta - te, can - ta - - - -
- ta - tion, O sing ye with ex - ul - ta - tion, O sing

47
S.
can - ta - te et ex - sul - ta -
O sing ye with ex - ul - ta -
te et ex - sul - ta - te, et ex - sul - ta - te
ye with ex - ul - ta - tion, with ex - ul - ta - tion,
A.
te et ex - sul - ta - te, can - ta - te et ex - sul - ta -
ye with ex - ul - ta - tion, O sing ye with ex - ul - ta -
et psal - li - te, et ex - sul -
T.
and praise the Lord, with ex - ul -
psal - li - te, can - ta - te et ex - sul - ta -
praise the Lord, O sing ye with ex - ul - ta -
B.
te, can - ta - te et ex - sul - ta -
ye, O sing ye with ex - ul - ta -
cresc.
f
52
S.
te et psal - li - te. Psal - li - te in ci - tha -
tion, and praise the Lord. Praise him on the mer - ry
et psal - li - te. Psal - li - te in ci - tha - ra, psal - li -
and praise the Lord. Praise him on the mer - ry harp, praise him
A.
te et psal - li - te. Psal - li - te in ci - tha -
tion, and praise the Lord. Praise him on the mer - ry
ta - te et psal - li - te. Psal - li - te in ci - tha -
T.
ta - tion, and praise the Lord. Praise him on the mer - ry
te et psal - li - te. Psal - li - te in ci - tha - ra, psal - li -
tion, and praise the Lord. Praise him on the mer - ry harp, praise him
B.
te et psal - li - te. Psal - li - te in ci - tha -
tion, and praise the Lord. Praise him on the mer - ry
mf marcato

57
S.
-ra, psal - li - te in ci - tha - ra, in ci - tha - ra et vo - ce, in
harp, praise him on the mer - ry harp, the mer - ry harp and voi - ces, the
-te in ci - tha - ra, in ci - tha - ra et vo - ce, in ci - tha - ra et
on the mer - ry harp, the mer - ry harp and voi - ces, the mer - ry harp and
A.
-ra, psal - li - te in ci - - tha - ra, in ci - tha -
harp, praise him on the mer - - ry harp, the mer - ry
T.
-ra, psal - li - te in ci - - tha - ra, in ci - tha - ra et vo - -
harp, praise him on the mer - - ry harp, the mer - ry harp and voice
-te in ci - tha - ra, in ci - tha - ra et vo - ce psal - mi, in
on the mer - ry harp, the mer - ry harp and voi - ces with a psalm, the
B.
-ra, psal - li - te in ci - - tha - ra,
harp, praise him on the mer - - ry harp,
più legato
62
S.
ci - tha - ra, in ci - tha - ra et vo - ce, in ci - tha - ra et vo -
mer - ry harp, the mer - ry harp and voi - ces, the mer - ry harp and voi -
vo - ce psal - mi, in ci - tha - ra et vo - - ce, in ci - tha -
voi - ces with a psalm, the mer - ry harp and voi - - ces, the mer - ry
A.
-ra et vo - ce psal - mi, in ci - tha - ra, in ci - tha - ra et
harp and voi - ces with a psalm, the mer - ry harp, the mer - ry harp and
T.
-ce psal - mi, in ci - tha - ra et vo - ce
with a psalm, the mer - ry harp and voi - ces
ci - tha - ra, in ci - tha - ra et vo - ce, in ci - tha - ra et
mer - ry harp, the mer - ry harp and voi - ces, the mer - ry harp and
B.
in ci - tha - ra et vo - ce psal - mi, in ci - tha - ra, in
the mer - ry harp and voi - ces with a psalm, the mer - ry harp, the
cresc.
f

67
S.
- ce psal - - - - - - mi: qui - - a, qui -
- ces with a psalm: won - - drous, won -
- ra et vo - ce psal - - mi: qui - - a, qui -
harp and voi - ces with a psalm: won - - drous, won -
A.
vo - - ce psal - - - mi: qui - - a, qui -
voi - - ces with a psalm: won - - drous, won -
T.
psal - mi, et vo - ce psal - mi: qui - - a, qui - - a
with a psalm, and with a psalm: won - - drous, won - - drous
vo - - ce psal - - - mi: qui - - a, qui -
voi - - ces with a psalm: won - - drous, won -
B.
ci - tha - ra et vo - ce psal - mi: qui - - a, qui -
mer - ry harp and voi - ces with a psalm: won - - drous, won -
73
S.
- a mi - - ra - bi - - li - a fe - - cit.
- drous are the works of the Lord God.
- a mi - - ra - - bi - - li - a fe - - cit.
- drous are the works of the Lord God.
A.
- a mi - ra - bi - - li - a fe - - - - cit.
- drous are the works of the Lord God.
T.
mi - ra - bi - - li - a fe - - - - - - cit.
are the works of the Lord God.
- a mi - ra - bi - - - - li - a fe - - cit.
- drous are the works of the Lord God.
B.
- a mi - ra - bi - - li - a fe - - cit.
- drous are the works of the Lord God.

33. Christe, adoramus te

(*Jesu, Saviour, to thy Name we pray*)

Antiphon at Feasts of the Holy Cross
English version by John Rutter

CLAUDIO MONTEVERDI
(1567–1643)

Note: Bars in this edition are of either four or six beats' length.

7
S.
ti - bi, et be-ne - di - ci-mus ti - bi,
bless thee, lo, we a - dore thee and bless thee,
ti - bi, et be-ne - di - ci-mus ti - bi, qui - a per
bless— thee, lo, we a - dore thee and bless thee, who by thy
A.
ti - bi, et be - ne-di - ci-mus ti - - bi, qui - a per san-ctam cru-cem
bless thee, lo, we a-dore thee and bless thee, who by thy ho - ly cross and
T.
ti - bi, et be-ne - di - ci-mus ti - bi, qui - a per san-ctam cru - - cem
bless thee, lo, we a - dore thee and bless thee, who by thy ho - ly cross and
B.
et be-ne - di - ci-mus ti - bi,
lo, we a - dore thee and bless thee,
mf
p
cresc.
6
[5♯]
12
S.
qui - a per san - ctam cru - - cem tu - am,
who by thy ho - ly cross and Pas - sion,
san - ctam cru - - cem tu - - - - - am,
ho - ly cross and Pas - - - - - sion,
A.
tu - - - am, per san - ctam cru - cem tu - am,
Pas - - - sion, thy ho - ly cross and Pas - sion,
T.
tu - am, per san - ctam cru - cem tu - am re - de - mi - sti
Pas - sion, thy ho - ly cross and Pas - sion hast re - deemed us
B.
qui - a per san - ctam cru - cem tu - am
who by thy ho - ly cross and Pas - sion
mf cresc.
f
p
[Solo]
[6]
[5♯]
[♯]
[6]

* Here and in bar 23, the ♯ figure has been interpreted as 4 - 3♯.

24
S.
Do - mi - ne, Do - mi - ne, mi-se - re - re no - bis,
Lord, we pray, Lord, we pray, look on us in mer - cy,
Do - mi - ne, Do - - mi - ne, mi - se - re - re no - bis,
Lord, we pray, Lord, we pray, look on us in mer - cy,
A.
Do - mi - ne, Do - - mi - ne, mi-se-re - re no - - - - - bis,
Lord, we pray, Lord, we pray, look on us in mer - - - - - cy,
T.
Do - mi - ne, Do - mi - ne, mi-se - re - re no - bis,
Lord, we pray, Lord, we pray, look on us in mer - cy,
B.
Do - mi - ne, Do - - mi - ne, mi - se-re - re no - bis,
Lord, we pray, Lord, we pray, look on us in mer - cy,
f
mp
6 6 6 6 ♯
27
S.
Do - mi-ne, Do - mi - ne, mi-se - re - - re no - bis.
Lord, we pray, Lord, we pray, look on us in mer - cy.
Do - mi - ne, Do - - mi - ne, mi - se - re - re no - bis.
Lord, we pray, Lord, we pray, look on us in mer - cy.
A.
Do - - mi - ne, Do - - mi - ne, mi - se - re - re no - bis.
Lord, we pray, Lord, we pray, look on us in mer - cy.
T.
Do - - mi - ne, Do - mi - ne, mi - se - re - re no - bis.
Lord, we pray, Lord, we pray, look on us in mer - cy.
B.
Do - - mi - ne, Do - - mi - ne, mi - se - re - re no - bis.
Lord, we pray, Lord, we pray, look on us in mer - cy.
f
mp
p
6 6 6 ♯

34. Ave verum Corpus

(*Jesus, Saviour, we behold thee*)

14th-century Eucharistic hymn
English version by John Rutter

W. A. MOZART (1756–91)
K618

*The accompaniment to this motet is for strings with organ continuo. The organ part shown here is a transcription of the string parts. Bass figuring, omitted here, is shown in the orchestral score. Score and parts are available on rental (see p. 378).
Original slurring (vocal and instrumental) is left unaltered.

In cru - - - ce pro ho - mi -
Thy cross all our wounds hath
pas - sum, im - mo - la - tum In cru - ce pro ho - mi -
suf - fered, for us of - fered, Thy cross all our wounds hath
im-mo - la - tum
for us of - fered,
- ne:
healed.
- ne:
healed.
Cu - jus la - tus
From thy bo - dy,
per - fo - ra - tum
pierced and bro - ken,
per - fo - ra - tum Un - da flu - xit et san - gui - ne:
pierced and bro - ken, Came forth wa - ter and pre - cious blood:

30
Es - to no - bis prae - gus - ta - tum In mor - - - - tis ex -
Be to us by thy ex - am - ple In death's hour of
Es - to no - bis prae - gus - ta - tum In mor - tis ex -
Be to us by thy ex - am - ple In death's hour of
in mor - - - - - - - - - - -
in death's
36
-a - - mi - ne,
trial our food,
in mor - - - - - - -
in death's
-a - mi - ne,
trial our food,
- tis ex - a - mi - ne.
hour of trial our food.
41
- tis ex - a - mi - ne.
hour of trial our food.
tr

35. Exsultate Deo

(*Come rejoice and sing*)

Psalm 81: 1–3
Translation by John Rutter

G. P. da PALESTRINA
(1525–94)

11
S.
ad - - ju - to - ri no - - stro: ju - bi - la - te De - -
un - - to God our help - - er: sing un - to the God - -
A.
-o, ad - ju - to - - - ri no - stro: ju - bi - la - te De - o,
ye un - to God our help - er: sing un - to the God,
ad - - ju - to - ri no - stro: ju - bi - la - te
un - - to God our help - er: sing un - to the
T.
- ju - to - - - - - - - ri no - - stro:
- to God our help - - er:
B.
no - stro, ad - - - ju - to - ri no - stro: ju - bi - la - te De - -
help - er, un - - - to God our help - er: sing un - to the God
ritmico
16
S.
- o Ja - - - - - - - - - cob,
- of Ja - - - - - - - - - cob,
A.
De - o Ja - cob, ju - bi - la - te De - - o
God of Ja - cob, sing un - to the God of
De - o Ja - - cob, De - o Ja - cob, ju - bi -
God of Ja - - cob, God of Ja - cob, sing un-
T.
ju - bi - la - te De - - o Ja - cob, ju - bi - la - te De - o
sing un - to the God of Ja - cob, sing un - to the God of
B.
- o Ja - - cob, ju - bi - la - te De - - o
of Ja - - cob, sing un - to the God of

21
S.
ju - bi - la - te De - - o Ja - cob. Su - mi - te psal - -
sing un - to the God of Ja - cob. Praise him with sing - -
A.
Ja - cob, ju - bi - la - te De - o Ja - - cob.
Ja - cob, sing un - to the God of Ja - - cob.
- la - te De - - o Ja - cob. Su - mi - te psal - mum
- to the God of Ja - cob. Praise him with sing - ing,
T.
Ja - cob, ju - bi - la - te De - o Ja - cob, De - o Ja - -
Ja - cob, sing un - to the God of Ja - cob, God of Ja - -
B.
Ja - cob, De - o Ja - cob. Su - mi - te psal - -
Ja - cob, God of Ja - cob. Praise him with sing - -
mf
26
S.
- mum et da - te tym - pa - num, su - mi - te psal - mum et da - te tym - pa -
- ing, praise God with pipe and drum, praise him with sing - ing, praise God with pipe and
A.
Su - mi - te psal - mum, su - mi - te psal - mum et da - te tym - pa -
Praise him with sing - ing, praise him with sing - ing, praise God with pipe and
et da - te tym - pa - num, su - mi - te psal - mum et
praise God with pipe and drum, praise him with sing - ing, praise
T.
- cob. Su - mi - te psal - mum et da - te, et
- cob. Praise him with sing - ing, with sing - ing, praise
B.
- mum et da - te tym - pa - num:
- ing, praise God with pipe and drum:

31
S.
-num, tym - pa - num: psal - te - ri - um ju - cun - - dum cum ci - tha - ra,
drum, pipe and drum: with lute and mer - ry harp in tune - ful sweet ac - cord,
A.
-num, et da - te tym - pa - num: psal - te - ri - um ju - cun - dum, psal -
drum, praise God with pipe and drum: with lute and mer - - ry harp, with
da - te tym - pa - num: psal - te - ri - um ju - cun -
God with pipe and drum: with lute and mer - ry harp
T.
da - te tym - pa - num: psal - te - ri - um ju - cun -
God with pipe and drum: with lute and mer - ry harp
B.
psal - te - ri - um ju - cun - - dum cum ci - tha - ra,
with lute and mer - ry harp in tune - ful sweet ac - cord,
più legato
36
S.
psal - te - ri - um ju - cun - - dum
with lute and mer - ry harp in
A.
-te - ri - um ju - cun - dum cum ci - tha - ra, cum ci -
lute and mer - ry harp in tune - ful ac - cord, tune - ful
- dum cum ci - tha - ra, cum ci - tha -
in tune - ful ac - cord, tune - ful ac -
T.
- - dum cum ci - - tha - ra, psal - te - ri - um ju - cun - dum
in tune - ful ac - cord, with lute and mer - ry harp in
B.
psal - te - ri - um ju - cun - - dum
with lute and mer - ry harp in

41
S.
cum ci - tha - ra. Buc - ci - na - te
tune-ful ac - cord. Sound his prais - es
A.
- tha - ra. Buc - ci - na - te, buc - ci - na -
ac - cord. Sound his prais - es, sound his prais -
- ra. Buc - ci - na - te, buc - ci - na - te
- cord. Sound his prais - es, sound his prais - es
T.
cum ci - tha - ra. Buc - ci - na - te, buc - ci -
tune - ful ac - cord. Sound his prais - es, sound his
B.
cum ci - tha - ra. Buc - ci - na - te, buc - ci - na - te
tune - ful ac - cord. Sound his prais - es, sound his prais - es
f marcato
46
S.
in Ne - o - me - ni - a tu - ba,
in the new moon with loud trum - pet,
A.
- te in Ne - o - me - ni - a tu -
- es in the new moon with loud trum -
in Ne - o - me - ni - a tu - ba, tu -
in the new moon with loud trum - pet, trum -
T.
-na - te in Ne - o - me - ni - a tu -
prais - es in the new moon with loud trum -
B.
in Ne - o - me - ni - a tu - ba,
in the new moon with loud trum - pet,

50
S.
tu - - - ba, tu - - - ba: in -
trum - - - pet, trum - - - pet: up -
A.
- - ba, tu - - - - - ba, tu - ba: in -
- - pet, trum - - - - - pet, trum - pet: up -
- - ba, tu - - - - - - - - - ba:
- - pet, trum - - - - - - - - - pet:
T.
-ba, tu - - - ba, tu - ba: in -
-pet, trum - - - pet, trum - pet: up -
B.
tu - - - ba:
trum - - - pet:
mf
54
S.
- si - gni di - - - e, in - si - gni di - e, in -
- on your feast day, up - on your feast day, up -
A.
- si - gni di - e, in - si - gni di - - - - - e,
- on your feast day, up - on your feast day,
in - si - gni di - e, in - si - gni di - e so - lem - ni -
up - on your feast day, up - on your feast day and at the
T.
- si - gni di - e so - lem - ni - ta - tis ve -
- on your feast day and at the time ap - point -
B.
in - si - gni di - e so - lem - ni - ta -
up - on your feast day and at the time

59
S.
-si - gni di - - e so - lem - ni - ta - - - tis ve - strae, in -
-on your feast day and at the time ap - point - ed, up -
A.
in - si - gni di - - e so - lem - ni - ta - tis ve - strae, in -
up - on your feast day and at the time ap - point - - ed, up -
-ta - tis ve - - - - - strae, in -
time ap - point - - - - - ed, up -
T.
- - strae, so - lem - ni - ta - tis ve - - strae, in - -
- - ed, and at the time ap - point - - ed, up - -
B.
- tis ve - strae, in - -
ap - point - ed, up - -
f
63
S.
- si - gni di - e so - lem - ni - ta - - tis ve - - - - strae.
-on your feast day and at the time ap - point - - - - ed.
A.
- si - gni di - e so - lem - - ni - ta - tis ve - - strae.
-on your feast day and at the time ap - point - - ed.
- si - gni di - e so - lem - ni - ta - - - tis ve - - strae.
- on your feast day and at the time ap - point - - ed.
T.
- si - gni di - e so - lem - ni - ta - - tis ve - - strae.
-on your feast day and at the time ap - point - - ed.
B.
- si - gni di - e so - lem - ni - ta - tis ve - - - - strae.
- on your feast day and at the time ap - - point - - - ed.

36. Tu es Petrus

(Thou art Peter)

Matthew 16: 18–19
English version by John Rutter

G. P. da PALESTRINA
(1525–94)

13
S.
su - per hanc pe - - - - - tram ae - di - fi - ca - bo Ec - cle -
rock and foun - da - - - - - tion where - on is rest - ing the Church
su - per hanc pe - - - - - tram
rock and foun - da - - - - - tion
A.
su - per hanc pe - - - - - tram ae - di - fi - ca - bo Ec - cle -
rock and foun - da - - - - - tion where - on is rest - ing the Church
T.
ae - di - fi - ca - bo Ec - cle -
where - on is rest - ing the Church
B.
su - per hanc pe - tram
rock and foun - - - - - da - tion
ae - di - fi - ca - bo Ec - cle -
where - on is rest - ing the Church
più f
18
- si - am me - am,
which I shall build,
ae - di - fi - ca - bo Ec - cle - si -
where - on is rest - ing the Church which
- si - am me - am, ae - di - fi - ca - bo Ec -
which I shall build, where - on is rest - ing the
- - si - am me - - - am, ae - di - fi - ca - bo Ec - cle - si -
which I shall build, where - on is rest - ing the Church which
ae - di - fi - ca - bo Ec - cle - si -
where - on is rest - ing the Church which
- si - am me - am,
which I shall build,

23
S.
ae - di - fi - ca - bo Ec - cle - si - am
where - on is rest - ing the Church which I
-am me - - - am, ae - di - fi - ca - bo
I shall build, where - on is rest - ing
A.
-cle - - si - am me - am, ae - di - fi - ca - bo
church which I shall build, where - on is rest - ing
T.
-am me - - - - am, ae - di - fi - ca - bo Ec - cle - - si -
I shall build, where - on is rest - ing the Church which
-am me - am, ae - di - fi - ca - - -
I shall build, where - on is rest - - -
B.
ae - di - fi - ca - bo Ec - cle -
where - on is rest - ing the Church
28
S.
me - am, Ec - cle - si - am me - - - am, et
shall build, the Church which I shall build; the
Ec - cle - si - am me - - - - am,
the Church which I shall build;
A.
Ec - cle - si - am me - - - am,
the Church which I shall build;
T.
-am, Ec - cle - si - am me - - am, et
I, the Church which I shall build; the
-bo Ec - cle - si - am me - - am, et por -
-ing the Church which I shall build; the gates
B.
- si - am me - - - am,
which I shall build;
mf

33
S.
por-tae in-fe-ri, et por-tae in-fe-
gates of dark-est hell, the gates of dark-est
et por-tae in-fe-ri,
the gates of dark-est hell,
A.
et por- tae in-fe-ri,
the gates of dark-est hell,
T.
por-tae in-fe-ri, et por- tae in-fe-
gates of dark-est hell, the gates of dark-est
B.
tae in-fe-ri, et por- tae in-fe-
of dark-est hell, the gates of dark-est
et por- tae in-fe-ri,
the gates of dark-est hell,
38
S.
-ri, et por-tae in-fe-ri non prae-va-le-bunt,
hell, the gates of dark-est hell shall have no pow-er,
et por-tae in-fe-ri non prae-va-le-bunt, non prae-va-
the gates of dark-est hell shall have no pow-er, shall have no
A.
et por- tae in-fe-ri non prae-va-le-bunt, non prae-va-
the gates of dark-est hell shall have no pow-er, shall have no
T.
-ri, et por- tae in-fe-ri non prae-va-le-bunt
hell, the gates of dark-est hell shall have no pow-er
B.
-ri non prae-va-le-bunt, non prae-va-
hell shall have no pow-er, shall have no
et por- tae in-fe-ri non prae-va-le-bunt,
the gates of dark-est hell shall have no pow-er,
marcato
cresc.
f

44
S.
non prae - va - le - bunt ad - ver - sus e -
shall have no pow - er a - gainst my king -
- le - bunt ad - ver - sus e - - - - - am:
pow - er a - gainst my king - - - - dom:
A.
- le - bunt ad - ver - sus e - - - - - am, non prae - va - le - bunt ad - ver - sus e -
pow - er a - gainst my king - - - - dom, shall have no pow - er a - gainst my king -
T.
ad - ver - sus e - - - - - am, non prae - va - le - bunt ad - ver - sus e -
a - gainst my king - - - - dom, shall have no pow - er a - gainst my king -
B.
- le - bunt ad - ver - sus e - am:
pow - er a - gainst my king - dom:
non prae - va - le - bunt ad - ver - sus e -
shall have no pow - er a - gainst my king -
50
S.
- - - am: et ti - bi
- - - dom: and I shall
et ti - bi da - bo
and I shall make thee
A.
- - - am: et ti - bi da - bo cla - ves, et ti - bi
- - - dom: and I shall make thee, and I shall
T.
- - - am: et ti - bi da - bo, et ti - bi
- - - dom: and I shall make thee, and I shall
B.
et ti - bi da - bo, et ti - bi
and I shall make thee, and I shall
- - - am: et ti - bi
- - - dom: and I shall
mf più legato

55
S.
da - bo cla - ves re - gni cae - lo - - - - - - - rum,
make thee guard and keep - er of hea - - - - - ven's gate,
cla - ves re - gni cae - lo - - - - - - - rum,
guard and keep - er of hea - - - - ven's gate,
A.
da - bo cla - ves re - gni cae - lo - - - - - - rum,
make thee guard and keep - er of hea - - - - ven's gate,
T.
da - bo cla - ves
make thee guard and
B.
da - bo cla - ves
make thee guard and
da - bo cla - ves
make thee guard and
60
S.
et ti - bi da - -
and I shall make
et ti - bi da -
and I shall make
A.
re - gni cae - lo - - - - - rum, et ti - bi da -
keep - er of hea - - - - ven's gate, and I shall make
T.
re - gni cae - lo - - - - - - rum,
keep - er of hea - - - - ven's gate,
B.
re - gni cae - lo - - - - - - rum,
keep - er of hea - - - - ven's gate,
re - gni cae - lo - - - - - - rum,
keep - er of hea - - - - ven's gate,

65
S.
-bo, et ti - bi da - bo, et ti -
thee, and I shall make thee, and I
-bo, et ti - bi da - bo, et
thee, and I shall make thee, and
A.
-bo, et ti - bi da - bo, et ti - bi da - bo
thee, and I shall make thee, and I shall make thee
T.
et ti - bi da - bo, et ti -
and I shall make thee, and I
B.
et ti - bi da - bo, et ti - bi da - bo, et ti -
and I shall make thee, and I shall make thee, and I
et ti - bi da - bo
and I shall make thee
cresc.
70
S.
- bi da - bo cla - ves re - gni, cla -
shall make thee guard and keep - er, guard
ti - bi da - bo cla - ves re - gni cae - lo - rum, cla -
I shall make thee guard and keep - er of hea - ven's gate, guard
A.
cla - ves re - gni cae - lo - rum, cla -
guard and keep - er of hea - ven's gate, guard
T.
- bi da - bo cla - ves re - gni cae - lo - rum,
shall make thee guard and keep - er of hea - ven's gate,
B.
- bi da - bo cla - ves re - gni cae - lo - rum, cla -
shall make thee guard and keep - er of hea - ven's gate, guard
cla - ves re - gni cae - lo - rum,
guard and keep - er of hea - ven's gate,
f
mf

75
- ves re - gni cae - lo - rum, cla - ves re - gni cae -
and keep - er of hea - ven's gate, guard and keep - er of
S.
- ves re - gni cae - lo - - - - - rum, cla - ves re - gni cae -
and keep - er of hea - - - - ven's gate, guard and keep - er of
A.
- ves re - gni cae - lo - - - - - rum, cla - ves re - gni
and keep - er of hea - - - ven's gate, guard and keep - er
T.
cla - ves re - gni cae -
guard and keep - er, guard and
B.
- ves re - gni cae - lo - - - - - rum, cla - ves re - gni cae -
and keep - er of hea - - - ven's gate, guard and keep - er of
cla - ves re - gni cae -
guard and keep - er of
f
80
FINE
S.
- lo - - - - - - - rum, cae - lo - - rum.
hea - - - - - - ven's gate, of hea - ven's gate.
- lo - - - - rum, cae - lo - - - - - rum.
hea - ven's gate, of hea - - - ven's gate.
A.
cae - lo - - - - - - rum.
of hea - - - ven's gate.
T.
- lo - rum, cae - - - - - lo - - rum.
keep - - er of hea - ven's gate.
B.
- lo - rum, cae - - - - - - lo - rum.
hea - ven's gate, hea - - - - - - - ven's gate.
- lo - - - - - rum, cae - - - lo - - rum.
hea - - - - - ven's, hea - - - ven's gate.
FINE
cresc.
ff

Secunda Pars
85
S.
A.
T.
B.
Quod - cum - que li - ga - ve-ris su - per ter - -
Here on earth what - ev - er law thou or - dain - -
Quod - cum - que li - ga - ve-ris su - per ter - -
Here on earth what - ev - er law thou or - dain - -
Quod - cum - que li - ga - ve-ris su - per
Here on earth what - ev - er law thou or - - -
Quod - cum - que,
Here on earth
Quod - cum - que,
Here on earth
Quod - cum - que,
Here on earth
mf
92
S.
A.
T.
B.
- - - ram,
- - - est,
- - - ram,
- - - est,
ter - - ram, quod - cum - que li - ga - ve-ris su - per
-dain - - est, what - ev - - er, what - ev - er law thou or - - -
quod - cum - que li - ga - ve-ris su - per ter - -
what - ev - - er, what - ev - er law thou or - dain - -
quod - cum - que li - ga - ve-ris su - per ter - -
what - ev - er, what - ev - er law thou or - dain - -
quod - cum - que li - ga - ve-ris su - per
what - ev - - er, what - ev - er law thou or - - -

98
S.
e - rit li - ga - tum et in cae - lis,
it shall be or - dained ev'n in hea - ven,
e - rit li - ga - tum et in cae - lis, e - rit li - ga -
it shall be or - dained ev'n in hea - ven, it shall be or -
A.
ter - ram, e - rit li - ga -
- dain - est, it shall be or -
T.
- ram, e - rit li - ga - tum et in cae - lis, li - ga -
- est, it shall be or - dained ev'n in hea - ven, be or -
B.
- ram, e - rit li - ga - tum et in cae - lis,
- est, it shall be or - dained ev'n in hea - ven,
ter - ram, e - rit li - ga -
- dain - est, it shall be or -
cresc.
f
mf
cresc.
104
S.
et in cae - lis. Et quod - cum - que, et quod - cum - que, et quod-
ev'n in hea - ven. And what - ev - er, and what - ev - er, and what-
- tum et in cae - lis. Et quod - cum - que,
- dained ev'n in hea - ven. And what - ev - er,
A.
- tum et in cae - lis. Et quod - cum - que, et quod-
- dained ev'n in hea - ven. And what - ev - er, and what-
T.
- tum et in cae - lis. Et quod - cum - que
- dained ev'n in hea - ven. And what - ev - er
B.
Et quod - cum - que, et quod-
And what - ev - er, and what-
- tum et in cae - lis. Et quod - cum - que,
- dained ev'n in hea - ven. And what - ev - er,
f
mf
cresc.
f

110
S.
-cum-que sol-ve-ris su - per ter - ram, et quod-cum-que sol - ve-ris,
-ev - er thou dost grant here up-on earth, and what-ev - er thou dost grant,
et quod-cum-que sol - ve-ris su -
and what-ev - er thou dost grant here
A.
-cum-que sol-ve-ris su - per ter - ram, et quod-cum-que sol - ve-ris
-ev - er thou dost grant here up-on earth, and what-ev - er thou dost grant
T.
sol-ve-ris su - per ter - ram, et quod-cum-que sol-ve-ris su -
thou dost grant here up-on earth, and what-ev - er thou dost grant here
B.
-cum-que sol-ve-ris su - per ter - ram,
-ev - er thou dost grant here up-on earth,
et quod-cum-que sol-ve-ris
and what-ev - er thou dost grant
marc.

116
S.
e-rit so-lu-tum, e-rit so-lu-tum et
it shall be grant-ed, it shall be grant-ed there
-per ter-ram, e-rit so-lu-tum,
up-on earth, it shall be grant-ed,
A.
su-per ter-ram, e-rit so-lu-tum, e-rit so-lu-tum, e-rit so-lu-tum
here up-on earth, it shall be grant-ed, it shall be grant-ed, it shall be grant-ed
T.
-per ter-ram, e-rit so-lu-tum, e-rit so-lu-tum, e-rit so-lu-tum
up-on earth, it shall be grant-ed, it shall be grant-ed, it shall be grant-ed
B.
e-rit so-lu-tum, e-rit so-lu-tum
it shall be grant-ed, it shall be grant-ed
su-per ter-ram, e-rit so-lu-tum,
here up-on earth, it shall be grant-ed,
mf più legato

122
S.
in cae - lis, e - rit so - lu - tum et in cae -
in hea - ven, it shall be grant - ed there in hea -
e - rit so - lu - tum et in
it shall be grant - ed there in
A.
et in cae - lis, e - rit so - lu - tum et
there in hea - ven, it shall be grant - ed in
T.
et in cae - lis, e - rit so - lu - tum et in
in hea - ven, it shall be grant - ed there in
B.
et in cae - lis, et in
there in hea - ven, there in
e - rit so - lu - tum
it shall be grant - ed
f
127
D. S. al Fine
(back to p. 262)
S.
- lis, et in cae - lis.
- ven, in hea - ven.
cae - lis, et in cae - lis. Et ti - bi da -
hea - ven, in hea - ven. And I shall make
A.
in cae - lis, et in cae - lis. Et ti - bi da - bo
hea - ven, there in hea - ven. And I shall make
T.
cae - lis, et in cae - lis. Et ti - bi da -
hea - ven, there in hea - ven. And I shall make
B.
cae - lis. Et ti - bi da -
hea - ven. And I shall make
et in cae - lis.
in hea - ven.
D. S. al Fine
(back to p. 262)
mf

37. Sicut cervus

(Like as the hart)

Psalm 42: 1
English translation by John Rutter*

G. P. da PALESTRINA
(1525–94)

* Based on the 1662 Book of Common Prayer

12
- - - qua - rum, si - - - cut
- - - ter - brooks, like as
-cut cer - vus de - si - de - rat ad fon - tes a - qua -
as the hart de - sir - eth the wa - - - ter - brooks, like as the
fon - tes a - - - qua - - - - - - - - - - -
wa - ter-brooks, like as
si - - cut cer - vus de - si - de-rat ad
like as the hart de - sir - eth the
dim.
p
cresc.
mp
17
cer - vus de - si - de-rat ad fon - tes a - - - - qua - -
the hart de - sir - eth, de - sir - eth the wa - -
-rum, de - si - de-rat ad fon - tes a - qua - - - -
hart de - sir - eth, de - sir - eth the wa - - - -
- rum, de - si - de - rat ad fon - tes a -
the hart de - sir - eth, de - sir - eth the
fon - tes, de - si - de - rat ad fon - tes a - qua -
wa - ter-brooks, the hart de - sir - - eth the wa - ter -
cresc.
mf

22
- - - rum: i - - - ta
- ter - - brooks: so my
- - - - - - - - - - rum:
- - - - - - - ter - - brooks:
-qua - - rum: i - - - ta de - - si - - de-rat,
wa - ter - brooks: so my soul long - - eth for
-rum: i - - - ta de - - - si - - - - -
- brooks: so my soul long - - - - -
dim.
p
28
de - si - - - - - - - de - rat,
soul long - - - - - eth for thee,
i - - ta de - - - si - - - - - - de-rat, i - -
so my soul long - - - eth for thee, long - -
i - ta de - si - de - rat, i - - ta de - si -
thee, so longs my soul for thee, so my soul long-
- - de - rat, i - - ta de - - si -
- eth for thee, so my soul long -

34
i - - ta de - si - de-rat
so my soul long - eth,
- ta, i - - ta de- - si - de-rat
- eth, so my soul long - eth,
- de-rat, de-si-de-rat, i - - ta de - si -
- eth for thee, for thee, O God, so my soul long -
- - - de - rat, i - -
- - eth for thee, so
cresc.
mp
40
a - - ni-ma me - - a ad te, De - - -
so my soul long - - eth for thee, O
a - - ni-ma me - a ad te, De -
so my soul long - eth, long - - eth for
- de-rat a - ni-ma me - - - a
- eth, long - - eth, so my soul long - - eth
-ta de - si - de-rat, de - si-de-rat a - ni -
my soul long - eth, long - eth, long - eth, so my
cresc.
mf

46
- us, a - ni - ma me - - a
God, so my soul long - - eth
- us, a - - ni - ma me - a ad te, De - us,
thee, so my soul long - eth, long - eth for thee,
ad te, De - - - - - - - - - us, a - ni-
for thee, O God, O God, so my
- ma me - a ad te, De - - - us, a - ni - ma me - a
soul long - eth for thee, O God, so my soul long - eth
52
ad te, De - - - - - - us.
for thee, O God.
ad te, De - - us, ad te, De - - - - - us.
for thee, O God, for thee, O God.
- ma me - a ad te, De - - us, ad te, De - - us.
soul long - eth for thee, O God, for thee, O God.
ad te, De - - us, ad te, De - - - - - - us.
for thee, O God, for thee, O God.
dim.
p

à Hélène

38. Salve Regina

Antiphon of the BVM

FRANCIS POULENC
(1899–1963)

Translation of text: Hail, holy Queen, Mother of mercy: hail, our life, our sweetness and our hope. We cry to you, exiles, children of Eve. We sigh to you, mourning and weeping in this vale of tears. Turn then, O our Advocate, your merciful eyes towards us. And, after this exile is over, show us Jesus, the blessed fruit of your womb. O kind, O holy, O sweet Virgin Mary.

Note: Poulenc's slurring has been left unaltered.

19
E - ja er - go,
f
p doux
-go, Ad-vo-ca - ta nos - tra, il - los tu-os mi-se-ri-cor-des
f
p doux
24
mf
(S.)
mf très lié
(A.)
p très lié
6
4
o - cu-los ad nos con-ver - te. Et Je - sum, Et Je - sum,
(T.)
(B.)
mf
mf très lié
p très lié
28
p
court
pp très doux
be - ne-dic-tum fruc-tum ven - tris tu - i, no - bis post hoc ex - si - li -
p
court
pp très doux
ex - si - li-um
33
mf
p très doux
-um, no-bis post hoc ex - si - li - um, no-bis post hoc os-ten - de. O cle-mens: O
mf
p très doux

Noizay, Mai 1941

39. Bogoroditsye Dyevo

(*Ave Maria*)

Words from the Liturgy of Vespers
English version by Bill Tamblyn

SERGEI RACHMANINOV (1873–1943)
Op. 37 no. 6

* Translated from the Russian. In the autograph the marking was 'Andante, leggiero, molto dolce'.

Note: See p. vii for pronunciation guide. The symbol ŏ indicates a sound nearer to 'a' than to 'o'.

11
pp
pp molto dolce
yu. Bŏ - - gŏ - ro - - di -
is with you. Hail O Vir - gin
p
yu. Bla - gŏ - slŏ - vyen - - - - na Tyi
is with you. A - mong all wo - - - - men you
yu. Bŏ - - gŏ - ro - - di -
is with you. Hail O Vir - gin
yu.
is with you.
16
-tsye Dye - vo, ra - - dui - ssya,
Mo - - ther. Hail Mo - ther, full of grace,
ff
vzhe - nakh, i bla - gŏ - slŏ - vyen Plod chrye - va Tvŏ - ye - go, ya -
are blest, and blest is the fruit of your womb, fruit of your womb, born
-tsye Dye - vo, ra - - dui - ssya,
Mo - - ther. Hail Mo - ther, full of grace,
ya -
born

20
ff
p
mf
ra - - - dui - ssya, ya - - ko Spa - - - - ssa
full of grace, born the Sa - - - - viour
- ko Spa - - ssa rŏ - di - la, ya - ko Spa - ssa rŏ - di -
the Sa - - viour, born the Sa - - - viour, born the Sa - viour of our
ra - - - dui - ssya, ya - - ko Spa - - ssa rŏ - di -
full of grace, born the Sa - - viour of our
- ko Spa - - ssa rŏ - di - la, ya - - ko Spa - ssa
the Sa - - viour, born the Sa - - viour, born the Sa - viour
23
pp
ppp
poco marcato
rŏ - - - di - la ye - ssi dush na - shikh.
of our souls, Sa - viour of our souls.
- la ye - ssi dush na - shikh.
souls, Sa - viour of our souls.
- la, ya - ko Spa - ssa rŏ - di - la ye - ssi dush na - shikh.
souls, born the Sa - viour of our souls, Sa - viour of our souls.
rŏ - - - di - la ye - ssi dush na - shikh.
of our souls, Sa - viour of our souls.

40. Abendlied

(*Bide with us*)

Luke 24: 29
English translation by John Rutter

JOSEF RHEINBERGER (1839–1901)
Op. 69 no. 3

7
S.
uns, denn es will A - bend wer - - den, denn es will
us, for eve - ning sha - dows dark - - en, for eve-ning
uns, denn es will A - bend wer - - den,
us, for eve - ning sha - dows dark - - en,
A.
bleib' bei uns, denn es will A - bend wer - - den,
bide with us, for eve-ning sha - dows dark - - en,
T.
denn es will A - bend wer - -
for eve-ning sha - dows dark - -
bleib' bei uns, denn es will, denn es will A - bend
bide with us, bide with us, for eve-ning sha - dows
B.
uns, denn es will A - bend, A - bend wer - - den,
us, for eve-ning sha - dows, sha - dows dark - - en,
f
13
S.
A - bend wer - den, A - - bend wer - - den;
sha - dows dark - en, sha - - dows dark - - en,
denn es will A - bend wer - - den, A - bend wer - den;
for eve-ning sha - dows dark - - en, sha - dows dark - en,
A.
denn es will A - bend wer - - - den;
for eve-ning sha - dows dark - - en,
T.
-den, denn es will A - - bend wer - - den;
-en, for eve - ning sha - - dows dark - - en,
wer - - den, will A - - - bend wer - - den;
dark - - en, the sha - - - dows dark - - en,
B.
denn es will A - - - bend wer - - den;
for eve-ning sha - - - dows dark - - en,
ff
dim.

19
S.
und der Tag hat sich ge - nei - - - get, sich ge - nei - - - - - -
and the day will soon be o - - - ver, soon be o - - - - - -
und der Tag hat sich ge - nei - - - - - - get, sich ge -
and the day will soon be o - - - - - - ver, soon be
A.
und der Tag hat sich ge - nei - -
and the day will soon be o - -
T.
und der
and the
und der Tag hat sich ge - nei - - - - - -
and the day will soon be o - - - - - -
B.
und der Tag hat sich ge -
and the day will soon be
25
dim.
p
S.
- get, sich ge - nei - get, bleib' bei uns,
- ver, soon be o - ver, bide with us,
- nei - - - - - - - - - get, bleib' bei uns,
o - - - - - - - - - ver, bide with us,
A.
- get, hat sich ge - nei - get, o bleib' bei uns,
- ver, will soon be o - ver, Lord, bide with us,
T.
Tag hat sich ge - nei - - - - - - get, bleib' bei
day will soon be o - - - - - - ver, bide with
- get, hat sich ge - nei - - - get, o bleib' bei
- ver, will soon be o - - - ver, Lord, bide with
B.
- nei - get, sich ge - nei - - - get, bleib' bei
o - ver, soon be o - - - ver, bide with

30
S.
denn es will A - bend wer - den,
for eve - ning sha - dows dark - en,
denn es will A - bend wer - den,
for eve - ning sha - dows dar - ken,
A.
denn es will A - bend wer - den,
for eve - ning sha - dows dark - en,
T.
uns, denn es will A - bend wer - den,
us, for eve - ning sha - dows dark - en,
f
uns, denn es will A - bend wer - den, und der
us, for eve - ning sha - dows dark - en, and the
B.
f
uns, denn es will A - bend wer - den, und der Tag hat sich ge -
us, for eve - ning sha - dows dark - en, and the day will soon be
f
35
S.
f
p
und der Tag hat sich ge - nei - - - get. O bleib' bei
and the day will soon be o - - - ver. Lord, bide with
f
und der Tag hat sich ge - nei - - - get.
and the day will soon be o - - - ver.
A.
f
und der Tag hat sich ge - nei - - - - - - - - - get.
and the day will soon be o - - - - - - - - - ver.
T.
f
p
und der Tag hat sich ge - nei - - - get. O
and the day will soon be o - - - ver. Lord,
Tag hat sich ge - neigt, hat sich ge - nei - - - get.
day will soon be o - ver, soon be o - - - ver.
B.
p
- nei - - - get, hat sich ge - nei - - - get. O
o - - - ver, will soon be o - - - ver. Lord,
p

40
S.
uns, o bleib' bei uns, o bleib' bei
us, O bide with us, O bide with
O bleib' bei uns, bleib, o bleib' bei
O bide with us, Lord, O bide with
A.
O bleib bei uns, bei uns, o bleib', o bleib' bei
Lord, bide with us, with us, O Lord, bide with
T.
bleib' bei uns, bei uns, denn es will A - bend wer - - -
bide with us, with us, for eve - ning sha - dows dark - - -
O bleib' bei uns, o bleib, o bleib' bei
Lord, bide with us, O Lord, bide with
B.
bleib', o bleib' bei uns, o bleib', o bleib' bei
bide, O bide with us, Lord, bide, O bide with
45
S.
uns, denn es will A - bend wer - - - den.
us, for eve - ning sha - dows dark - - - en.
uns, denn es will A - bend wer - - - den.
us, for eve - ning sha - dows dark - - - en.
A.
uns, denn es will A - bend wer - - - den.
us, for eve - ning sha - dows dark - - - en.
T.
-den, denn es will A - bend wer - - - den.
- en, for eve - ning sha - dows dark - - - en.
uns, denn es will A - bend wer - - - den.
us, for eve - ning sha - dows dark - - - en.
B.
uns, denn es will A - bend wer - - - den.
us, for eve - ning sha - dows dark - - - en.

41. Unser lieben Frauen Traum

(Our Lady's dream)

Words: German traditional
English version by Catherine Winkworth

MAX REGER (1873–1916)
Op. 138 no. 4

33
S.1
S.2
A.
T.
B.1
B.2
f
Herr Je - sus Christ der Hei - land ist un - ser Heil und Trost: Mit sei - ner
Lord Je - sus Christ, our sav - ing health, hears us when we call: By his most
40
ritardando
pp
mp
ff
S.1 uns all er - lost.
re - deemed us all.
bit - tern Mar - ter hat er uns all er - lost, hat er uns all er - lost.
bit - ter Pas - sion He hath re - deemed us all, He hath re - deemed us all.

42. O salutaris Hostia

(Lord, who for us was sacrificed)

Words by St Thomas Aquinas (1225–74)
English version by John Rutter

GIOACHINO ROSSINI
(1792–1868)

Andantino
sotto voce
SOPRANO ALTO
TENOR BASS
O sa - lu - ta - ris Hos - ti - a, Quae cae - li pan-dis os - ti-um,
Lord, who for us was sa - cri - ficed, Thou o - pened hea-ven's por - tals wide,
5
ff
pan - dis os - ti - um, Bel - la, bel - la pre - munt hos - ti - li - a,
hea - ven's por - tals wide; Guard us, guard us now from our foes, O Christ,
10
pp
pre - munt hos - ti - li - a, Da ro - bur, fer au - xi - li - um, Da ro - bur, fer au -
guard us from our foes, O Christ, Thy strength and sav - ing help pro - vide, thy strength and sav - ing
15
f
- xi - li - um, fer au - xi - li - um. O sa - lu - ta - ris Hos - ti - a,
help pro - vide, sav - ing help pro - vide. Lord, who for us was sa - cri - ficed,

20
ff
Quae cae - li pan - dis os - ti - um, pan - dis os - ti - um, Bel - la pre - munt hos -
Thou o - pened hea - ven's por - tals wide, hea - ven's por - tals wide; Guard us from all our
ff
25
pp
f
- ti - li - a, hos - ti - li - a, Da ro - bur, da ro - bur, fer au -
foes, O Christ, from all our foes. Give strength, Lord, give strength, Lord, grant thy
pp
f
30
p
- xi - li - um, Da ro - bur, da ro - bur, fer au - xi - li -
sav - ing help, Give strength, Lord, give strength, Lord, grant thy sav - ing
p
35
S.
cresc.
f
- um. Da ro - bur, da ro - bur, au -
help. Give us thy strength, grant us thy
A.
cresc.
f
- um. Da ro - bur, fer au - xi - li - um, au -
help. Give us thy strength, grant us thy help, thy
T.
cresc.
f
- um. Da ro - bur, fer au - xi - li - um, au -
help. Give us thy strength, grant us thy help, thy
B.
cresc.
f
- um. Da ro - bur, fer au - xi - li - um, au -
help. Give us thy strength, grant us thy help, thy
cresc.
f

40
ff
S.
-xi - li - um, Da ro - bur, da ro - bur, da ro - bur, fer au - xi - li - um,
sav - ing help: Give strength, Lord, give strength, Lord, give strength, and grant thy sav - ing help,
A.
- xi - li - um, Da ro - bur, da ro - bur, da ro - bur, fer au - xi - li - um,
sav - ing help: Give strength, Lord, give strength, Lord, give strength, and grant thy sav - ing help,
T.
-xi - li - um, Da ro - bur, da ro - bur, da ro - bur, fer au - xi - li - um,
sav - ing help: Give strength, Lord, give strength, Lord, give strength, and grant thy sav - ing help,
B.
-xi - li - um, Da ro - bur, da ro - bur, da ro - bur, fer au - xi - li - um,
sav - ing help: Give strength, Lord, give strength, Lord, give strength, and grant thy sav - ing help,
46
pp
au - xi - li - um, Da ro - bur, da ro - bur, fer au - xi - li -
thy sav - ing help, give strength, Lord, give strength, Lord, grant thy sav - ing
51
Più lento
-um, Da ro - bur, da ro - bur, fer au - xi - li - um.
help, Give strength, Lord, give strength, Lord, grant thy sav - ing help.

43. Psalm 23

(*Gott ist mein Hirt*)

German version by Moses Mendelssohn
English version by John Rutter*

FRANZ SCHUBERT
(1797–1828)

* Based on the 1662 Book of Common Prayer

10
pp
Hirt, mir wird nichts man - - - - - geln, er
shep - herd: I shall lack no - - - - - thing. He
13
la - gert mich auf grü - ne Wei - de, er lei - tet mich an
feed - eth me in pas - tures green, yea, he lead - eth me be -
pp
er lei - tet mich an
he lead - eth me be -
lei - - - tet mich, er
lead - - - eth me, he
16
stil - len Bä - chen, er la - gert mich auf grü - ne Wei - de, er
-side still wa - ters, he feed - eth me in pas - tures green, yea, he
stil - len Bä - chen, er la - gert mich auf grü - ne Wei - de, er
-side still wa - ers, he feed - eth me in pas - tures green, yea, he

19
ppp
lei - tet mich an stil - len Bä - - chen,
lead - eth me be - side still wa - - ters.
ppp
ppp
22
p
er labt mein schmacht-en-des Ge - müt, er
The Lord re - stor - eth all my soul; he
p
p
25
cresc.
führt mich auf ge-rech-tem Stei - ge zu sei - nes
lead - eth me in paths of right-eous-ness to praise his
fz
fz
cresc.
cresc.
ff
fz

28
fz fz fz pp
Na - mens Ruhm. Und wall' ich auch im
ho - ly Name. Yea, though I walk through
[dim.] p decresc. pp
32
dim.
To - des-schat-ten - Ta - le, so wall' ich oh - ne Furcht, denn
death's dark sha - dowed val - ley, yet I will fear no e - vil, for
mf
36
p pp
du be - schüt - zest mich, und wall' ich auch im
thou dost shel - ter me, yea, though I walk through

39
dim.
To - des - schat - ten - Ta - le, so wall' ich oh - ne
death's dark sha - dowed val - ley, yet I will fear no
dim.
dim.
42
f
pp
p
Furcht, denn du be - schüt - zest mich, dein Stab
e - vil, for thou dost shel - ter me: thy rod
f
p
(A.2) p
dein
thy
f
p
46
und dei - ne
and staff, thy Stü - tze sind mir
rod and staff they
dein Stab und dei - ne
thy rod and staff, thy
Stab und dei - ne
rod and staff, thy

* See Commentary (p. 375).

59
pp
Fein - de zu, du salbst mein Haupt mit Ö - le, und
all my foes, thou hast an - oint - ed my head with oil, and
pp
Freu - den - mahl,
ta - ble for me
Be - cher
shall be
62
pp
f
pp
p
schenkst mir vol - le, vol - le Be - cher ein, mir
my cup shall be full, it shall be full. Thy
pp
f
pp
p
pp
f
pp
p
65
fol - get Heil und Se - lig - keit in die - sem Le - ben
good - ness and thy mer - cy, they shall ev - er fol - low
pp

68
nach, einst ruh' ich ew' - ge Zeit dort in des
me; Yea, I shall dwell for ev - er in the
pp
71
ppp
Ew' - - - gen Haus, mir fol - get Heil und
house of the Lord: thy good - ness and thy
ppp
ppp
74
Se - lig - keit in die - - - sem Le - ben
mer - cy shall ev - - - ver fol - - low
im
shall
in die - - - sem Le - - ben
shall ev - - - ver fol - - low

77
morendo
nach, einst ruh' ich ew' - ge Zeit
me: yea, I shall dwell ev - er - more,
morendo
nach, einst ruh' ich ew' - ge Zeit
me: yea, I shall dwell ev - er - more,
morendo
80
dort in des Ew' - - - - - - - gen
dwell there for ev - - - - - - - er - -
in des
for
dort in des
dwell there for
83
f
[pp]
Haus.
-more.
f
[pp]
f
pp

44. Psalm 100

(*Jauchzet dem Herrn*)

English version by John Rutter

HEINRICH SCHÜTZ (1585–1672)
SWV 36

See Commentary (p. 376) for prefatory information.

13
die - net dem Her - ren mit Freu - - - - - - den,
serve him with glad - ness, with glad - - - - - - ness;
mit Freu - - -
with glad - - -
18
kommt vor sein An-ge-sicht, kommt vor sein
come ye be - fore his face, come ye be -
- - - - den, kommt vor sein An-ge-sicht,
- - - - ness; come ye be - fore his face,

22
An-ge-sicht,
-fore his face,
kommt vor sein An-ge-sicht mit Froh-lock-en,
come ye be-fore his face with re-joi-cing,
mit Froh-
with re-
kommt vor sein An-ge-sicht
come ye be-fore his face,
mit Froh-lock-en,
with re-joi-cing,
[#]
27
Her-re Gott
Lord he is
-lock-en.
-joi-cing.
Er-ken-net dass der Her-re Gott ist, er hat
Ac-know-ledge that the Lord he is God, he cre-
mit Froh-lock-en.
with re-joi-cing.
più legato
f marc.
6 6 7 6 # # 6

* Conductors may wish to shorten this chord to one beat.

44
sei - ner Wei - de, und zu Scha - fen sei - ner Wei - de. Ge - het zu
of his pas - ture, and the sheep of his pas - ture. En - ter in -
Scha - fen sei - ner Wei - de, und zu Scha - fen sei - ner Wei - de.
sheep of his pas - ture, and the sheep of his pas - ture.
dim.
p
f
[♯]
49
sei - nen To - ren ein, ge - het zu sei - nen To - ren ein mit
- to Je - ho - vah's gates, en - ter in - to Je - ho - vah's gates with
Ge - het zu sei - nen To - ren ein, ge - het zu sei - nen To - ren ein
En - ter in - to Je - ho - vah's gates, en - ter in - to Je - ho - vah's gates
♯
♯
[♮]

54
Dan - - - - - - - ken,
thanks - - - - - - gi - ving,
zu sei - nen Vor-
and in - to his
mit Dan - - - - - - ken,
with thanks - - - - - - gi - ving,
[6♯] ♯ 4 3[♯] [6♯] ♯ 4 3[♯] ♯ ♯ ♯
59
Lo - - - - - ben,
prais - - - - - es,
mit Lo -
with prais -
- hö - fen mit Lo - ben, mit Lo - ben,
courts with prais - es, with prais - es,
mit Lo - - - - - ben,
with prais - - - - - es,
mit Lo - ben, mit Lo - ben,
with prais - es, with prais - es,
4 3[♯] 4 3[♯]

- - - - ben,
- - - - es,
64
-ben, mit Lo - ben,
- es, with prais - es,
dan - ket ihm,
thank the Lord,
mit Lo - - - - ben,
with prais - - - - es,
mit Lo - ben, mit Lo - ben,
with prais - es, with prais - es,
dan - ket ihm,
thank the Lord,
[𝅗𝅥. = 𝅗𝅥 of preceding]
4 3
4 3
6
6
70
lo - bet, lo - bet sei - nen
praise his ho - ly Name for
dan - ket ihm,
thank the Lord,
lo - bet sei - nen Na - - men,
praise his Name for ev - - er,
lo - bet, lo - bet sei - nen
praise his ho - ly Name for
lo - bet, lo - bet sei - nen
praise his ho - ly Name for
dan - ket ihm,
thank the Lord,
lo - bet sei - nen Na - men,
praise his Name for ev - er,
[𝅗𝅥 = 𝅗𝅥. of preceding]
lo - bet, lo - bet sei - nen
praise his ho - ly Name for
♮
♯
6
♯
♯

75
lo - bet, lo - bet sei - nen
praise his ho - ly Name for
lo - bet, lo - bet sei - nen
praise his ho - ly Name for
lo - bet sei - nen Na - men,
praise his Name for ev - er,
lo - bet sei - nen
praise his Name for
lo - bet, lo - bet sei - nen
praise his ho - ly Name for
lo - bet, lo - bet sei - nen
praise his ho - ly Name for
lo - bet, lo - bet sei - nen
praise his ho - ly Name for
lo - bet, lo - bet sei - nen
praise his ho - ly Name for
lo - bet sei - nen Na - men,
praise his Name for ev - er,
lo - bet, lo - bet sei - nen Na - men,
praise his ho - ly Name for ev - er,
6 6 ♮ ♮ ♯ ♮ ♯ [♯] [6] [♯]
79
Na - men. Denn der Herr ist freund - lich,
ev - er. For the Lord is gra - cious,
lo - bet, lo - bet sei - nen
praise his ho - ly Name for
lo - bet sei - nen Na - men. ist
praise his Name for ev - er. is
lo - bet, lo - bet sei - nen
praise his ho - ly Name for
mf
♮ ♯ 6

85
ist freund - lich, und sei - ne Gna - de wäh - ret e - - wig,
is gra - cious, and ev - er - last - ing is his mer - - cy:
freund - lich, und sei - ne Gna - de wäh - ret e - -
gra - cious, and ev - er - last - ing is his mer -
cresc.
f
92
und sei - ne Wahr-heit für und für, und sei - ne Wahr-heit für und für,
his truth shall stand for ev - er - more, his truth shall stand for ev - er - more,
-wig, und sei - ne Wahr-heit für und für, und sei - ne Wahr-heit für und
- cy: his truth shall stand for ev - er - more, his truth shall stand for ev - er -
[5 2] 6 [4 3] [4 3] [4 3] [4 3]

97
und sei - ne Wahr - heit für und für.
his truth shall stand for ev - er - more.
für, und sei - ne Wahr - heit für und für.
- more, his truth shall stand for ev - er - more.
104
Eh - - - - re, Eh - re sei dem Va - ter,
Glo - - - - ry, glo - ry to the Fa - ther,
Eh - - - - re, Eh - re sei dem Va - ter,
Glo - - - - ry, glo - ry to the Fa - ther,
(f)

110
Eh - re sei dem Va - ter und dem Sohn
glo - ry to the Fa - ther, and to the Son,
und dem Sohn
and to the Son,
Eh - re sei dem Va - ter und dem
glo - ry to the Fa - ther, and to the
und dem
and to the
6 7 6[♯] 7 6[♯]
115
und auch dem heil' - - - gen Gei - ste,
and to the Ho - - - - ly Spi - rit,
und auch dem heil' - - gen Gei - - ste,
and to the Ho - - ly Spi - - rit,
heil' - gen
Ho - ly
Sohn, dem heil' - - - gen Gei -
Son, the Ho - - - - ly Spi -
Sohn, dem heil' - - gen Gei - -
Son, the Ho - - ly Spi - -
dem heil' - gen Gei - -
the Ho - ly Spi - -
mf
5 6 ♯ 5 2 6 6 5 ♯ 5 6 ♯ 5 2 6 6 5 ♯

120
dem heil' - - - - - gen Gei - ste,
the Ho - - - - - ly Spi - rit,
dem heil' - - gen Gei - - ste,
the Ho - - ly Spi - - rit,
dem heil' - gen Gei - - ste,
the Ho - ly Spi - - rit,
- ste,
- rit,
dem heil' - - - - - gen Gei -
the Ho - - - - - ly Spi -
- ste,
- rit,
dem heil' - - gen Gei - -
the Ho - - ly Spi - -
- ste,
- rit,
dem heil' - gen Gei - -
the Ho - ly Spi - -
♯ [♮] [6] 5 6 ♯ 6 5 ♯ 5 6 ♯ 6 5 ♯
125
wie es war im An - fang, jetzt und im - mer - dar
as in the be - gin - ning, now and ev - er - more,
- ste,
- rit,
- ste,
- rit,
wie es war im An - fang, jetzt und im - mer -
as in the be - gin - ning, now and ev - er -
- ste,
- rit,
6[♯] 6[♯] 6 ♯ 6

130
und von E - wig - keit
now and ev - er - more,
zu E - wig - keit.
and ev - er - more.
A - - - - -
A - -
A - - - - -
- dar
- more,
und von E - wig - keit
now and ev - er - more,
zu E - wig - keit.
and ev - er - more.
cresc.
f
♮ 6 6 6 6[♯] 6 6[♯]
135
- - men,
a - - - - - - - men,
- - men,
a - - - - men,
- - men,
a - - - - - - - men,
A - - - - - men,
a - - - - - -
A - - - men,
a - - -
A - - - - - - men,
a - - - - - -
5 6
4 3
4 3[♯] ♯
5 6
4 3
4 3[♯]

139
a - - - - - - men, a - - - - - - - -
a - - - men, a - - - -
a - - - - - - men, a - - - - - - - -
-men, a - - - - - - men, a - -
-men, a - - - men,
-men, a - - - - - - men, a - -
4 3[♯]
143
-men,
a - - - - - - - - - - men.
-men,
-men,
- - - - men,
a - - - - - - men.
a - - - men,
- - - - men,
4 3

45. Selig sind die Toten

(*Blessed are the faithful*)

Revelation 14: 13
English version by John Rutter

HEINRICH SCHÜTZ (1585–1672)
SWV 391

* May alternatively be sung by baritones, with all tenors singing Tenor 1 part.

8
S.
se - blest
A.
die in dem Her - ren ster - ben, se -
whose earth - ly life is end - ed, blest
T.
die in dem Her - ren ster - ben,
whose earth - ly life is end - ed,
Her - ren ster - ben, se - lig
life is end - ed, blest are
B.
die in dem Her - ren ster - ben, se -
whose earth - ly life is end - ed, blest
mp
6 6 ♮ ♯
14
S.
- lig sind, se - lig sind, se - lig sind die To - ten, die in dem
are they, blest are they, bless - ed are the faith - ful, whose earth - ly
se - lig sind, se - lig sind, se - lig sind die To - ten,
blest are they, blest are they, bless - ed are the faith - ful,
A.
- lig sind, se - lig sind die To - ten,
are they, bless - ed are the faith - ful,
T.
se - lig sind, se - lig sind die To - ten,
blest are they, bless - ed are the faith - ful,
sind, se - lig sind, se - lig sind die To - ten,
they, blest are they, bless - ed are the faith - ful,
B.
- lig sind, se - lig sind die To - ten,
are they, bless - ed are the faith - ful,
[6] 5 6 ♯ ♮

20
S.
Her - ren ster - - ben, ster - - - - - ben,
life is end - - ed, end - - - - - ed,
die in dem Her - ren ster - - ben,
whose earth-ly life is end - - ed,
A.
die in dem Her-ren ster - ben,
whose earth-ly life is end - ed,
T.
die in dem Her - ren ster - - - - - - - ben,
whose earth-ly life is end - - - - - - - ed,
die in dem
whose earth-ly
die in dem Her-ren ster -
whose earth-ly life is end -
B.
die in dem
whose earth-ly
6 6 5 6 6
26
S.
die in dem Her-ren ster -
whose earth-ly life is end -
die in dem Her - ren ster - - ben,
whose earth-ly life is end - - ed,
A.
die in dem Her - ren ster - - ben,
whose earth-ly life is end - - ed,
T.
Her - ren ster - ben,
life is end - ed,
die in dem Her-ren ster - ben, die in dem
whose earth-ly life is end - ed, whose earth - ly
-ben,
-ed,
die in dem Her-ren ster - ben,
whose earth-ly life is end - ed,
die in dem
whose earth-ly
B.
Her - ren ster - - - - - - ben,
life is end - - - - - - ed,
die in dem Her-ren ster -
whose earth-ly life is end -
6 8 7 7 6[♯] 6 5 6 5 6

32
S.
-ben, die in dem Her - - - - ren ster - - ben, von nun
- ed, whose earth - ly life is end - - ed, from hence - - - -
die in dem Her - ren ster - - ben, ster - - - - ben, von nun
whose earth - ly life is end - - ed, end - - - - ed, from hence -
A.
die in dem Her - ren ster - - ben von nun
whose earth - ly life is end - - ed, from hence -
T.
Her - ren ster - ben, die in dem Her - ren ster - - ben, von nun
life is end - ed, whose earth - ly life is end - - ed, from hence - -
Her - ren ster - ben,
life is end - ed,
B.
-ben,
- ed,
6 5 6 [4] 6 6 5 7 6 7 6[♯] 7 6
38
S.
an. Ja, der Geist spricht, ja, der Geist spricht:
- forth. Yea, the Lord saith, yea, the Lord saith:
an. Ja, der Geist spricht, ja, der Geist
- forth. Yea, the Lord saith, yea, the Lord
A.
an. Ja, der Geist spricht, ja, der Geist
- - - forth. Yea, the Lord saith, yea, the Lord
T.
an. Ja, der Geist spricht, ja, der Geist
- forth. Yea, the Lord saith, yea, the Lord
Ja, der Geist spricht, ja, der Geist
Yea, the Lord saith, yea, the Lord
B.
Ja, der Geist spricht, ja, der Geist
Yea, the Lord saith, yea, the Lord
mf
mp
4 ♯ ♯ ♮ [6] 4 3 4 ♯

* See Commentary (p. 376).

62
S.
- beit, ih - rer Ar - - beit,
- bours, all their la - - bours,
Ar - - beit,
la - - bours,
und ih - re Wer - ke fol - gen
yea, and their works do fol - low
A.
- beit, ih - - rer Ar - - - - beit,
- bours, all their la - - - - bours,
und ih - re Wer - ke
yea, and their works do
T.
von ih - rer Ar - beit,
from all their la - bours,
Ar - beit, Ar - - - - beit, und ih - re Wer - ke fol - gen ih - nen
la - bours, la - - - - bours, yea, and their works do fol - low af - ter
B.
- - - beit, Ar - - - beit,
- - - bours, la - - - bours,
dim.
p
mp
4 ♮ 6[♭] 6 [5]
♯ 4 4 ♯
67
S.
und ih - re Wer - ke fol - gen ih - nen,
yea, and their works do fol - low af - ter,
ih - nen nach,
af - ter them,
und ih - re Wer - ke fol - gen ih - nen
yea, and their works do fol - low af - ter
A.
fol - gen ih - nen nach,
fol - low af - ter them.
T.
und ih - re Wer - ke fol - gen ih - nen nach,
yea, and their works do fol - low af - ter them,
und ih - re Wer - ke
yea, and their works do
nach, und ih - re Wer - ke fol - gen ih - nen nach,
them, yea, and their works do fol - low af - ter them,
B.
und ih - re Wer - ke fol - gen ih - nen nach,
yea, and their works do fol - low af - ter them,
[♯] ♯ 6

71
S.
fol - gen ih - - - - nen nach. Sie ru - hen von
fol - low af - - - - ter them. They rest now from
nach, fol - gen ih - - nen nach. Sie ru - hen von ih - rer
them, fol - low af - - ter them. They rest now from all their
A.
sie ru - hen von ih - rer
They rest now from all their
T.
fol - gen ih - nen, fol - gen ih - nen nach, sie ru - hen,
fol - low af - ter, fol - low af - ter them, they rest now,
sie ru - hen,
they rest now,
B.
fol - gen ih - nen nach, sie ru - hen,
fol - low af - ter them, they rest now,
p
6 6
79
S.
ih - rer Ar - beit, sie ru - hen, sie ru - hen von ih - rer Ar -
all their la - bours, they rest now, they rest now from all their la -
Ar - - beit, sie ru - hen, sie ru - hen von ih - rer
la - - bours, they rest now, they rest now from all their
A.
Ar - - - beit, sie ru - hen, sie ru - hen von ih - rer Ar -
la - - - bours, they rest now, they rest now from all their la -
T.
sie ru - hen von ih - rer
they rest now from all their
sie ru - hen, sie ru - hen
they rest now, they rest now
B.
sie ru - hen von ih - rer Ar -
they rest now from all their la -
cresc.
mp
6 6 4 ♯ ♯ ♯ [♮] ♯ ♯ ♮ ♯ [6♮] 4
♯ 4 ♯

88
S.
- beit, ih - rer Ar - - beit,
- bours, all their la - - bours,
Ar - - beit,
la - - bours,
und ih - re Wer - ke fol - gen ih - nen
yea, and their works do fol - low af - ter
A.
- beit, ih - - rer Ar - - - - beit,
- bours, all their la - - - - bours,
T.
Ar - - beit, ih - - rer Ar - - - - beit,
la - - bours, all their la - - - - bours,
und ih - re
yea, and their
von ih - rer Ar - - beit,
from all their la - - bours,
und ih - re Wer - ke fol - gen
yea, and their works do fol - low
B.
- - beit, Ar - - beit,
- - - bours, la - - bours,
dim.
p
mp
4 ♮ 6 3 6 4 4 3
93
S.
und ih - re Wer - ke fol - gen ih - nen nach,
yea, and their works do fol - low af - ter them,
fol - gen
fol - low
nach,
them,
und ih - re Wer - ke fol - gen ih - nen nach,
yea, and their works do fol - low af - ter them,
A.
und ih - re Wer - ke fol - gen ih - nen nach, und ih - re Wer - ke fol - gen ih - nen
yea, and their works do fol - low af - ter them, yea, and their works do fol - low af - ter
T.
Wer - ke fol - gen ih - - - - nen nach,
works do fol - low af - - - - ter them,
ih - - - nen nach,
af - - - ter them,
und ih - re Wer - ke fol - gen
yea, and their works do fol - low
B.
und ih - re Wer - ke fol - gen ih - nen nach,
yea, and their works do fol - low af - ter them,
cresc.
mf
♯ 6 ♮ ♯

97
S.
ih - - nen nach, und ih - re Wer - ke fol - gen ih - -
af - - ter them, yea, and their works do fol - low af - -
fol - gen ih - - - nen nach, und ih - re Wer - ke fol - gen
fol - low af - - - ter them, yea, and their works do fol - low
A.
nach, fol - gen ih - - - - nen nach,
them, do fol - low af - - - ter them,
T.
fol - gen ih - nen nach, ih - nen nach,
fol - low af - ter them, af - ter them,
ih - nen, fol - gen ih - nen nach, fol - gen ih - nen, fol - gen
af - ter, fol - low af - ter them, fol - low af - ter, fol - low
B.
fol - gen ih - - - - nen
fol - low af - - - - ter
dim.
mp cresc.
mf
6 5 # [6] 6 # 4 # 6 6
101
S.
- - - nen nach, fol - gen ih - nen, ih - nen nach.
- - - ter them, fol - low af - ter, af - ter them.
ih - - nen nach, und ih - re Wer - ke fol - gen ih - nen nach.
af - - ter them, yea, and their works do fol - low af - ter them.
A.
fol - gen ih - - - - nen nach, ih - - - nen nach.
fol - low af - - - - ter, af - - - ter them.
T.
und ih - re Wer - ke fol - gen ih - nen nach, fol - gen ih - nen nach.
yea, and their works do fol - low af - ter them, fol - low af - ter them.
ih - - nen nach.
af - - ter them.
B.
nach, fol - gen ih - - - - nen nach.
them, fol - low af - - - - ter them.
mp cresc. mf
6 3 6 4 4 3 6 6

46. Ave Maria

The Angelic Salutation

IGOR STRAVINSKY
(1882–1971)

47. Laudate Dominum

(*O praise the Lord our God*)

Psalm 117
Translation by John Rutter

J. P. SWEELINCK
(1562–1621)

6
S.
o - mnes gen - - tes: lau - da - - te
all ye peo - - ple: praise him, ye
Do - mi - num o - mnes gen - - - - - tes:
Lord our God, all ye peo - - - - - ple:
A.
- tes, o - mnes gen - tes, o - mnes gen - tes: lau - da - - te e - um, lau -
- ple, all ye peo - ple, all ye peo - ple: praise him, ye na - tions, praise
T.
Do - mi - num o - mnes gen - - - tes: lau -
Lord our God, all ye peo - - - ple: praise
B.
o - mnes gen - - - - - tes: lau - da - - te e - um,
all ye peo - - - - - ple: praise him, ye na - tions,
6
9
S.
e - um, lau - da - te e - um, lau - da - - te
na - tions, praise him, ye na - tions, praise him, ye
lau - - da - - te e - - um, lau - da - te e - -
praise him, ye na - tions, praise him, ye na - -
A.
- da - - te e - um, lau - da - - te e - um, lau -
him, ye na - tions, praise him, ye na - tions, praise
T.
- da - - te e - um, lau - da - te e - um, lau - da -
him, ye na - tions, praise him, ye na - tions, praise him,
B.
lau - da - - te e - um,
praise him, ye na - tions,
[7 6] 6 [7 6]

11
S.
e - - um o - mnes po - - - pu - li,
na - tions, praise his ho - - - ly Name,
-um, lau - da - - - te e - um o - mnes
- tions, praise him, ye na - tions, praise his
A.
- da - te e - - - - - um o - mnes po - -
him, ye na - - - - - tions, praise his ho - -
T.
- te e - - - um o - mnes po - - - pu -
ye na - - - tions, praise his ho - - - ly
B.
lau - da - - - te e - um
praise him, ye na - tions,
[♮] [7 6♮]
13
S.
o - mnes po - - - pu - - - li, o - mnes po - - - pu -
praise his ho - - - ly Name, praise his ho - - - ly
po - - - - pu - li, o - mnes po - - - pu - -
ho - - - ly Name, praise his ho - - - ly
A.
- pu - li, o - mnes po - - - pu - li, po - - pu -
- ly Name, praise his ho - - - ly Name, ho - - ly
T.
- li, o - mnes po - pu - - li, o - - - mnes po - pu -
Name, praise his ho - ly Name, praise his ho - ly
B.
o - mnes po - - pu - li.
praise his ho - - ly Name.
[♭ 4 3♮ ♮] [6 4 5 ♮]

15
S.
- li. Quo - ni - am, quo - ni - am con - fir - ma - ta
Name. For the Lord, for the Lord shew - eth ev - er
- li. Quo - ni - am, quo - ni - am con - fir - ma - ta est,
Name. For the Lord, for the Lord shew - eth ev - er more,
A.
- li. Quo - ni - am, quo - ni - am,
Name. For the Lord, for the Lord,
T.
- li. Quo - ni - am con - fir - ma - ta est, con - fir -
Name. For the Lord shew - eth ev - er more, shew - eth
B.
Quo - ni - am, quo - ni - am con - fir - ma - ta est,
For the Lord, for the Lord shew - eth ev - er more,
mf più dolce
[6]
6 5 6 4
18
S.
est, con - fir - ma - ta est, con - fir - ma - ta est, con - - fir -
more, shew - eth ev - er more, shew - eth ev - er more, shew - - eth
quo - - ni - am con - fir - ma - ta est, con - fir - ma - ta
for the Lord shew - eth ev - er more, shew - eth ev - er
A.
quo - - ni - am con - fir - ma - ta est, con - fir -
for the Lord shew - eth ev - er more, shew - eth
T.
- ma - ta est, quo - - ni - am con - fir - ma - ta
ev - er more, for the Lord shew - eth ev - er
B.
quo - - ni - am con - - - - - -
for the Lord shew - - - - - -
6 5 6 4 ♯ 6 4 ♯ 6 4

20
S.
-ma - ta est, quo - ni - am con - - fir - ma - ta est
ev - er more, for the Lord shew - - eth ev - er more
est, con - fir - ma - ta est, con - fir - ma - ta est
more, shew - eth ev - er more, shew-eth ev - er more
A.
-ma - ta est, con - - fir - ma - ta est, con - fir - ma - ta est
ev - er more, shew - - eth ev - er more, shew-eth ev - er more
T.
est, con - fir - ma - ta est, con - fir - ma - ta est su - per
more, shew - eth ev - er more, shew-eth ev - er more un - to
B.
-fir - - - ma - - - - ta est
-eth ev - - - - - er more
mp
22
S.
su - per nos mi - se - ri - cor - di - a e - jus, mi - se - ri - cor - di - a e -
un - to us his lov - ing kind - ness and mer - cy, his lov - ing kind - ness and mer -
su - per nos mi - se - ri - cor - di - a e - - jus, quo - ni - am
un - to us his lov - ing kind - ness and mer - - cy, for the Lord,
A.
su - per nos mi - se - ri - cor - di - a e - jus, mi - se - ri - cor - di - a e -
un - to us his lov - ing kind - ness and mer - cy, his lov - ing kind - ness and mer -
T.
nos mi - se - ri - cor - - di - a e - jus, mi - se - ri - cor - di - a e -
us his lov - ing kind - - ness and mer - cy, his lov - ing kind - ness and mer -
B.
su - per nos mi - se - ri - cor - di - a e - - - - - - - jus,
un - to us his lov - ing kind - ness and mer - - - - - - cy,
legato

25
S.
-jus, quo - ni-am con-fir-ma-ta est su-per nos mi-se-ri-cor - di-a
-cy, for the Lord shew-eth ev-er more un-to us his lov-ing kind - ness and
quo - ni-am con-fir-ma-ta est su-per nos mi-se-ri-cor - di-a
for the Lord shew-eth ev-er more un-to us his lov-ing kind - ness and
A.
-jus, quo - ni-am con-fir-ma-ta est su-per nos mi-se-ri-cor - di-a
-cy, for the Lord shew-eth ev-er more un-to us his lov-ing kind - ness and
T.
-jus, quo - ni-am con-fir-ma-ta est su-per nos mi-se-ri-cor -
-cy, for the Lord shew-eth ev-er more un-to us his lov-ing kind -
B.
quo - ni-am con-fir-ma - ta est su-per nos mi-se-ri-cor - di-a
for the Lord shew-eth ev - er more un-to us his lov-ing kind - ness and
28
S.
e - jus: et ve-ri-tas Do - mi-ni,
mer - cy: and lo, the truth of the Lord,
e - jus: et ve-ri-tas Do - mi-ni, et ve-ri-
mer - cy: and lo, the truth of the Lord, and lo, the
A.
e - jus: et ve-ri-tas Do-mi-ni, et ve-ri-tas Do-mi-ni,
mer - cy: and lo, the truth of the Lord, and lo, the truth of the Lord,
T.
-di-a e-jus: et ve-ri-tas Do-mi-ni, et ve-ri-
-ness and mer-cy: and lo, the truth of the Lord, and lo, the
B.
e - jus: et ve-ri-tas Do-mi-ni,
mer - cy: and lo, the truth of the Lord,
più marcato
mf

31
S.
et ve-ri - tas Do-mi-ni, Do - mi-ni ma - net in ae -
and lo, the truth of the Lord, of the Lord shall en-dure for
-tas Do - mi-ni, et ve-ri - tas Do-mi-ni
truth of the Lord, and lo, the truth of the Lord
A.
et ve-ri-tas Do-mi - ni, et ve-ri - tas Do-mi-ni ma - net
and lo, the truth of the Lord, and lo, the truth of the Lord shall en-
T.
-tas Do-mi-ni, Do-mi-ni, et ve-ri-tas Do-mi-ni
truth of the Lord, and lo, the truth, and lo, the truth of the Lord
B.
et ve-ri-tas Do-mi-ni ma - net
and lo, the truth of the Lord shall en-
cresc.
[7 6♮ ♭ 6 3]
34
-ter - - num, ma-net in ae-ter - - - - num, et
ev - - er, shall en-dure for ev - - - - - er, and
ma-net in ae-ter - - - - num, ma-net in ae-ter-num,
shall en-dure for ev - - - - - er, shall en-dure for ev - er,
in ae-ter - num, ma - net in ae-ter-num, ma-net in ae-ter-num, et
-dure for ev - er, shall en-dure for ev - er, shall en-dure for ev - er, and
ma - net in ae-ter - num, et
shall en-dure for ev - er, and
in ae-ter - num, ma-net in ae-ter-num,
-dure for ev - er, shall en-dure for ev - er,
f
mf
[6] ♮ [6] [♭] ♮ ♮

37
S.
ve - ri - tas Do - mi - ni, et ve - ri - tas Do - mi - ni,
lo, the truth of the Lord and lo, the truth of the Lord,
et ve - ri - tas Do - mi - ni, et ve - ri -
and lo, the truth of the Lord, and lo, the
A.
ve - ri - tas Do - mi - ni, et ve - ri - tas Do - mi - ni, et ve - ri - tas Do - mi -
lo, the truth of the Lord, and lo, the truth of the Lord, and lo, the truth of the
T.
ve - ri - tas Do - mi - ni, et ve - ri - tas Do - mi - ni, Do - mi - ni,
lo, the truth of the Lord, and lo, the truth of the Lord, and lo, the
B.
et ve - ri - tas Do - mi - ni, et ve - ri -
and lo, the truth of the Lord, and lo, the
[6♮] [6] [6♮ 5 6] ♮ [♮] [♮]
40
S.
et ve - ri - tas Do - mi - ni ma-net in ae - ter -
and lo, the truth of the Lord shall en - dure for ev -
-tas Do - mi - ni, Do - mi - ni ma - net in ae - ter - num,
truth of the Lord, of the Lord shall en - dure for ev - er,
A.
-ni, et ve - ri - tas Do - mi - ni ma - net in ae - ter - num, ma -
Lord, and lo, the truth of the Lord shall en - dure for ev - er, shall
T.
et ve - ri - tas Do - mi - ni ma - net
truth, and lo, the truth of the Lord shall en -
B.
-tas Do - mi - ni ma - net in ae - ter - num,
truth of the Lord shall en - dure for ev - er,
cresc.
[5 6 6] [7 6♮] [♭ 6 3 6] ♮

43
S.
- - - - num, ma - net in ae - ter - num, ma - - net in ae -
- - - - er, shall en - dure for ev - er, shall en - dure for
ma - net in ae - ter - - - - num, ma - - net in ae - ter -
shall en - dure for ev - - - - - er, shall en - dure for ev -
A.
- net in ae - ter - num, ma - net in ae - ter - num, ma - net, ma -
en - dure for ev - er, shall en - dure for ev - er, en - dure, shall
T.
in ae - ter - num, ma - net in ae - ter - -
- dure for ev - er, shall en - dure for ev - -
B.
ma - net in ae - ter - num, ma - -
shall en - dure for ev - er, en - -
f
[6]
46
- ter - - - - - - - - - - - - - - num.
ev - - - - - - - - - - - - - - er.
- num, ma - - net in ae - ter - - num.
- er, shall en - dure for ev - - er.
- net in ae - ter - num, ma - net in ae - ter - num.
en - dure for ev - er, shall en - dure for ev - er.
- num, ma - - net in ae - ter - - - - - - - num.
- er, shall en - dure for ev - - - - - - - er.
- net in ae - - - - ter - - - num.
- dure for ev - - - - - - - - er.
cresc. al fine

48. Dostoino yest

(Hymn to the Virgin)

Words from the Liturgy of St John Chrysostom
English version by John Rutter

P. I. TCHAIKOVSKY
(1840–93)

Note: See p. vii for pronunciation guide. The symbol ŏ denotes a sound closer to 'a' than to 'o'.

11
dim.
Ma - ter Bo - ga na - - she-go, i Ma - ter Bo - - - ga
thee our Sa - viour Christ was born, of thee our Sa - - viour
dim.
Ma - ter Bo - ga na - she - go, i Ma-ter Bo - - - ga
thee our Sa - viour Christ was born, of thee our Sa - - viour
f
dim.
- roch - nu-yu, i Ma-ter Bo - ga na - she - go, Ma - - - ter Bo - ga
pur - est One, Of thee our Sa - viour Christ was born, of thee our Sa - viour
dim.
Ma - ter Bo - ga na - she - go, i Ma - ter Bo - - - ga
thee our Sa - viour Christ was born, of thee our Sa - - viour
dim.

15
p
ff
na - she - go; chest - nyei - shu - yu khe - ru - vim i slav - nyei - shu - yu byez sra-
Christ was born; A - bove all the che - ru - bim, and ex - cel - ling in glo - ry
p
ff
na - she - go; chest - nyei - shu - yu khe - ru - vim i slav - nyei - shu - yu byez sra-
Christ was born; A - bove all the che - ru - bim, and ex - cel - ling in glo - ry
p
ff
na - she - go; chest - nyei - shu - yu khe - ru - vim i slav - nyei - shu - yu byez sra-
Christ was born; A - bove all the che - ru - bim, and ex - cel - ling in glo - ry
p
ff
na - she - go; chest - nyei - shu - yu khe - ru - vim i slav - nyei - shu - yu byez sra-
Christ was born; A - bove all the che - ru - bim, and ex - cel - ling in glo - ry
p
ff

21
p
-vnye-ni - ya se - ra - fim; Byez ist - lye - ni - ya Bo - ga slo - va rozhd - shu - yu,
all the bright se - ra - phim; Bless - ed Vir - gin and Mo - ther of God's Ho - ly Child,
-vnye - ni - ya se - - ra - fim; Byez ist - lye - ni - ya Bo - ga slo - va rozhd - shu - yu,
all the bright se - - ra - phim; Bless - ed Vir - gin and Mo - ther of God's Ho - ly Child,
27
mf
su - shchu - yu Bŏ - gŏ - ro - dit - su, Tya vye - li - cha - yem, Tya vye - li - cha - yem,
Mai - den most pure and un - de - filed, We sing thy prai - ses, we sing thy prai - ses,
su - shchu - yu Bŏ - gŏ - ro - dit - su, Tya vye - li - cha - yem, Tya vye - li -
Mai - den most pure and un - de - filed, We sing thy prai - ses, we sing thy

34
Tya vye - li - cha-yem, vye - li - cha - yem, Tya vye - li - cha -
we sing thy prai - ses, sing thy prai - ses, we sing thy prai -
Tya vye - li - cha-yem, vye - li - cha - yem, Tya vye - li - cha -
we sing thy prai - ses, sing thy prai - ses, we sing thy prai -
- cha - - - - - - - - - - yem, Tya vye - li - cha -
prai - - - - - - - - - - ses, we sing thy prai -
Tya vye - li - cha-yem, vye - li - cha - yem, Tya vye - li - cha -
we sing thy prai - ses, sing thy prai - ses, we sing thy prai -
40
- - yem. I vsyekh, i vsya.
- - ses. A - men, a - - - men.
- - yem. I vsyekh, i vsya.
- - ses. A - men, a - - - men.
- - yem. I vsyekh, i vsya.
- - ses. A - men, a - - - men.
- - yem. I vsyekh, i vsya.
- - ses. A - men, a - - - men.

49. Ave Maria

The Angelic Salutation
English version by John Rutter

(*Hail, Virgin Mary*)

GIUSEPPE VERDI
(1813–1901)

11
ppp
dim. sempre
morendo
et be - ne - di - ctus fru - ctus ven - tris tu - i Je - sus.
e - qual in bless - ing is the Child thou bear - est, Je - sus.
et be - ne - di - ctus fru - ctus ven - tris tu - i Je - sus.
e - qual in bless - ing is the Child thou bear - est, Je - sus.
et be - ne - di - ctus fru - ctus ven - tris tu - i Je - sus.
e - qual in bless - ing is the Child thou bear - est, Je - sus.
a - ve Ma - ri - a.
hail, thou Vir - gin Ma - ry.
17
p
San - cta Ma - ri - a, Ma - ter De - i,
Ma - ry most ho - ly, God's pure Mo - ther,
SCALA ENIGMATICA
A - ve Ma -
Hail thou Vir -
San - cta Ma - ri - a, Ma - ter De - i, o - ra pro
Ma - ry most ho - ly, God's pure Mo - ther, O pray, pray for
San - cta Ma - ri - a,
Ma - ry most ho - ly,

22
p
o - ra pro no - bis, pro no - - - bis
pray for us sin - ners, O pray for
- ri - - - - - - a, a - - - ve,
- gin Ma - - - ry, hail thou,
p
no - bis pec - ca - to - ri - bus, nunc et in
us poor sin - ners ev - 'ry one, now and in our
p
Ma - ter De - i, o - ra pro no - - - - bis pec - ca -
God's pure Mo - ther, O pray for us poor sin - ners
p
27
pp
pec - ca - to - - ri - bus, nunc et in ho - - ra mor - tis
sin - ners ev - - 'ry one, both now and in our hour of
a - - ve Ma - - ri - - - - - - -
hail thou Vir - - - gin Ma - - -
pp
ho - ra mor - - - - - tis, et in ho - - ra mor - tis
hour of dy - - - - - ing, now and in our hour of
[pp]
- to - - - - - ri - bus, o -
ev - - - - - 'ry one, O
pp

32
p
no - strae. A - ve Ma - ri - a,
dy - ing. Hail, Vir - gin Ma - ry,
p
- a. A - ve Ma - ri - - - - - a,
- ry. Hail, Vir - gin Ma - - - - - ry,
Scala enigmatica
p
no - strae. A - - - - - - - - - - - ve
dy - ing. Hail, thou
p
dolce
- ra. A - ve Ma - ri - - a, gra - ti - a ple - na,
pray. Hail, Vir - gin Ma - - ry, mai - den most ho - ly,
p
37
gra - ti - a ple - na, Do - mi - nus te - cum, be - ne - di - cta tu in mu - li -
mai - den most ho - ly, God's grace is with thee, thou art great - ly blest a - bove all
gra - ti - - a ple - - na, Do - mi - nus te - cum, be - ne - di - cta
mai - den most ho - - ly, God's grace is with thee, thou art great - ly
Ma - - - - ri - - - - - - - a, a - - -
Vir - - - gin Ma - - ry, hail
Do - mi - nus te - cum, be - ne - di - cta tu in mu - li - e - ri - bus,
God's grace is with thee, thou art great - ly blest a - bove all wo - man - kind,

42
p
- e - ri - bus, et be - ne - di - ctus fru - ctus ven - tris tu - - - i
wo - man - kind, and e - qual in bless - ing is the Child thou
p
tu in mu - li - e - ri - bus, et be - ne - di - ctus fru - ctus
blest, God's grace is with thee, e - qual in bless - ing is the
p
- ve, a - - ve Ma - - ri - - -
thou, hail thou Vir - - gin
p
47
estremamente piano
Scala enigmatica
pp
Je - - - sus. A - - - - - - - - -
bear - - - est. Hail,
ven - tris tu - i Je - sus. San - cta Ma - ri - a, Ma - - -
Child thou bear - est, Je - sus. Ma - ry most ho - ly, Ma - - -
- - - - a. San - cta Ma - ri - a, Ma - ter
Ma - - - ry. Ma - ry most ho - ly, God's pure
A - ve Ma - ri - a. San - cta Ma - ri - a, Ma - ter
hail, Vir - gin Ma - ry. Ma - ry most ho - ly, God's pure
pp estremamente piano

52
un poco cresc.
- ve Ma - - - ri - - - - - - a,
Vir - - - gin Ma - - - - - - - ry,
- ter De - i, o - - - ra pro no - bis
- ry most ho - - ly, O pray, pray thou for
De - - - i, o - ra pro no - - - - - bis pec -
Mo - - - ther, O pray for us poor sin -
un poco cresc.
De - i, o - - - - ra pro no - - -
Mo - ther, O pray for us,
un poco cresc.
57
dim. poco a poco
a - - - ve, a - - - ve
hail, thou Vir - - - gin
dim. poco a poco
pec - - - ca - to - - - ri - bus, nunc et in
us poor sin - - - ners all, now and in our
dim. poco a poco
- ca - to - ri - bus, nunc et in ho - ra
- ners ev - 'ry one, both now and in our
dim. poco a poco
- bis pec - ca - to - - - ri - bus, nunc et in
pray for sin - - - ners all, both now and
dim. poco a poco

61
allarg.
p morendo
Ma - - - - ri - - - - - - - - a.
Ma - - - - - - - - - - - - - ry.
p morendo
ho - ra mor - - - tis no - - strae.
hour of dy - - - - ing, dy - - ing.
p morendo
mor - - - - tis no - - - - strae.
hour of dy - - - ing.
p morendo
ho - - ra mor - - - tis no - - - - strae.
in our hour of dy - - - - ing.
allarg.
p morendo
Vuota
66
pp
allarg.
A - - - - - - - - men. A - - - men.
pp
A - - - - - - - - men. A - - - - men.
pp
A - - - - - - - - men. A - - - - - men.
pp
A - - - - - - - - men. A - - - men.
allarg.
pp

50. Exsultate justi

(*Shout for joy, ye righteous*)

Psalm 33: 1–3
Translation by John Rutter

LODOVICO VIADANA
(*c.*1560–1627)

* ¢ in source. Note values in this section are unaltered.

13
-no in ci - - - - - - tha-ra, con-fi - te - mi-ni Do-mi - no
him with tune - - - - - ful harp, praise the Lord and re-joice in him
-no in ci - - - - - tha - ra, con-fi - te - mi-ni Do-mi - no in
him with tune - - - - - ful harp, praise the Lord and re-joice in him with
-no in ci - - - - tha - - ra, con-fi - te - mi-ni Do-mi - no in
him with tune - - - - ful harp, praise the Lord and re-joice in him with
-no, con-fi - te - mi-ni Do-mi - no in
him, praise the Lord and re-joice in him with
leggiero
f
mf
19
in ci - - - - tha - ra: in psal-te-ri-o de-cem chor-da-rum, in psal -
with tune - - - ful harp: bring the lute and be joy - ful be - fore him, bring the
ci - - - - - tha-ra: in psal - te - ri-o de-cem chor-
tune - - - - - ful harp: bring the lute and be joy - ful be -
ci - - - - - tha-ra: in psal - te - ri-o de-cem chor-
tune - - - - - ful harp: bring the lute and be joy - ful be -
ci - - - tha - - - ra: in psal-te-ri-o de-cem chor-da-rum, in psal -
tune - - - ful harp: bring the lute and be joy - ful be - fore him, bring the

24
-te - ri - o de - cem chor - da - - rum psal - li - te il - li,
lute and be joy - ful be - fore him, of - - fer your prai - ses,
-da - rum, in psal - te - ri - o de - cem chor - da - rum psal -
-fore him, bring the lute and be joy - ful be - fore him, of -
-da - rum, in psal - te - ri - o de - cem chor - da - rum psal - - li - te
-fore him, bring the lute and be joy - ful be - fore him, of - - fer your
-te - ri - o de - cem chor - da - - rum psal - li - te il - -
lute and be joy - ful be - fore him, of - - fer your prai - -
28
psal - - - - li - te il - - li. Can - ta - te
of - - - - fer your prais - es. Sing ye a
- li - te il - li, psal - li - te il - - - - - li.
fer your prai - ses, of - fer your prai - - - - - ses.
il - li, psal - - li - te il - - li, psal - li - te il - li.
prai - ses, of - - fer your prai - ses, of - fer your prai - ses.
- li, psal - - li - te il - - - - - - - li.
- ses, of - - fer your prai - - - - - - - ses.
f marcato

33
e - i, can - ta - te e - i can - ti-cum no -
new song, sing ye a new song un - to the Lord
Can - ta - te e - i, can - ta - te e - i can - - ti -
Sing ye a new song, sing ye a new song un - - to
Can - ta - te e - i, can - ta - te e - i can - - ti - cum
Sing ye a new song, sing ye a new song un - to the Lord
Can - ta - te e - i, can - ta - te e - i can - - ti -
Sing ye a new song, sing ye a new song un - - to
39
- - - - - - - vum: be - ne psal - li - te e -
God: raise your song to the High -
-cum no - - vum: be - ne psal - li - te e - i, be - ne
the Lord God: raise your song to the High-est, raise your
no - vum: be - ne psal - li - te e - i in vo -
your God: raise your song to the High - est, with heart
-cum no - - vum:
the Lord God:
mf più legato

44
-i in vo-ci-fe-ra-ti-o-ne,
-est, with heart and voice sing and praise him,
psal-li-te e-i in vo-ci-fe-ra-ti-o-ne, be-ne psal-li-te e-
song to the High-est, sing ye and praise him, and praise him, raise your song to the High-
-ci-fe-ra-ti-o-ne, be-ne
and voice sing and praise him, raise your
be-ne psal-li-te e-
raise your song to the High-
49
be-ne psal-li-te e-i, be-ne psal-li-te e-i in
raise your song to the High-est, raise your song to the High-est, with
-i, be-ne psal-li-te e-i, be-ne psal-li-te e-i
-est, raise your song to the High-est, raise your song to the High-est,
psal-li-te e-i, be-ne psal-li-te e-i
song to the High-est, raise your song to the High-est,
-i, be-ne psal-li-te e-i, be-ne psal-li-te e-i in
-est, raise your song to the High-est, raise your song to the High-est, with
f

55
vo - ci - fe - ra - ti - o - - ne, in vo - ci - fe - ra - ti - o - - - -
heart and with voice come praise him, with heart and with voice come praise
in vo - - ci - fe - ra - - ti - o - - ne,
with heart and with voice come praise him,
in vo - ci - fe - ra - ti - o - - ne, in vo - ci - fe - ra - ti -
with heart and with voice come praise him, with heart and with voice come
vo - ci - fe - ra - ti - o - - ne, in vo - ci - fe - ra - ti - o - - ne, in
heart and with voice come praise him, with heart and with voice come praise him, with
marcato
59
-ne, in vo - ci - fe - ra - - - ti - o - - - - - ne.
him, with heart and with voice come praise him.
in vo - ci - fe - ra - ti - o - ne, in vo - ci - fe - ra - ti - o - ne.
with heart and with voice come praise him, with heart and with voice come praise him.
-o - - - - - ne, in vo - ci - fe - ra - ti - o - ne.
praise him, with heart and with voice come praise him.
vo - ci - fe - ra - - - ti - o - - - - - - ne.
heart and with voice come praise him.

64
Ex - sul - ta - te, ju - sti, in Do - mi - no: re - ctos de - cet
Shout for joy, ye right - eous, be - fore the Lord: it be - comes the
Ex - sul - ta - te, ju - sti, in Do - mi - no: re - ctos de - cet
Shout for joy, ye right - eous, be - fore the Lord: it be - comes— the
Ex - sul - ta - te, ju - sti, in Do - mi - no: re - ctos de - cet
Shout for joy, ye right - eous, be - fore the Lord: it be - comes the
Ex - sul - ta - te, ju - sti, in Do - mi - no: re - ctos de - cet
Shout for joy, ye right - eous, be - fore the Lord: it be - comes the
Tempo I

70
col - lau - da - ti - o, col - lau - da - ti - o.
just to give him thanks, give him, give him thanks.
col - lau - da - ti - o, col - lau - da - ti - o.
just to give him thanks, give— him, give him thanks.
col - lau - da - ti - o, col - lau - da - ti - o.
just to give him thanks, give— him, give him thanks.
col - lau - da - ti - o, col - lau - da - ti - o.
just to give him thanks, give— him, give him thanks.
più f

51. Ave Maria

(*Hail, Virgin Mary*)

The Angelic Salutation
English version by John Rutter

attributed to
T. L. de VICTORIA (1548–1611)

9
in mu - li - e - - ri - bus, et be - ne - di - ctus
a - bove all wo - - man - kind, and bless - ed is the
in mu - li - e - - ri - bus, et be - ne -
a - bove all wo - - man - kind, and bless - ed
mu - li - e - - ri - bus, in mu - li - e - ri - bus, et
- bove all wo - - man-kind, a - bove all wo - man-kind, and
mu - li - e - - ri - bus, et be - ne -
- bove all wo - - man-kind, and bless - ed
mf
dolce sempre
14
fru - ctus ven - tris tu - i, Je - - - - - - sus Chri - -
ho - ly Child thou bear - est, Je - - - - - - sus our
- di - ctus fru - - ctus ven - tris tu - i, Je - sus Chri - - -
is he thou bear - est, thou bear-est, Je - sus our
be - ne - di - ctus fru - ctus ven - tris tu - i, Je - sus Chri - - -
bless - ed is the ho - ly Child thou bear - est, Je - sus our
- di - ctus fru - ctus ven - tris tu - i Je - - - - - sus Chri - - -
is the ho - ly Child thou bear - est, Je - - - - sus our
dim.

* $\frac{3}{1}$ in source. Original note values in this section quartered.

31
pec - ca - to - ri - bus, nunc et in ho - ra mor - tis no - - -
pray for sin - ners all, now and at death's hour, at death's last
pec - ca - to - ri - bus, nunc et in ho - ra mor - tis no - strae.
pray for sin - ners all, now and at death's hour, at death's last hour.
pec - ca - to - ri - bus, nunc et in ho - ra mor - tis no -
pray for sin - ners all, now and at death's hour, at death's last
pec - ca - to - ri - bus, nunc et in ho - ra mor - tis no - strae.
pray for sin - ners all, now and at death's hour, at death's last hour.
mp
mf
36
- strae. A - - - - - - - - men.
hour.
A - - - - - - - - men, a - men.
- strae. A - - - - - - men, a - men.
hour.
A - - - - - - - - men, a - men.
mp
dim.
p

52. O quam gloriosum

(*O how fair and glorious*)

Antiphon at Vespers, All Saints' Day
English version by John Rutter

T. L. de VICTORIA
(1548–1611)

12
Chri - - - - - - - sto, in quo, in quo cum
saints dwell, where - in, where - in the
quo cum Chri - - - - - sto, in quo cum Chri - - - - -
- in the saints dwell, where- in the saints
- - sto, in quo cum Chri - sto, in quo cum Chri -
dwell, where - in the saints dwell, where-in the saints
- - sto, in quo cum Chri - - sto, in
dwell, where-in the saints dwell, where-
cresc.
mf
17
Chri - - - - sto gau - - - dent, gau -
saints dwell, joy - - - ful, joy -
- sto, in quo cum Chri - sto gau - - - - - dent, gau - - - - - -
dwell, where-in the saints dwell, joy - - - - - ful, joy - - - - - -
- sto, in quo cum Chri - sto gau - - - - dent, gau - - - -
dwell, where-in the saints dwell, joy - - - - ful, joy - - - -
quo cum Chri - sto gau - - - - - dent, gau - - - - dent,
- in the saints dwell, joy - - - - - ful, joy - - - - ful
cresc.
f

22
- - dent o - - mnes San - - - cti, o - mnes
- - ful in their Sa - - - viour, in their
-dent, gau - - dent o - mnes San - - - cti, o - mnes
-ful, joy - - ful in their Sa - - - viour, in their
- - - - - dent o - mnes San - - - cti, o - mnes San -
- - - - - ful in their Sa - - - viour, in their Sa -
gau - dent o - - mnes San - - - cti, o - mnes
in their Lord and Sa - - - viour, in their
27
San - - - cti. A - mi - cti sto - lis al - -
Sa - - - viour, all clothed in shin - ing rai - -
San - - - cti. A - mi - cti sto - lis al - bis, a - mi - cti sto - lis al - -
Sa - - - viour, all clothed in shin - ing rai - ment, all clothed in shin - ing rai - -
- - - cti. A - mi - cti sto - lis al - bis, a - mi - cti sto - lis al - -
- - - viour, all clothed in shin - ing rai - ment, all clothed in shin - ing rai - -
San - - - cti. A - mi - cti sto - lis al - bis,
Sa - - - viour, all clothed in shin - ing rai - ment,
dim.
mp

32
- - - bis, a - mi - cti sto - lis al - - - bis,
- - - ment, all clothed in shin - ing rai - - - ment,
- - - bis, a - mi - - cti sto - lis al - bis, se - quun -
- - - ment, all clothed in shin - ing rai - ment, fol - low -
- - bis, a - mi - cti sto - lis al - bis, se - - quun -
- - ment, all clothed in shi - ning rai - ment, fol - - low -
a - mi - - cti sto - lis al - bis, se - quun -
all clothed in shin - ing rai - ment, fol - low -
cresc.
mf
mp
37
se - - - quun - tur A - - - - - - - - -
fol - - - low - ing af - - - - - - - - ter
- tur A - - - gnum, se - quun - tur A - - - -
- ing af - - ter the Lamb, fol - low - ing af - - - - ter
- tur A - - - - gnum, se - quun - - tur A - gnum, se -
- ing af - - - ter the Lamb, af - - - ter the Lamb, fol -
- tur A - - - - gnum, se - -
- ing af - - ter the Lamb, fol -

* See Commentary (p. 377–8).

52
-rit, quo - cum - que i - - - - - - - - - - - - e -
lead, wher - ev - er he shall
i - e - rit, quo - cum - que i - - - - e - rit, quo -
he shall lead, wher - ev - er he shall lead, wher -
- - - e - rit, quo - cum - que i - - - - - - e -
shall lead, wher - ev - er he shall
i - - e - - rit, quo - cum - que i - - e -
he shall lead, wher - ev - er he shall
mf
56
-rit.
lead.
cum - que i - - - - - - - - e - rit.
-ev - er he shall lead.
-rit, quo - cum - que i - - - - - e - rit.
lead, wher - ev - er he shall lead.
-rit, quo - cum - que i - - - - - - e - rit.
lead, wher - ev - er he shall lead.
dim.
mp

53. O vos omnes

(*O ye people*)

Responsory at Matins for Holy Saturday*
English version by John Rutter

T. L. de VICTORIA
(1548–1611)

* Lamentations 1: 12

13
et vi - de - - - - te Si est
look up - on me: Could there
- de - - - - - - - te Si est do - lor
- on me: Could there a - ny
- - - - - - - - te Si est do - lor si -
me: Could there sor -
- de - - - - - - - te Si est do - lor
- on me: Could there
mf
p
mf
f
19
FINE
do - lor si - - - mi - lis si - cut do - lor me - - us.
a - ny sor - - row be like un - to my sor - - row?
si - - - - - - mi - lis si - cut do - lor me - - us.
sor - - - - - row be like un - to my sor - - row?
- - mi - lis, si - mi - lis si - cut do - lor me - - us.
- - row be, sor - row be like un - to my sor - - row?
si - - - - - - mi - lis si - cut do - lor me - - us.
sor - - - - - row be like un - to my sor - - row?
FINE
mp
dim.
p

25
[SOLO]
At - ten - di - te, u - ni - ver - si po - - - pu - li, et vi - de -
Be - hold and see, all ye peo - ple come, give heed, and con - sid -
[SOLO]
At - ten - di - te, u - ni - ver - si po - - pu - li, et vi -
Be - hold and see, all ye peo - ple come, give heed, and con -
[SOLO]
At - ten - di - te, u - ni - ver - si po - - - pu - li,
Be - hold and see, all ye peo - ple come, give heed,
mp
cresc.
mf
mp
'Si est dolor'
D.S. al Fine
32
- te do - lo - rem me - um, do - lo - rem me - - um.
- er my grief and sor - row, my grief and sor - - row.
- de - te do - lo - - rem me - - um, do - lo - rem me - - um.
- sid - er my grief and sor - - row, my grief and sor - - row.
do - lo - rem me - um, do - lo - - rem me - - um.
my grief and sor - row, my grief and sor - - row.
'Si est dolor'
D.S. al Fine
cresc.
mf
dim.

54. Jesu, dulcis memoria

(Jesu, sweet are those thoughts of thee)

Office hymn for the Feast of the Holy Name
attributed to St Bernard of Clairvaux (12th cent.)
Translation by John Rutter

attributed to
T. L. de VICTORIA (1548–1611)

8
gau - - - - - - di - a, gau - - - - - - - di - a:
hearts most joy - ful - ly, most joy - - - - - - ful - ly;
- - - - - - di - a, gau - - - - - - di - a:
hearts most joy - ful - ly, joy - - - - - - ful - ly;
gau - - - - - di - a, cor - - - - - di gau - di - a:
joy - - - - - ful - ly, most joy - - ful - ly;
- a, ve - - ra cor - - di gau - - - di - a:
- ly, fill our hearts most joy - - - ful - ly;
mf
dim.
mp
12
Sed su - per mel et o - - - - - mni - a,
Yet sweet - er far that bliss will be,
Sed su - - per mel et o - - - - - mni - a, su -
Yet sweet - - er far that bliss will be, sweet -
Sed su - - - per mel et o - - - - mni - a, su -
Yet sweet - - er far that bliss will be, sweet -
Sed su - per mel et o - - mni - - - a,
Yet sweet - er far that bliss will be,

16
su - per mel et o - mni - a, E - jus dul - cis
sweet - er far that bliss will be Ev - er - more thy
- per mel et o - mni - a, E - jus dul -
- er far that bliss will be Ev - er -
- per mel et o - mni - a, E - jus
- er far that bliss will be Ev - er -
et o - mni - a, E -
that bliss will be Ev -
dim.
p
20
prae - sen - ti - a, dul - cis prae - sen - ti - a.
face to see, thy bless - ed face to see.
- cis prae - sen - ti - a, dul - cis prae - sen - ti - a.
- more thy face to see, thy bless - ed face to see.
dul - cis prae - sen - ti - a, dul - cis prae - sen - ti - a.
- more thy face to see, thy bless - ed face to see.
- jus dul - cis prae - sen - ti - a.
- er - more thy face to see.

COMMENTARY

Notes

1. Psalms are numbered according to Protestant usage.
2. Specific references to musical notes in the scores are given thus: bar number (Arabic), stave number counting down from top stave in each system (Roman), symbol number in the bar (Arabic). For example, in the Allegri *Miserere*, 2 iv 3 refers to the tenor D in the second bar.
3. Pitch and rhythmic references are given in terms of the editions in this book, not in terms of the original sources. Where editions are transposed and note values shortened, so are all references to variants.
4. The Helmholtz system of pitch notation has been used whenever it is important to specify the octave of a particular note (but not otherwise). The seven notes upwards from the C an octave below middle C are shown thus: *c d e f g a b*, the seven notes upwards from middle C thus: *c' d' e' f' g' a' b'*, and the next octave thus: *c'' d''* etc.

1. Allegri: *Miserere*

Gregorio Allegri was a singer, composer, and priest, who lived and worked throughout his life in Rome. From 1629 until his death he was a member of the papal choir, for which he wrote his *Miserere*, the single work upon which his present-day fame rests. Its text (Psalm 51 without a doxology) was customarily appended to the combined office of Matins and Lauds on the last three days of Holy Week. On those three days the service was known as Tenebrae (Latin for 'darkness'), and in the papal chapel and elsewhere it was observed on the previous evenings (that is, on Wednesday, Thursday, and Good Friday) around the hour when dusk fell. During the singing of the psalms, candles in the church were extinguished one by one, leaving a single candle alight but hidden behind the altar by the time the *Miserere* was sung. From around 1666 Allegri's setting was performed annually by the papal choir, and was reserved for their exclusive use; reputedly, excommunication was the penalty for copying the manuscript. The English music historian Charles Burney managed to obtain a copy when he visited Rome in 1770, and he published it (along with four other pieces performed by the papal choir in Holy Week) on his return home in 1771. Other editions soon began to appear, which did nothing to dispel a widespread mystique attached to Allegri's actually fairly simple *falso bordone* composition, since none of these early editions included the ornamentation ('*abbellimenti*') and special nuances of expression added by the singers of the papal choir in accordance with what was believed to be a secret oral tradition. Visitors flocked to hear the *Miserere* performed each Holy Week in Rome, their numbers reaching a peak in the years between the end of the Napoleonic Wars in 1815, and 1870, when the papal choir was effectively disbanded. Spohr, in 1817, and Mendelssohn, in 1831, left especially full written accounts of what they heard, with musical examples.

In modern times the Allegri *Miserere* has enjoyed a fresh wave of popularity, but the problem confronting the editor of any new edition is that the form in which the work is now so widely known has been altered and added to over the years, somewhat like an old building: for example, the soprano soloist's top C in the four-voiced verses is not to be found in any performing edition until 1951. Thanks to the survival of a pair of Vatican manuscripts dating from Allegri's time (Codices 205–6) it is possible to restore the *Miserere* to something like its original state (albeit without the vocal embellishments that may always have been an integral part of its performance)—but the altered, 'patchwork' version has so firmly displaced the original as to have become a classic in its own right. For that reason, the version given in this volume is essentially the familiar patchwork; for the 'original' Allegri *Miserere*, see the edition by Julius Amann (Schott, 1936) which is based solely on Vatican Codices 205–6. A new critical edition by Hugh Keyte is presently in progress; unlike Amann's, it includes *abbellimenti* based on the performing practice of the papal choir, as transcribed by the former director, Domenico Mustafà, in 1892.

The elements of the modern patchwork *Miserere* were assembled by Sir Ivor Atkins in his edition of 1951, which adapted Allegri's music to fit the English translation of the 1662 Book of Common Prayer. Atkins took the music of the five-voiced verses and the concluding nine-voiced half-verse from Burney, but for the four-voiced verses he turned to a musical example found in the first and second editions of *Grove's Dictionary*. Under the entry 'Miserere', the Victorian music historian W. S. Rockstro wrote at length about Allegri's setting, illustrating the four-voiced verses with a version of his own which appears to have been assembled quite conjecturally. This grafted together the opening from Burney (bars 15–17 of the edition in this volume), an embellished cadence as given in an Italian edition of 1840 (Alfieri: bars 18–21), two bars of Burney (bars 22–3), and finally (bars 24–8) a second embellished cadence, including the top C, as written out in a letter by Mendelssohn, who had been present at the 1831 Holy Week ceremonies in Rome. Thus, one of the elements in the Atkins patchwork was itself a patchwork—one, moreover, based on a twofold misunderstanding. By the nineteenth century, the papal choir was singing the *Miserere* settings of Allegri (and the rather similar one by Bai, which made use of the same embellishments) at pitches higher than the notated G minor. Mendelssohn heard it in C minor, not Burney's G minor, and so 'his' section (starting on the last beat of bar 23) is a fourth too high if inserted into a *Miserere* performed in G minor. Rockstro also misunderstood the placement of Mendelssohn's passage, which rightly belonged midway through the four-voiced verses, in the same place as the Alfieri cadence, not at the end. For the non-polyphonic verses of the psalm Atkins followed Rockstro in adopting a

Gregorian chant (Tone II), another decision with a shaky historical basis: in psalm-compositions, any verses not set to polyphony would indeed have been chanted monophonically, but in the papal chapel (by the nineteenth century, at least) they were chanted on a single note, the dominant, rather than to a Gregorian psalm-tone. If a psalm-tone is to be used, it would be logical to choose the *Tonus peregrinus,* on which Allegri's polyphonic verses are based, rather than the unrelated Tone II. Both chants are given in the present edition; if preferred, the choir can simply sing a unison D. Atkins assigned the five-voiced sections to full choir, the chant verses to tenors and basses, and the four-voiced verses to soloists; in fact, all the verses were sung by soloists. The *Miserere* should be sung *a cappella*: no accompaniment was ever used in the papal chapel.

To summarize, the sources of the present edition are as follows: five- and nine-voiced verses from Burney, *La musica che si canta annualmente nelle funzioni della settimana santa nella cappella pontificia composta dal Palestrina, Allegri, e Bai* (London, 1771); first four-voiced verse from W. S. Rockstro, article 'Miserere' in *Grove's Dictionary of Music and Musicians*, 1st edition (London 1880); later four-voiced verses extrapolated from the same source; monophonic verses, Tone II and *Tonus peregrinus* as given in the *Liber Usualis*.

A fuller account of this complex history is given in the separate octavo of the *Miserere* (Oxford Choral Classics, OCCO 5). The editor gratefully acknowledges the researches and generous assistance of Hugh Keyte, the source of some of the information in this note.

2. Anerio (F.): *Christus factus est*

Like his younger brother Giovanni, Felice Anerio was a composer and priest whose sacred music follows closely in the tradition of Palestrina. Born in Rome, he sang as a boy in the choir of S. Maria Maggiore, and then in the papal Cappella Giulia under Palestrina. On the death of the latter in 1594 he was appointed composer to the papal choir, for which he wrote masses, motets, and other polyphonic music. *Christus factus est*, perhaps his best-known piece, does not appear in any of the volumes of his work published in his lifetime; the earliest extant source dates from 1840, and all others derive from it. The chromatic *musica ficta* (notably in bars 9, 12, 30, and 36) may have been added by the nineteenth-century editor; if not, it shows an influence of early baroque madrigal style not found in Palestrina. *Source: Raccolta di mottetti a quattro voci . . . dall' Abate Pietro Alfieri* (Rome, 1840).

3. Arensky: *Otche nash (The Lord's Prayer)*

Born in Novgorod, Arensky studied composition at the St Petersburg Conservatory with Rimsky-Korsakov, though his style was more strongly influenced by Tchaikovsky. From 1882 to 1894 he taught harmony and counterpoint at the Moscow Conservatory, establishing a strong reputation as composer, pianist, and conductor. In 1895 he became director of the Imperial Court Chapel in St Petersburg, which may have occasioned the writing of one of his few liturgical works, the *Four sacred choruses from the Liturgy of St John Chrysostom,* op. 40, published in 1897. *Otche nash* is no. 3 of the set. *Source:* first edition (Jurgenson, Moscow, 1897).

4. Bach: *O Jesu Christ, meins Lebens Licht*, BWV 118

This lovely motet is all too often overlooked in Bach's sacred output. Despite being recognizably a motet (as that term was understood in eighteenth-century Protestant Germany) and being explicitly described by Bach on its title page as 'motetto', it was mistakenly included among his cantatas in the old Bach-Gesellschaft edition, presumably because of its independent instrumental accompaniment. As a result it lay hidden among the 200 or so real cantatas until the Neue Bach Ausgabe put matters right by placing it in their volume of motets. Even now, it is generally omitted from recordings and publications of Bach's other six motets, for which reason alone it is worth including here. Bach wrote it in 1736 or 1737 for a funeral service in Leipzig. The accompaniment was originally scored for an outdoor group comprising two *litui* (curved trumpets used at funerals), a cornetto, and three trombones, which suggests processional performance. Only one stanza of the hymn text is given in Bach's manuscript, but Behm's hymn (subtitled 'for the dying') has fourteen more, enough to accommodate even the longest procession. Ten years later Bach rescored it for indoor use: the *litui* were retained, woodwind doubled the voice parts *ad libitum*, and the cornetto and trombone parts were reassigned to strings and continuo. (This second version is the one available on rental. Flugelhorns may be used as a modern replacement for the extinct *litui.*) The chorale melody upon which the motet is based comes from a Leipzig hymnal of 1625, *As hymnodus sacer*. Mendelssohn later used this melody in his oratorio *St Paul*; his version, with an altered last line, is the one usually found in modern hymnals, under the name *Breslau. Source: BG*, vol. xxiv. Also consulted: *Neue Bach-Ausgabe*, III/i.

5. Brahms: *Warum ist das Licht gegeben dem Mühseligen?*, op. 74 no. 1

This intense, deeply-felt motet—considered by more than one authority to be Brahms's finest—would undoubtedly be more often performed were it not for the dauntingly chromatic appearance of its first twenty-four bars. Choir directors need to look beyond this anguished opening to the more melodiously diatonic sections which follow; these breathe the same autumnal air of gentle consolation as the *Requiem*. The motet convincingly unites Brahms's interest in contrapuntal devices and archaic structural models (in this case including Bach's motets) with his own song-like style. It was written in 1877 or 1878 (possibly as a memorial to his friend Hermann Goetz who had died young in 1876) around the same time as the shorter *O Heiland, reiss die Himmel auf*; the two motets were published as a pair in 1879. Brahms compiled the text with care, writing humorously of it to a friend that 'my bible knowledge should perhaps be praised'. Much of the music is a reworked version of the then unpublished (and now partly lost) *Missa canonica* which Brahms had written in 1856: for example, the opening phrase of the second section 'Lasset uns unser Herz' was originally set to the words 'Benedictus qui venit in nomine Domini'. This refitting process accounts for some occasional infelicities of verbal accentuation in the motet. (For a full account of the relationship between the *Missa canonica* and the motet, see Robert Pascall's relevant article in the symposium *Brahms 2*, edited by Michael Musgrave, Cambridge University Press, 1987.) The melody of the final chorale (its text being Luther's paraphrase of the *Nunc dimittis*) is traditionally also ascribed to Luther. *Source:* first edition (Simrock, Berlin, 1879).

6. Brahms: *Ach, arme Welt*, op. 110 no. 2
This brief, chorale-like setting belongs to a set of three motets written in 1889, shortly after the *Fest- und Gedenksprüche*, op. 109; they were Brahms's last choral compositions. The anonymous text is an old German hymn. Comparisons can be made between the opening phrase of the melody and the chorale *Es ist genug*, used by Bach in his Cantata no. 60. *Source*: first edition (Simrock, Berlin, 1890).

7. Brahms: *Geistliches Lied*, op. 30
Brahms wrote this in 1856 as one of a number of compositions which he and his friend Joachim exchanged for mutual criticism, both men having the aim of improving their (in Brahms's case already considerable) contrapuntal mastery. The *Geistliches Lied* wears its learning lightly: despite being a strict double canon in the vocal parts, with canonic writing in the organ too, the music projects a mood of gentle, lyric serenity, clearly foreshadowing the *Requiem*. *Source*: first edition (Breitkopf & Härtel, 1864).

8. Bruckner: *Ave Maria*
This, the best-loved of Bruckner's three settings of the text, was written in 1861 while the composer was organist of Linz Cathedral. He had just completed a five-year course of contrapuntal study during which he was forbidden by his teacher, Sechter, to write 'free' compositions. Released from the ban, his creativity flowered in this simple yet powerful motet, rooted clearly in the Viennese tradition but pointing towards Bruckner's symphonic achievements to come. *Source:* first edition (Wetzler, Vienna, 1887, published as no. 2 of 2 *Kirchen-Chöre*). Also consulted: *Anton Bruckner, Sämtliche Werke*, vol. 21. *Variants:* 34: *dim.* absent in other sources / 38 iv 2: *SW* has a *divisi*, B♭ and *f*, rather than the single *f* / 46 ii, iii, iv 2: accent absent in other sources / 47 iii 1–2: tie absent in other sources.

9. Bruckner: *Christus factus est*
By the time Bruckner wrote this impressive Gradual setting, he was living in Vienna and devoting most of his energy to symphonic writing; his later pieces of church music were, however, carefully considered and significant. *Christus factus est* dates from 1884, the period of the Seventh Symphony and the *Te Deum*. The score bears a dedication to Father Oddo Loidol, a Benedictine monk of Kremsmünster. *Source:* first edition (Rättig, Vienna, 1886, published as no. 1 of *Vier Graduale*).

10. Bruckner: *Os justi*
Bruckner wrote this Gradual setting in July 1879 for the choir of St Florian, the monastery near Linz where he had spent so many of his formative years; the score bears a dedication to Ignaz Traumihler, the choir director there. Also on the title page is the description 'Lydisch', meaning that the music is in the Lydian mode (which Bruckner adheres to strictly: there are no accidentals), and 'alla cappella' [*sic*]. The occasion for which the piece was written was the Feast of St Augustine (28 August), and Bruckner at first set the text only as far as 'in corde ipsius', believing that to be what was required. Traumihler then informed him that, for liturgical use, he needed to add the phrases 'et non supplantabuntur gressus ejus. Alleluia. Inveni David servum meum, oleo sancto meo unxi eum. Alleluia.' Bruckner dealt with this in a slightly makeshift way by amending the repeated chords at the end of the composition to include the first of these phrases, adding the monophonic 'Alleluia' in Gregorian style, then a brief monophonic setting with organ of 'Inveni David', followed by a reprise of the 'Alleluia'. The 'Alleluia' is printed here because its performance at the end of the polyphony has become almost customary, but with little justification: it is the start of the monophonic 'Inveni David' setting, not the conclusion of *Os justi*. *Source*: No. 3 of *Vier Graduale* (Rättig, Vienna, 1886). For a complete list of sources, see *Gesamtausgabe* (ed. Nowak). *Note:* Bruckner notated the 'Alleluia' all in semibreves, as shown.

11. Bruckner: *Locus iste*
This simple Gradual setting, aptly described by Deryck Cooke as 'an exquisite personal distillation of Mozart's church style', was written in Linz in 1869 but not published until 1886, as no. 2 of the *Vier Graduale* already referred to. *Source:* as for *Christus factus est*.

12. Buxtehude *(attrib.)*: *Magnificat*
This charming little work, a favourite in Germany though less well known elsewhere, survives only in a single, manuscript source: a set of parts and a score from the extensive collection of Gustav Düben, who was Kapellmeister at the German church in Stockholm from 1663 till his death in 1690. Düben knew Buxtehude (who lived in Lübeck), and over 100 Buxtehude pieces are in his collection; but the *Magnificat* cannot be shown to be one of them. The manuscript did not originally bear the name of any composer, although Buxtehude's name has been added in square brackets on the title page by a later hand. The basis of the attribution appears to be solely that Bruno Grusnick, the editor of the first modern edition (Bärenreiter, 1931), believed that the music bore all the marks of Buxtehude's style. A more recent scholar, Martin Geck (in his article 'Das Vokalwerk Dietrich Buxtehudes', *Die Musikforschung*, xiv, 1961) pointed out the obvious: the *Magnificat* does not actually resemble any known work by Buxtehude. Its lilting triple-time melodies with frequent hemiolas, its simple diatonic harmony with much use of thirds, and its clear sectional structure, are all features of the Franco–Italian middle baroque *bel canto* style of Carissimi and Lully which was widely imitated, but not by Buxtehude. The authorship of the *Magnificat* remains in doubt, but there is no doubt of its delightful melodic appeal and endearing simplicity. The scoring is for 2 violins, 2 violas, cello, bass, and continuo, but the violas are optional: the score (written in German organ tablature) omits them, and the texture is satisfactorily complete with just the two violins and *basso continuo*. There are no solo/tutti indications in the source, but solo voices are the preferable option in the sections editorially marked thus.

Source: Uppsala, Düben collection, *Vokalmusik i Handskrift* 69:17. The score and parts concur well. Slurs are in the parts only (there is no way of showing them in the tablature used for the score). SSATB clefs are used for the voice parts, modern clefs for the string parts. Modern key and time signatures are used throughout. *Variants:* 25 i 5: 2nd soprano '-a' underlaid to first note of 26 in part / 68 i 1: 1st soprano has *d''* not *e''* in part (*e''* in score) / 80 i 3: 2nd soprano has G♮ in part (G♯ in score) / 175 i 2: G♮ in part (G♯ in score).

13. Casals: *O vos omnes*
Pablo Casals is remembered principally as the foremost cellist of his generation, but was active throughout his life as a composer, though his output was small. *O vos omnes*, believed to date from 1932, is one of a number of sacred pieces he wrote for the Benedictine monks of Montserrat, an abbey near his native city of Barcelona. Originally for tenors and basses, it was recast by the composer for mixed choir and published in that form in 1965 in New York. *Source:* Published edition, Tetra/Continuo Music Group.

14. Fauré: *Cantique de Jean Racine*, op. 11
From 1854 till 1865 Fauré was a pupil at the Ecole Niedermeyer in Paris, a newly-founded school for training future church musicians. He composed the *Cantique* in his final year and entered it for the school's composition prize, which it won. Some ten years later it was published in a church music series called *Echo des Maîtrises*; this series was edited by Romain Bussine, co-founder with Saint-Saëns of the Société Nationale de musique, an organization dedicated to the promotion of French music. In 1905 the *Cantique* was orchestrated, though (as with other Fauré works) there is doubt whether Fauré himself did the orchestration. Racine's text comes from his collection *Hymnes traduites du bréviaire romain.* The Latin hymn from which it is translated, *Consors paterni luminis*, is in the Ambrosian style but of unknown authorship.
Source: first edition (Schoen, Paris, *c.*1875).

15. Franck: *Panis angelicus*
The origin of this renowned piece was said by Franck's biographer Léon Vallas to have been an organ improvisation played by Franck in 1861 during a Christmas service at the church of Sainte-Clotilde in Paris, where he was organist. Its first appearance in print was in 1872, as an interpolated movement for use during Communion, in Franck's *Messe à trois voix*. The Mass, originally for choir and orchestra, had been written in 1860 without the extra movement, but the 1872 publication was of Franck's own reduced scoring for organ, harp, cello, and bass; *Panis angelicus* was now included, scored just for tenor solo, organ, harp, and cello. (Franck is not known to have rescored it for orchestra.) A choral arrangement of *Panis angelicus* by L. Michelot was published in Franck's lifetime, and there have been numerous others since. The text is the sixth verse of Aquinas's Corpus Christi hymn *Sacris solemniis*. This verse had gained currency in the nineteenth century because it was used as part of the afternoon devotion of Rosary and Benediction. *Source:* first edition (Bornemann, Paris, 1872). The choral arrangement and organ transcription are editorial.

16. Gabrieli (G.): *Jubilate Deo*
Like his uncle Andrea, Giovanni Gabrieli's last and most important post was as organist of S. Marco in his native city of Venice. Prior to this, he held a court post in Munich. Once appointed to S. Marco in 1585, he composed prolifically for the lavish vocal and instrumental resources available to him there, generally dividing his forces into *cori spezzati*, multiple choirs spaced apart; many of his motets were written for the great festivals of church and state for which Venice was renowned. Following the death of Doge Grimani in 1605, there were cutbacks in the musical establishment at S. Marco, and *Jubilate Deo*, written in a fairly simple chanson- and madrigal-influenced style for single choir, would seem to belong to this post-1605 period. It did not appear in print until shortly after Gabrieli's death, in three separate collections published in Germany (where the composer's reputation was honoured more than in Italy). Although untypical of Gabrieli in the sense that it is not polychoral, *Jubilate Deo* is one of his most attractive and often-performed works. Its text is compiled mainly from the psalms, in the manner of a litany. Gabrieli made two other settings of the same text, which suggests that it was associated with a regular Venetian festival such as the Feast of the Ascension. The climax of this ceremony involved the Doge casting a ring into the sea as a symbol of Venice's union with it; this would explain the inclusion of the line 'Deus Israel conjungat vos' (taken from a nuptial blessing in the Vulgate version of the Book of Tobit). *Source: Reliquiae sacrorum concentuum Giovan Gabrielis . . . Nürnberg, P. Kauffmann, 1615.* Also consulted: *Promptuarii musici III* (Strasbourg, 1613) and *Florilegii Musici Portensis . . . M. Erhardo Bodenschatzio* (Leipzig, 1621). The *basis generalis* part is only in the 1621 source. *Variants:* 22 i and iv 1–5: these parallel octaves (left unaltered) are in all sources / 56 viii 1: D in all sources, but B♭ has been preferred as a more exact imitation of bass 1 two bars earlier, also avoiding an unlikely close low chord spacing / 148 iii 1: E♮ in all sources / 158–9 v: all sources have the following, probably corrupt, version:

The altered version in this edition avoids the parallel octaves with alto 1 and restores a more exact motivic imitation with altos 1 and 2.
Note: The lowest sounding voice in the organ part (irrespective of clef and stave) is the 1621 *basis generalis*; the other voices are an editorial realization of it, even though, in the interests of easy legibility, they are not printed small. Figuring in the source is very sparse and has been editorially supplemented without the normal square brackets. Instrumental parts for this motet (doubling the voice parts) are available on rental from the publisher.

17. Gesualdo: *O vos omnes*
Gesualdo is remembered as much for the single sensational act of murdering his adulterous wife and her lover as he is for his music. Otherwise, his life as Prince of Venosa was that of an Italian noble amateur of music, similar to those who were writing the first operas in Florence at about the

same time. His preferred form was the madrigal, of which he published six books, but he also left two books of *cantiones sacrae* and a volume of music for Holy Week. His madrigals are noted for their eccentric and adventurous chromaticism, which is found to a lesser extent in his sacred music also. *O vos omnes* (a text he later set for six voices in his Holy Week volume of 1611) was published in his first book of *cantiones sacrae* in 1603. The poignant text, popular with composers of the Counter-Reformation period, is set to music of eloquence and dramatic power, cast in the same responsorial form used by Victoria. *Source: Sacrarum cantionum liber primus* (Naples, 1603). The repeated section is written out in full in the source; the final ♯ to the alto C (bar 25) and the cancelling ♮ to the 2nd tenor F (bar 25) are missing in the repeat, but probably no difference was intended. In the source, the final note of the piece is a long without fermata.

18. Glinka: *The Cherubic Hymn (Izhe kheruvimyi)*
Glinka is acknowledged as the founding father of the Russian national school of composition. Church music did not play a large part in his career, although in 1856, the year before his death, he took counterpoint lessons in Berlin with the aim of forging a new style for sacred composition. His *Cherubic Hymn* dates from much earlier: it was written in 1837, the year that the Tsar appointed him Kapellmeister to the imperial chapel in recognition of the success of his opera *A life for the Tsar* (premièred in 1836). Glinka did not find the post congenial, and resigned after two years. None the less, the *Cherubic Hymn*—curiously reminiscent of S. S. Wesley and even of Pearsall's madrigal *Lay a garland*—has earned a well-merited place in the repertory of Russian liturgical music. *Source: Tsyerkovno-Pyevchyeskii Sbornik*, vol 2. (St Petersburg, 1903) *Variants:* 23–27 ii–v: crescendo mark missing (supplied by analogy with bars 8–12) / 38–42: ditto / 48: time sig. **C** in source.
Note: This edition in D major has been transposed up a tone from the original key, C major. If low basses are available, C major or D♭ major would be preferable.

19. Grieg: *Ave maris stella*
This enchanting miniature, dating from 1898, is Grieg's own choral arrangement of a solo song with piano which he wrote in the same year and published as one of a pair of sacred songs—his only sacred pieces apart from the *Four Norwegian psalms* written shortly before his death. The text of *Ave maris stella*, in its solo version, was a Danish poem by Thor Lange, but for the choral version Grieg reverted to the familiar Latin text. The poetic image of Mary as a star guiding mortal souls across the ocean of life no doubt held special significance for Grieg, who was born and lived for much of his life near the North Sea port of Bergen. *Source:* no. 2 of *To religiøse Kor* (Wilhelm Hansen, Copenhagen, 1899). The metronome marking is supplied from an autograph MS in the Bergen Public Library.

20. Guerrero: *Ave Virgo sanctissima*
During his lifetime and for at least 200 years after his death, Guerrero was one of the most widely published and performed composers of the Spanish Renaissance, second only to Victoria in reputation. From 1551 until his death he worked at Seville Cathedral, first as assistant director of music, then from 1574 as director. He travelled widely, and his music circulated in several countries; it was much performed in the Spanish–American colonies. He wrote mainly vocal music, sacred and secular. Among his 150 or so published motets, *Ave Virgo sanctissima* (1566) enjoyed exceptional popularity. In fact it is slightly unusual among Guerrero's motets, its two top voice parts being in strict canon throughout. Starting from bar 22, at the word 'salve', the music quotes the first four notes of the Gregorian antiphon *Salve Regina* (*Liber Usualis*, p. 276), a reference that would have been familiar to Guerrero's listeners. The anonymous text was used as a Marian antiphon for Thursdays and Saturdays in some pre-Tridentine liturgies. *Source: Motteta Francisci Guerreri in Hispalensi Ecclesia musicorum praefecti . . . Venetiis apud Filios Antonii Gardani, 1570. Variants:* 14–21, all voices: 'mari stella' in source / 68–70 v: 'olens' seems to be deliberately omitted because of the shortness of the musical phrase and has not been reinserted in this edition.

21. Handl: *Pater noster*
Jacob Handl (sometimes known as Gallus) was born in Slovenia. In his youth he left his homeland, living for a while at the monastery of Melk in Austria before becoming a singer at the Imperial chapel in Vienna. In 1575 he embarked upon a period of travel around central Europe, then in 1580 became choirmaster to the Bishop of Olomouc, settling finally in Prague in 1586 as director of music at the church of St Jan. His compositions, mainly vocal, were widely known and highly regarded in his own day. Handl published most of them himself in a number of substantial volumes: there are four books of motets, arranged according to the church's year. *Pater noster* is one of his many polychoral pieces, owing something both to the Venetian model of Willaert and to the more Netherlandish style of Josquin and Lassus. *Source: Tomus Primus Operis musici cantionum . . . Iacobo Hándl. Praga 1586. Variants:* 11 vi 2: *eb'* in source, amended here to *ab* by analogy with bar 6 / 43 v 2: *db* in source / 46 i 2: ditto / 61 iv 1: *ab* in source / 73–4 i: last two notes underlaid to 'amen' in source / 73–4 iii: ditto

22. Hassler: *Dixit Maria*
One of three musical brothers born in Nuremberg, Hassler studied under Andrea Gabrieli in Venice before returning to Germany where, in 1586, he was appointed chamber organist to the wealthy Fugger family in Augsburg. He published his first collection of sacred music, dedicated to his patron Octavian II Fugger, in 1591; it was evidently successful, with a new edition appearing in Nuremberg in 1597. Hassler seems to have had a restless and entrepreneurial streak, moving to new posts in Nuremberg in 1601 and Dresden in 1608, while being involved in instrument making and music publishing. Much of his music is popular in style: *Dixit Maria* (from the 1591 collection) is written in the secular style of a canzona or chanson rather than a motet, with a typical ABB structure, an attractive melody starting with the characteristic long–short–short canzona rhythm, and simple, clear

counterpoint. The piece is designated for the Feast of the Annunciation. *Source: Cantiones sacrae, de festis praecipuis totius anni. Editio altera, Noribergae, 1597.*

23. John IV, King of Portugal: *Crux fidelis*

This favourite polyphonic setting of the eighth stanza of the hymn *Pange lingua* was first published in an eleven-volume collection of 'musique ancienne' issued in Paris in 1843–5, where it is given a date of 1615 and ascribed to John IV, King of Portugal. He was indeed a composer, but as he was born in 1604, the date, at least, is unlikely. All but this and one other of his compositions were said to have been destroyed with the royal library in the Lisbon earthquake and fire of 1755, so there is scant basis for stylistic comparison, but it must be seriously doubted whether *Crux fidelis* was written in the seventeenth century at all. Its chromaticism extends to notes and chords so far on the flat side (at the original given pitch, a tone lower than in this edition) as to be modally far-fetched for all except an experimenter of Gesualdo-like boldness. Eleven dominant seventh chords—to use an anachronistic term—occur in the piece's 31 bars. The effect is more like the consciously 'churchy' sacred music of Liszt than the work of a younger contemporary of Monteverdi. Moreover, the 2½-beat note in the soprano in bar 22 would have been unlikely in the early seventeenth century, when dots were still the only means of prolongation. None of this is to question the excellence of *Crux fidelis*, but rather to open up the issue of its true origin. *Source: Recueil des morceaux de musique ancienne executés aux concerts de Musique Religieuse et Classique fondée à Paris en 1843 . . . Et sous la Direction de M. le Prince de la Moskowa* (Vol. 6, Pacini, Paris, 1843–5). All other editions appear to derive from this one. In the present edition, dynamic markings in the source have been omitted. With the exception noted below, underlay is preserved as given in the source (some later editions 'correct' it to accord with Renaissance principles). *Variants:* 14 ii 3: C is sharpened in source / 16–17 ii: 'flo-re__ ger-mi--ne' in source / 16 iii 3: ♪D not C in source.

24. Josquin Desprez: *Ave Maria*

Josquin has always been regarded as the greatest composer of his generation, the fullest embodiment of the ideals of the Renaissance and one of the most impressive and prolific exponents of both sacred and secular vocal music. Believed to have been born in north-eastern France, his first documented appearance is as a member of Milan Cathedral choir (from 1459), followed by a period in the service of Cardinal Ascanio Sforza in Rome and in the choir of the papal chapel there. He developed associations with French courts and with the Italian court of Ferrara, the latter coming to an end in 1504 when the court was dissolved due to the threat of plague. Josquin returned to north-eastern France, spending his remaining years as a canon of the cathedral of Notre Dame in Condé, his compositions known and revered throughout Europe. Of his 100 or so surviving motets, *Ave Maria*, probably written shortly before 1500, is one of the loveliest and most celebrated. As early as 1502 it was chosen by the Venetian publisher Petrucci to open his first collection of motets, and it is extant in at least ten other sixteenth-century sources. Distinctive features of Josquin's style are in evidence, including the use of contrasting pairs of voices, canon (bars 48–61, between soprano and tenor), and paraphrased Gregorian chant (the pre-Tridentine sequence *Ave Maria*), though this appears only at the opening as a kind of prelude to the main part of the motet, which is a free setting of a five-versed poem starting with the words 'Ave cujus conceptio' (bar 16). The verses deal in turn with the five Marian feasts—Conception, Nativity, Annunciation, Purification, and Assumption—and at the end the prayer 'O Mater Dei, memento mei' is added. The poem is found in a number of French and Belgian books of hours and was used as a votive antiphon. (Some sources of Josquin's setting substitute a different first verse, beginning 'Ave coelorum domina'.) *Sources:* For a full list, see *Josquin, Werken, Motetten I : 2*, ed. A. Smijers. The present edition is based principally on Petrucci, *Motetti* (1502).

Variant: 35 ii: All sources have a scarcely credible reading here:

This results in consecutive unisons with the tenor on the third beat. The tenor has to be correct because it is a point of imitation, but the alto can be more confidently amended, especially since in all other voices the syllable '-ens' is set to a ♩ or a 𝅗𝅥 (minimum likely values for the last note of a phrase). The amended reading also makes the stepwise rise on the word 'verum' consistent with the tenor and bass on the same word.

Note: Exceptionally, ligatures in the source are shown by slurs in this edition.

25. Lassus: *Adoramus te, Christe*

The sacred music of Lassus is often held up alongside that of Palestrina as one of the twin peaks of the late sixteenth century. Although this is not unjust, the backgrounds and careers of the two composers differed, and this was reflected in their music. Whereas Palestrina spent all his life in or near Rome and devoted himself predominantly to sacred music, Lassus was a cosmopolitan who travelled widely and wrote vocal music in every genre, sacred and secular. Born in Mons (now in Belgium) he was a choirboy in the service of Ferrante Gonzaga, Duke of Mantua, whose retinue he accompanied to Italy. His first important adult post was as choirmaster at the church of St John Lateran in Rome (1553–5). After various travels, in 1556 he joined the court of Albrecht V of Bavaria in Munich, first as a singer, later as *maestro di cappella*. He remained there for the rest of his life—though continuing to visit other musical centres—composing prolifically, and enjoying widespread fame. After his death, his two sons published much of his music (some of which had already appeared in his lifetime) in a massive collection, the *Magnum Opus Musicum*. *Adoramus te, Christe*, like many of Lassus's huge total of 500 or so motets, is known only from this publication, and there is no certain way of dating it. After a flirtation with reform, the Bavarian court had returned to Catholicism by the 1560s, and Latin motets were required throughout Lassus's 30-year tenure of office there. *Adoramus te* is based on the Gregorian chant set to those words as a Responsory at the Feast of the Finding of the Holy Cross, 3 May (*Liber Usualis*, p. 1458). *Source: Magnum Opus Musicum Orlandi de Lasso* (Munich, 1604).

26. Lassus: *Ave verum Corpus*

Lassus's treatment of this familiar eucharistic text is serene and elegiac, with imaginative use of the six-voiced texture to create expressive interplay between high and low voices, and restrained word-painting at the words 'unda fluxit sanguine'. The motet was first published in a 1582 collection issued in Munich, and reprinted in the posthumous collection of 1604. *Source: Magnum Opus Musicum Orlandi de Lasso* (Munich, 1604). Also consulted: *Mottetta typis nondum uspiam excusa* (Munich, 1582), which concurs closely with the 1604 source.

27. Lassus: *Timor et tremor* and *Exaudi Deus*

This celebrated two-section motet first appeared in 1564, in a collection published in Nuremberg. Its text was compiled from the psalms, possibly by Lassus himself; this was a not uncommon Renaissance practice (see Gabrieli, *Jubilate Deo*), enabling the composer to make a particular expressive, religious, or sometimes political point. In this case, Lassus portrays in vividly madrigalian fashion the contrast between human fear and uncertainty, and the firm trust that may be placed in God. *Sources: Op. cit.*, 1604, and *Thesauri musici Tomus tertius continens optimas sex vocum cantiones sacres . . .* (Nuremberg, 1564). *Variants:* 18–21 v: 1564 text is 'Miserere mei', 1604 as given here / 63–4 v: 1564 text is 'Quoniam', 1604 as given here.

28. Lotti: *Crucifixus a 8*

Lotti, believed to have been born in Venice, lived and worked for most of his life there, gaining the prestigious position of *maestro di cappella* at S. Marco in 1736. Among his prolific output there is a large quantity of church music that was admired for its contrapuntal mastery and the elegance of its voice writing. Nevertheless it is his fate to be remembered today mainly for this eight-voiced *Crucifixus*, which is part of a *Credo* written during a period of employment at the court of Dresden in 1717–19 (two other Lotti *Crucifixus* settings, for six and ten voices respectively, are also sometimes performed). The piece is often sung *a cappella*, but Lotti wrote a figured bass part for it, and organ accompaniment would have been expected. *Source:* Dresden ms. score (*Mus. 2159/D/5*) containing complete *Credo* by Lotti, 18th century, possibly holograph. Accidentals and figuring have been amended to accord with the key signature of the present edition. *Variant:* 15 vi 3: A♮ in source, but figuring has 6♭, so A♭ has been preferred.

29. Mendelssohn: *Psalm 43*, op. 78 no. 2

In 1840 Friedrich Wilhelm IV acceded to the throne of Prussia and asked Mendelssohn to be head of an Academy of the Arts in Berlin, the aim of which was to revitalize the artistic life of the kingdom. One of Mendelssohn's duties was to conduct a newly-formed Berlin cathedral choir, and during his tenure of office starting in 1843 (which ended prematurely in 1844, along with his other Berlin obligations, as a result of disputes and frustrations) he wrote a number of sacred pieces for the choir. Op. 78 consists of three *a cappella* psalm-settings, of which Psalm 43, written in January 1844, is considered the finest. Its first two sections show a tight motivic integration probably inspired by Bach; the third section, which serves as a confident coda, is a reworked version of the final section of Mendelssohn's Psalm 42 setting of 1837. The composer himself may have been responsible for fitting the English text, which closely follows the 1662 Book of Common Prayer. *Source: Werke*, ed. Rietz, vol. xiv.

30. Mendelssohn: *Verleih uns Frieden*

In 1830 Franz Hauser, a Viennese singer and Bach enthusiast, sent a Lutheran hymnal, the *Lutherisches Liedbüchlein,* to Mendelssohn, who was in Italy as part of his Grand Tour. This treasury of words and music inspired Mendelssohn to compose six chorale cantatas, two motets, and the present hymn-setting—which takes only Luther's text, the music being entirely Mendelssohn's own. He wrote to Hauser in January 1831: 'I intend to set the little song 'Verleih uns Frieden' as a canon with cello and bass', and by February the piece was complete. In the event, the canonic opening was for divided cellos, its theme both recalling the second subject from the *Hebrides* overture of 1830 and anticipating the opening clarinet motif from another overture, *Die schöne Melusine* (1833). *Source:* Facsimile of autograph MS, in *AMZ* xli, supplement for June 1839. This gives the German text only. In the Rietz Collected Edition, the Latin text, *Da nobis pacem,* which was the source of Luther's hymn, is added.

31. Monteverdi: *Beatus vir*

Monteverdi wrote church music throughout his long career, first while he was employed at the court of Mantua, then during his years as *maestro di cappella* at S. Marco in Venice, but much of it is hard to date because it was published in two large collections—the celebrated *Vespers* (1610) and the *Selva morale e spirituale* (1641)—which gathered together compositions written over a period of years. *Beatus vir*, a favourite among Monteverdi's sacred pieces, was published in the *Selva morale*. It calls for only modest instrumental forces, just two violins and *basso continuo* with three *ad libitum* instruments doubling voice parts. The origins of this Vesper psalm setting lie in a canzonetta, *Chiome d'oro*, published in Monteverdi's Seventh Book of Madrigals in 1619, a light-hearted secular duet with two violin parts and ostinato bass similar to *Beatus vir*, though shorter and less ambitiously worked-out structurally. Like so many other composers before and since, Monteverdi did not hesitate to introduce secular material into his sacred music; the catchy tunefulness of *Beatus vir* must have set even the sternest ecclesiastical toes tapping.

The tempo of the piece needs careful planning. If the *proportio sextupla* notation of the middle section is to be taken seriously, its 𝅗𝅥. must equal the 𝅗𝅥 of the outer sections. The tempo of the middle section must be slow enough to accommodate the virtuosic passage to the words 'exaltabitur in gloria' (bars 182–97). A pulse of 𝅗𝅥. = 42 would result in ♩ = 84 for the outer sections, a fairly serene speed. Monteverdi's notation provides no justification for taking bars 182–97 slower than bars 62–181. Conductors may wish to consider assigning bars 182–97 to soloists, in the interests of greater possible rapidity. *Source: Selva morale e spirituale di Claudio Monteverde . . .* (Magni, Venice, 1641) *Variants:* 2 i and ii: last two notes of bar are equal ♪s in source / 5–7 iv and v: tenor parts here are interchanged in this edition / 7 i and 8 ii: last two notes of the bar are equal ♪s in source / 23 i: ditto / 57 iv 2: F not E in source / 80 ii 1: 𝅗𝅥. in source / 84 iv 3: C in source / 133 iii 1, 2: ♩ ♩ in source / 151 iv 1: 𝅗𝅥. in source / 188 vi 1: Vln 2 *a'* not *c''* in source / 198 i: last two notes of bar are equal ♪s in source / 199 i and ii: ditto / 210 ii: this bar appears a 3rd higher in source (in unison with S1) / 232 iii: last two notes of bar are *d' d'* in source, but *c' a* (following Vln 2 an octave lower) seems a better and more likely reading / 232 v 6: *a* in source / 236 v 5: ♯ missing in source.

32. Monteverdi: *Cantate Domino*
This festive motet was published in 1620 in a collection issued by Monteverdi's former pupil from Mantua days, Bianchi. The collection comprised 31 motets: 24 by Bianchi himself, one by Losio, and six by Monteverdi, whose contributions may well have been recently written for the great Venetian religious festivals. *Cantate Domino* may have been intended for one of the two feasts of the Holy Cross, though the text, being a compilation, could not strictly be proper to any church occasion. The continuo bass is rarely independent of the vocal bass, so the motet can be performed *a cappella*, but accompaniment by organ would have been assumed. *Source: Libro primo de motetti . . . di Giulio Cesare Bianchi* (Magni, Venice, 1620) *Variants:* The voice name 'Tenor Sec[ondo]' appears to be an error, since logically this voice should appear above the 'Quinto'. / 7 iii 1: *a'* in source / 65 v 2: *a* in source / 67 ii and iv: parallel octaves on beats 2–3 (C–B) are left unaltered.

33. Monteverdi: *Christe, adoramus te*
Also from Bianchi's 1620 collection, this motet is headed 'Nella elevatione di N.[ostro] Signore', meaning it is to be sung at the elevation of the host during mass. The text is proper to the feasts of the Holy Cross (3 May and 14 September), especially important occasions in the Venetian calendar after 1617: in that year a relic of what was held to be the Holy Cross was found by workmen excavating in S. Marco. *Source:* as for *Cantate Domino*. *Variant:* 20 vii: Bass line in the source is:

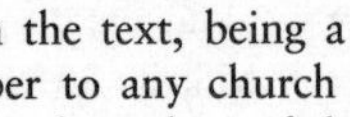

This has been amended to concur with bar 13, which is otherwise identical in all respects to bar 20.
Note: The marking 'Solo' in bar 22 (applicable also in bar 15) is probably just an indication to the continuo player that only one voice part is singing at that point, but it could mean that a soloist sings 'redemisti mundum'.

34. Mozart: *Ave verum Corpus*
Mozart's manuscript of this much-loved motet bears the inscription 'Baaden 17 Juni 1791'. During that early summer, his wife Constanze was taking the waters at the little spa town of Baden near Vienna. Mozart visited her there and became friendly with the local church choirmaster Anton Stoll, for whom he wrote the motet. Its text, a hymn in honour of the Blessed Sacrament, sometimes ascribed to Pope Innocent VI (d. 1342), is appropriate to the feast of Corpus Christi, which in 1791 fell on 23 June. This was no doubt the occasion for the composition. *Source:* facsimile of autograph manuscript. The vocal parts are written in open score, in SATB clefs.

35. Palestrina: *Exsultate Deo*
Palestrina's life and work centred around Rome. He was born in the nearby town of Palestrina, from which he took his name, trained as a choirboy in the Roman church of S. Maria Maggiore, appointed to prominent positions in the Roman musical establishment, and brought to international fame by his numerous publications, issued in the first instance from Rome. In 1551 he was appointed *maestro* of the Cappella Giulia, the choir of St Peter's Basilica, and in 1555 he sang for a few months in the Sistine choir until the introduction of a celibacy rule by the new pope led to his dismissal as a married man. Periods of directorship at the church of St John Lateran, where Lassus had preceded him (1555–60) and at his old church of S. Maria Maggiore (1561–6) were followed by a return in 1571 to the Cappella Giulia, where he remained till his death. His stream of publications began with a successful book of madrigals in 1555; by the time of his death there were seven books of masses, six of motets, and sundry other volumes of liturgical music and madrigals. Among his 375 or so motets, *Exsultate Deo* has always been a favourite. With its joyous tunefulness and vivid word-painting depicting musical instruments, it refutes the inaccurate myth of Palestrina as a cold, bloodless master of abstract polyphony, a myth due in part to the reverence surrounding him even in his lifetime and to the use of his music ever since as a model in the teaching of counterpoint. *Source: Motettorum liber quintus* (Rome, 1584).

36. Palestrina: *Tu es Petrus* and *Quodcumque ligaveris*
The text of this resplendent pair of motets would have held obvious significance for Palestrina during his years at St Peter's; he wrote two settings, of which the present one is the better known. It was published in 1572, the year after his return to the Basilica, and he thought highly enough of it to base a later, very grand mass setting for triple choir on it. The text of the *prima pars* was proper to all feasts of St Peter, but the complete text was the Tract for the feast of St Peter's Chair at Rome (January 18). *Source: Motettorum quae partim quinis, partim senis, partim octonis vocibus concinantur . . . liber secundus* (reprint of 1572 publication, Venice, 1580).
Variant: 90 ii 2 (2nd of two ♪s) C in source, amended to B♭ by analogy with 96 iv.

37. Palestrina: *Sicut cervus*
This has always been one of the most familiar of Palestrina's motets, frequently reprinted and anthologized since the nineteenth century, and justly held up as a model of Renaissance imitative polyphony. Its psalm text was appropriately appointed as the first part of the Tract at the blessing of the font on Holy Saturday. The rest of the Tract, beginning *Sitivit anima mea*, was set by Palestrina

as a *secunda pars* (not printed here) of *Sicut cervus. Sitivit anima mea* is, in effect, a separate motet, so the general practice of performing *Sicut cervus* on its own is not objectionable except in a strictly liturgical context. This is a different case from *Tu es Petrus* and *Quodcumque ligaveris*, which form a musically interlocked ABCB pair and should be performed together if possible. *Source: Motettorum quatuor vocibus . . . liber secundus* (reprint of 1581 publication, Venice, 1596).

38. Poulenc: *Salve Regina*
The death of a friend in a car accident in 1936 and a subsequent visit to the shrine of Rocamadour turned Poulenc's thoughts towards the composition of sacred music, which was not a genre he had previously cultivated. Starting with the *Litanies à la Vierge Noire* (1936) he wrote a remarkable series of sacred works large and small, to which he attached considerable importance. The *Salve Regina* and another *a cappella* motet, *Exultate Deo*, were written in 1941 at Poulenc's country home at Noizay in Touraine, both pieces being inspired by archaic models. *Exultate Deo* is directly modelled on Palestrina's setting of the same text, but the more homophonic *Salve Regina* is simply given a serenely antique flavour influenced by Gregorian chant, spiced with touches of Poulenc's own distinctive harmonic language. The dedicatee of the piece was Hélène de Wendel, a cultured and music-loving friend who helped to edit Poulenc's letters for publication after his death. *Source:* Published edition, Salabert.

39. Rachmaninov: *Bogoroditsye Dyevo (Ave Maria)*, op. 37 no. 6
The fifteen *a cappella* pieces making up the *All-Night Vigil* were written early in 1915. Rachmaninov had set the Liturgy of St John Chrysostom in 1910, and a performance which he conducted in 1914 convinced him that he should write another and (to him) more satisfactory work for the Russian Orthodox Church. The *All-Night Vigil* was an immediate success at its première by the Moscow Synodal Choir in 1915, but the suppression of the Church following the 1917 revolution prevented it achieving wide recognition until the 1960s. The *Ave Maria* concludes Vespers, the first part of the Vigil (Matins forms the second part). In accordance with Orthodox practice, Rachmaninov based his music on traditional chants, but the *Ave Maria* is one of six movements where the chants were, in his words, 'conscious counterfeits' which he himself invented.
Source: Published edition, Boosey & Hawkes.

40. Rheinberger: *Abendlied*, op. 69 no. 3
Born in Liechtenstein, Rheinberger lived and worked from 1851 in Munich, becoming a much-valued teacher at the conservatory, a church organist, conductor of the Munich Choral Society, and composer of a large number of works in many genres, of which only the organ sonatas now remain in the general repertory. He took a strong interest in the composition and practice of sacred music, and in 1877 was made Kapellmeister to the Munich court, the post once occupied by Lassus. *Abendlied* is no. 3 of *Drei geistliche Gesänge*, a set of three *a cappella* sacred pieces published in 1873 and dedicated to a choral society in Berlin. As with Stanford's *Three Motets*, op. 38, academic mastery of contrapuntally-influenced voice writing is combined with an authentically personal and Romantic expressiveness, to memorable effect. Conductors may wish to temper the composer's surprisingly loud dynamic markings to the reflective character of the music.
Source: first edition (Simrock, Berlin, 1873).

41. Reger: *Unser lieben Frauen Traum*, op. 138 no. 4
Like Rheinberger, Reger was a south German Catholic organist-composer whose prolific output of music, covering most genres, has never been wholeheartedly revived. Born in Bavaria, he studied under the noted theorist Riemann, and lived successively in Munich, Leipzig, Meiningen (where he was conductor of the court orchestra), and Jena. In his day he enjoyed an international success comparable with Richard Strauss's which did not, however, long outlive his premature death. The *Acht geistliche Gesänge*, op. 138, written in 1914, are among the last of his thirty or so choral compositions. *Unser lieben Frauen Traum*, no. 4 of the set, is clearly in the tradition of the Brahms *Marienlieder* but not without its own graceful charm and simplicity, well in keeping with the folk-like character of the text.
Source: first edition (Simrock, Berlin, 1916).

42. Rossini: *O salutaris Hostia*
By 1857, when Rossini wrote this devout miniature, he was in retirement, composing now and again either for his own amusement or (as in this case) at the request of friends. The manuscript of *O salutaris Hostia*, dated 29 November 1857, bears the inscription 'Petit souvenir offert à mon ami J. d'Ortigue'. D'Ortigue was a music critic, church music scholar, and co-founder with Baron Niedermeyer of a journal devoted to sacred music, *La maîtrise*. Rossini's motet was published in the December issue of the journal. The text (the fifth verse of Aquinas's eucharistic hymn *Verbum supernum prodiens*), was commonly used at the blessing of the sacrament. *Source:* facsimile of autograph manuscript, contained in *G. Rossini: sa vie et son oeuvre* (A. Azevedo, Paris, 1864). The score is written in SATB clefs.

43. Schubert: *Psalm 23 (Gott ist mein Hirt)*
Schubert composed this setting of Moses Mendelssohn's German version of Psalm 23 in December 1820. It was written for a soirée given in Vienna by four musical sisters, Anna, Barbara, Katharina and Josephine Fröhlich; Anna taught singing at the Vienna conservatory, and the soirée was for her singing pupils. The setting was subsequently performed a number of times as an examination piece for quartets of conservatory students, and at public concerts. It quickly became a favourite. Unusually for Schubert, it was soon published: Diabelli issued a score and separate vocal parts in 1832, as op. 132. The autograph manuscript and Diabelli's edition concur quite well, with the exception of bar 50, where the B♮s on the first beat are not in the autograph. The editor of the old *Gesamtausgabe* considered that B♭ should therefore be adopted, but the 1832 edition, which has B♮, must also be taken seriously. Schubert obviously cannot have overseen this posthumous publication, but its source text was probably the

performing material (score and vocal parts) copied out for the first performances he heard, in which any accidentals inadvertently omitted in the original manuscript could have been added. B♮ does seem a better reading, forming a more exact sequence with the A♮ in bar 52. Even if not originally intended, B♮ could have been an afterthought.

A familiar Schubert editing problem arises with the *decrescendo* hairpins in bar 13 and parallel places. It is not clear whether these are indeed *decrescendi* (>), or accents (>) applying to the first of the two notes they appear over. In the piano part, they are written only under the left-hand stave: where a dynamic marking applies to both hands, Schubert generally writes it under both piano staves. Therefore, in the piano part to this edition they have been interpreted as accents applying to the bass notes (by analogy with bars 44–7), but in the vocal parts they are shown as *decrescendi*, on the grounds that, to present-day performers, accents indicate something sharper than the gentle shading-off within each pair of notes which was no doubt the nuance Schubert wanted.

Sources: (1) autograph manuscript (Wiener Stadtbibliothek, MH 188/c) and (2) first edition (Diabelli, Vienna, 1832). The voice parts are shown in open score. *Variants: General:* Schubert's markings *dimin.*, *ligato*, and *emoriendo* have been normalized. In the piano part, the division of notes between the staves has been altered where appropriate, to reflect division between the hands, and some notational abbreviations have been opened out. Bars 21–2 of the piano accompaniment are awkward to play (unlike the parallel bars, 64–5) because of the lack of a third triplet on each beat, but the notes are carefully placed in the MS. and Schubert's rhythmic intention seems clear. *Specific:* 9 pno: < is in (2) but not (1) / 11 pno: <> is in (2) but not (1) / 19 and 62 i: S.2 B♭♭ is shown as A♮ in (1) / 38–9 pno: r.h. slur is divided into two in both sources thus: ♩♩| ♩♩♩♩, amended by analogy with bars 31–2 / 39 ii and pno: *dim.* one beat later in both sources / 50 i 1: S.1 has B♭ in (1), B♮ in (2) / 50 pno: top note of first r.h. chord B♭ in (1), B♮ in (2) / 60 and 61 pno: <> supplied by analogy with bars 17–18.

44. Schütz: *Psalm 100 (Jauchzet dem Herrn)*, SWV 36

Schütz's position as the first German-speaking composer of international repute, and the greatest of his century, is not disputed, but his legacy of some 500 works is only now becoming widely known outside Germany. Born in the little town of Köstritz, not far from Leipzig, he studied first at Kassel and then with Giovanni Gabrieli in Venice, a fruitful period which came to an end with Gabrieli's death in 1612. He returned to Kassel, but his talents were spotted by the Elector of Saxony, who secured his services for the Dresden court in 1617. With the exception of brief interludes serving temporarily at courts in Hildesheim and in Denmark, Schütz spent the rest of his long life in or around Dresden, in charge of music at court through the difficult period of the Thirty Years' War but maintaining a prolific output of published collections of his work, the majority of it sacred music for Lutheran use. *Psalm 100* (which also exists in an earlier version for three choirs) comes from his first collection, the *Psalmen Davids* of 1619, in which the influence of Venetian polychoral writing is successfully blended with a more square-cut German style of text setting. *Source: Psalmen Davids sampt etlichen Moteten und Concerten* (Dresden, 1619). Each of the two choirs (named *Proposta* and *Riposta*) has its own *basso continuo* part, conflated into one in the present edition. Original clefs SATB in each choir, with key signature of one flat, time signatures ¢3 and (bar 9) ¢. Note values in the present edition have been quartered in bars 1–8 and 68–71, unaltered elsewhere. Original *BC* parts (only) are barred, once for every two bars of present edition. Original pitch a tone lower than present edition. *Variants:* 54, Ch. I: alto and bass rhythm 𝅗𝅥. ♫ in source (also in *BC*) / 56, Ch. II: ditto / 75 ii 3: tenor C (not D) in source, conflicting with bass figure 6 / 147: in source, final bar is followed by a blank bar with fermata, possibly the result of Ch. II following Ch. I in exact canon here.

45. Schütz: *Selig sind die Toten*, SWV 391

This dignified and consolatory motet, one of the relatively few by Schütz to be widely known and appreciated, was first published in the *Geistliche Chormusik* of 1648, an important collection of 29 of the composer's motets. They represent a turning away from the Venetian extravagance of Schütz's earlier work, with more emphasis on traditional imitative polyphony, which the composer's preface to the volume recommends as a discipline for budding composers. *Selig sind die Toten* is indeed just as imitative in style as any Renaissance motet, though the strong expressive contrasts between the slow-moving sections and the more active treatment of the words 'und ihre Werke folgen ihnen nach' belong clearly to the Baroque era. Schütz discusses the issue of instrumental accompaniment in his preface, stating that the *basso continuo* has been included because it is considered desirable, not out of necessity. Hence, he sanctions performance either with organ continuo or (unusually for the seventeenth century) *a cappella*. *Source: Geistliche Chor-Music . . . erster Theil, op.11* (Dresden, 1648). In the *BC* part, some long notes are shown as two shorter tied ones in order to pinpoint changes of figuring. These have been normalized. In bars 44–5 the parallel octaves E–D between S.2 and T.1 are vexatious because they are unlikely to be right but hard to amend with confidence. If the first S.2 note in bar 45 were amended to *a*', a more exact imitation between S.1 and S.2 would be restored, with a falling fifth on 'Geist spricht' in both voices; the resulting parallel fifths by contrary motion with the *BC* part would be permissible, but the direct parallel fifths with the vocal bass would not.

46. Stravinsky: *Ave Maria*

In 1926 Stravinsky rejoined the Russian Orthodox Church, from which he had been estranged for some twenty-five years. The main musical fruit of his reconversion was the *Symphony of Psalms*, but he also wrote three short unaccompanied sacred choruses, of which the *Ave Maria* (1934) was the last. Originally in Slavonic (to the text *Bogoroditsye Dyevo*), it was adapted by the composer to the Latin text in 1949. *Source:* Published edition, Boosey & Hawkes.

47. Sweelinck: *Laudate Dominum*

Born in the Netherlands, Sweelinck spent his whole working life in Amsterdam, where he became organist of the Oude Kerk and a renowned teacher. As a composer, he wrote keyboard music, madrigals, and chansons, but his *magnum opus* was a four-volume collection of polyphonic settings of all 150 psalms in the French translation of Marot and De Bèze, a work spanning his entire creative life. He published only one volume of Latin motets, the five-voiced *Cantiones sacrae* of 1619: the Netherlands then being officially Calvinist, these 37 pieces (including the famous *Hodie Christus natus est*) would have been intended for private rather than liturgical use, at least in Sweelinck's own country. The sparkling *Laudate Dominum* indeed calls for the lightness and agility associated with secular rather than liturgical music-making. The *basso continuo*, although not independent from the vocal bass, indicates that accompaniment was expected. *Source: Cantiones sacrae* (Antwerp, 1619).

48. Tchaikovsky: *Dostoino yest (Hymn to the Virgin)*
Tchaikovsky first tried his hand at church music with the *Liturgy of St John Chrysostom* in 1878. The success of this work prompted the Tsar to ask Tchaikovsky, at an audience early in 1884, to write more for the church. The *Nine liturgical choruses*, written during the composer's wanderings round Europe in that year, were his response. Balakirev, director of the imperial chapel choir, was sent three (and probably later all) of the set to perform for the Tsar. *Dostoino yest* is no. 5 of the nine choruses. *Source:* first edition (Jurgenson, Moscow, 1885). The music is written in open score in SATB clefs, with a piano reduction (adjusted in places in the present edition). Performance in the Orthodox Church would, however, have been unaccompanied.

49. Verdi: *Ave Maria*
This is the first of the *Quattro pezzi sacri*, four very diverse compositions completed in 1898 which form Verdi's swan-song; the other three are the *Stabat Mater* for chorus and orchestra, the *Laudi alla Vergine Maria* for four unaccompanied female voices, and the *Te Deum* for double chorus and orchestra. The *Ave Maria* has a curious history. The *scala enigmatica* on which it is based was submitted anonymously to a music magazine, the *Gazzetta Musicale*, and Verdi took up the challenge of treating it as a *cantus firmus* in what turned out to be a harmonically adventurous little setting that bears the composer's distinctive stamp. Thanks to his expert voice writing, it is easier to sing than it at first sight appears. *Source:* first edition (Ricordi, Milan, 1898).

50. Viadana: *Exsultate justi*
Viadana took his name from the small town near Parma where he was born, and is believed to have studied composition with Costanzo Porta, a friar and renowned musician. Viadana also became a friar, holding both musical and ecclesiastical posts at different times in his life. From 1594–7 he was *maestro di cappella* at Mantua Cathedral, and thereafter worked in Cremona, Concordia (near Venice), and at Fano Cathedral, before taking up a monastic appointment and eventually retiring to a monastery. Although not an exceptionally prolific composer, his works, both sacred and secular, were widely published and popular with their attractive and up-to-date style. *Exsultate justi* comes from his most famous publication, the *Cento concerti ecclesiastici* of 1602. This collection is often cited as the first documented use in sacred music of a *basso continuo*. The continuo is essential in some pieces, but in others, including the present motet, it just doubles the vocal bass and can be omitted, though in the preface Viadana advises against this. The style of *Exsultate justi*, with its tunefulness, word-painting, sectional repeat and not too strenuous counterpoint, owes more to secular than to sacred models, perhaps the secret of its perennial appeal. *Source: Cento concerti ecclesiastici* (Venice, 1602).

51. Victoria *(attrib.)*: *Ave Maria*
Victoria has long been regarded as the greatest Spanish Renaissance composer, despite being both less prolific and less versatile than many of his contemporaries: virtually his entire output, all of it Latin church music, is contained in only eleven volumes, all published in his lifetime. He began his musical life as a choirboy at Avila Cathedral, then moved to Rome to study at the Jesuit Collegio Germanico; he may have received tuition from Palestrina. He was made director of music at the Collegio in 1573, and was ordained priest in 1575. In 1576 he joined St Philip Neri's community, later taking chaplaincies at two Roman churches. Despite growing European fame from his compositions, he wanted to return to a quieter life in his native Spain, and in 1587 he accepted Philip II's offer to become chaplain to his sister, the Dowager Empress Maria, who lived in retirement at the convent of Descalzas Reales in Madrid. Victoria remained at the convent, first as choirmaster and later as organist, until his death. Among his works are numerous settings of Marian texts. This gentle, gracious *Ave Maria* is one of his most often-performed pieces, though doubts have been cast on its authenticity as it was never published in Victoria's lifetime. Pedrell included the piece in his complete edition only because it had appeared in an important nineteenth-century anthology, Proske's *Musica divina* (vol. 4), the earliest known source. Proske died during the preparation of this volume, and his successor editor stated in the commentary that he was unable to find the source from which the *Ave Maria* had been taken (the only such case in the volume), which raises the possibility that the piece was a pious invention of Proske's own. The opening intonation and much of the outline of the polyphony are closely based on the Gregorian antiphon at Second Vespers for the Feast of the Annunciation (*Liber Usualis*, p. 1416). *Source: Musica divina*, vol. 4, ed. Proske (Ratisbon, 1863).

52. Victoria: *O quam gloriosum*
Designated in the part-books as a motet 'in Festo omnium Sanctorum', *O quam gloriosum* was published in 1572 in Victoria's first book of motets, which was reprinted a number of times. It was later used by Victoria as the basis of a mass setting, published in 1583. Both the motet and the mass are among the most-performed of Victoria's works. *Source: Thomæ Ludovici de Victoria Abulensis Motecta . . .* (Rome, 1583: reprint of 1572 publication). *Variants:* 18–19 iii: underlay is clearly thus in source. Some editions alter it to 'Chri-sto gau - - - | dent', which is dubious, because elsewhere 'gaudent' starts only on weak beats. The rising scale on beat 3 of bar 18 might appear to

be the start of the new point of imitation, but the underlay goes against this interpretation. / 47 iv 2: the editorial ♯ should be viewed with caution. It does make the phrase consistent with its later appearances, but at the expense of creating a tritone G♯–D with the soprano on the second beat. If, however, the soprano 𝅗𝅥 was intended to be shortened in performance to ♩, being the last note of a phrase (a view held by some scholars), then no tritone is created except by reverberation, and the ♯ is more admissible.

53. Victoria: *O vos omnes*
Victoria set this poignant Holy Week text twice, first as an individual motet (published in 1572), and then as the fourteenth of eighteen Tenebrae Responsories which formed part of his monumental *Officium Hebdomadae Sanctae* [Office of Holy Week] published in 1585. The present setting, considered the finer of the two, is the second one. As set by Victoria, it was the fifth Responsory at Matins (the first part of Tenebrae) for Holy Saturday, actually observed on Good Friday evening (see notes on the Allegri *Miserere*); the text recurs later in the Office as an antiphon. The correct pitch of Victoria's setting is a matter of doubt. It is notated a fifth higher than given here, and the part-books designate it 'quattuor vocibis paribus' [for four equal voices]. Some scholars believe that this high notated pitch was dictated by modal convention, and that all the Tenebrae Responsories should be sung at a lower pitch by male voices AATB. The present pitch, suitable for SATB, represents a compromise. *Source: Officium Hebdomadae Sanctae* (Rome, 1585).

54. Victoria *(attrib.)*: *Jesu, dulcis memoria*
This polyphonic hymn setting is found under Victoria's name in two nineteenth-century collections, Alfieri's *Raccolta di mottetti* of 1840 (also the source of Anerio's *Christus factus est*), and the Prince of Moscow's collection of 1843–5 (from which the John of Portugal *Crux fidelis* comes). There is no earlier extant source, and on stylistic grounds it appears very unlikely that Victoria can have written the piece, exquisite as it is: it belongs rather to Monteverdi's generation, or later. Pedrell included it in the complete edition of Victoria, his version being the basis of most later editions. Three variant readings from Alfieri have been adopted in the present edition.
Sources: See above. *Variants:* 16 iii: '-per' is underlaid one note earlier in Pedrell / 19 iii: Pedrell has a two-beat note on '-jus' followed by a two-beat rest / 22–3 iv: Pedrell has '-sen-' as a four-beat note, '-ti-' as a two-beat note.
Note: The text as given in the *Liber Usualis* has 'cordis' not 'cordi', but 'cordi' is found in several sources of this hymn.

INDEX OF ORCHESTRATIONS

4. Bach: O Jesu Christ, meins Lebens Licht
2 litui (may be taken by flugelhorns, trumpets, oboes or other suitable instruments), 2 ob (optional), cor anglais (optional), bsn (optional), strings, continuo
Note: the litui parts are shown in two versions, for B flat or for C instrument.

12. Buxtehude: Magnificat
Vln 1, vln 2, vla 1 (optional), vla 2 (optional), vc, cb, continuo

14. Fauré: Cantique de Jean Racine (orchestrated by John Rutter)
Harp, vla 1, vla 2, vc 1, vc 2, cb
Note: The viola parts may be doubled by violins 1 and 2 (parts available)

15. Franck: Panis angelicus
Harp, organ, solo cello

16. Gabrieli: Jubilate Deo
Eight instruments (strings, wind, or brass). Parts are provided for C, B flat and (inner voices) F instruments.
Possible modern brass combination: 3 tpt, hn, 3 tbn, tba

30. Mendelssohn: Verleih uns Frieden
2 fl, 2 cl, 2 bsn, strings, organ (optional)

31. Monteverdi: Beatus vir
Vlns 1 and 2 (soli or tutti), 3 tbns (optional), vc, cb (optional), continuo
Note: the optional trombone parts may alternatively be taken by two violas and a cello.

34. Mozart: Ave verum Corpus
Strings, organ (optional). Organ plays from vocal score.

Scores and parts of all the above are available on rental from the publisher.